Lonergan and Feminism

While Bernard Lonergan's work has been develpoed and applied to a range of cultures and ideas, few scholars have addressed the question of whether it is subject to feminist critique. And few feminists have employed the transcendental method of Lonergan to aid the feminist scholarly agenda.

This collection of ten essays initiates dialogue among scholars interested in Lonergan and concerned with feminism, and engages several fields of enquiry: philosophy, natural science, human science, ethics, and theology. Frederick E. Crowe deals with the challenges involved when one applies the work of a generalist, such as Lonergan, to a particular set of concerns, such as those of feminists. Three articles by philosophers – Paulette Kidder, Michael Vertin, and Elizabeth Morelli – treat questions of epistemology and gender. Cynthia Crysdale discusses women's ways of knowing from a social-scientific perspective. Articles by Tad Dunne and Denise Carmody deal with the question of authenticity and the criteria by which feminist truths are delineated. Michael Shute examines Lonergan's work on 'emergent probability' in light of eco-feminist critiques of the 'great chain of being.' Mary Frohlich addresses the question of the theological significance of sexuality. Charles Hefling examines Lonergan's Christology in reference to the feminist question of whether a male saviour can save women.

Lonergan invites his readers to engage in an experiment in cognitive self-appropriation – *Lonergan and Feminism* encourages this experiment.

(Lonergan Studies)

CYNTHIA CRYSDALE is a member of the Department of Religion and Religious Education, Catholic University of America.

Cynthia S.W. Crysdale, Editor

Lonergan and Feminism

UNIVERSITY OF TORONTO PRESS

Toronto Buffalo London

© University of Toronto Press Incorporated 1994
Toronto Buffalo London
Printed in Canada

ISBN 0-8020-5024-7 (cloth)
ISBN 0-8020-7432-4 (paper)

Printed on acid-free paper

Lonergan Studies series

Canadian Cataloguing in Publication Data

Main entry under title:

Lonergan and feminism

(Lonergan studies)
Includes bibliographical references and index.
ISBN 0-8020-5024-7 (bound) ISBN 0-8020-7432-4 (pbk.)

1. Lonergan, Bernard J. F. (Bernard Joseph Francis),
1904–1984 – Criticism and interpretation.
I. Crysdale, Cynthia S. W., 1953–   . II. Series.

BX4705.L7133L65 1994   261.8'3442   C94-930931-1

Contents

One offsets decline by following through on one's discoveries. For when one makes a discovery, when one comes to know what one did not know before, often enough one is advancing not merely from ignorance to truth but from error to truth. To follow up on such discovery is to scrutinize the error, to uncover other connected views that in one way or another supported or confirmed it. These associates of the error may themselves be errors. They will bear examination. In the measure they come under suspicion and prove to be erroneous, one can move on to their associates, and so make the discovery of one error the occasion of purging many.

Bernard Lonergan, *Method in Theology*

Foreword

At the beginning of his book *Insight* Bernard Lonergan makes a claim breath-taking in its sweep. Understand what understanding is, he writes, and you will possess in principle an understanding of all that there is to understand. Some, no doubt, have found that claim offputting, an instance of what they take to be the overweening arrogance typical of white, male, Eurocentric intellectuals, while for others Lonergan's claim displays the simplicity of genius. In this context it seems relevant to note that much later in the same work, when he turns to consider the ways in which the course of human history is distorted by the flight from understanding, Lonergan himself constructs a technically precise concept of bias. Arising at the interstices between psyche and spirit, between ego and community, between intersubjectivity and the good of order, and between common sense and detached intelligence, in a host of ways bias skews the drive to understand and thus undercuts the exercise of freedom that, for Lonergan, is the principle of genuine human, historical progress. Bias can rob individual living of its zestful drama when it entraps people in the repetitive banalities of neurosis. Raising egoism to an art form, it animates the often sophisticated and ingenious schemes of the criminal element within society. In its group form bias can lock entire societies into a relatively short cycle of alternating power shifts among competing vested interests, while its general form establishes a vortex that can suck whole civilizations into a downward spiral of meaninglessness. If, for Lonergan, freedom is the root of progress, bias is the enemy.

Further analysing the longer cycle through which civilizations decline, Lonergan identifies one dynamic that he finds especially pernicious. Egoism and the self-interest of groups can pervert praxis, giving rise to a situation that embodies not intelligence and responsibility but their opposite. Such a distorted situation in turn calls forth pseudo-theory, theory that draws its plausibility from the facts of the situation to which it corresponds and that, rather than criticizing that situation, accepts it in its distortion as a given, as simply the way things are. Theory of this sort renders distortion normative. In this way are born the false beliefs that canonize the status quo, beliefs that preclude authenticity and smother freedom. Such false beliefs, once they achieve the status of what passes as self-evident, contribute mightily to an ever-broadening morass of moral impotence. Yet this is not the last word. Pain cannot be repressed completely and forever, and for at least this reason the longer cycle of decline bears within it the principle of its own reversal.

Certainly women's pain has found voice of late, voice eloquent and powerful as it unmasks the oppressive and demeaning elements in what has long been taken for granted about women and their place. No longer mute, that pain has unleashed not only a torrent of protest but also a broad, sophisticated quest for understanding. For the sake of transforming the present, feminists turn their gaze upon the past and upon those classic texts, both literary and religious, that have shaped the present through the traditions and institutions issuing from them.

David Tracy, a member of the first generation of Lonergan's students, as Cynthia Crysdale charts them, alerts us to the ambiguity of every classic. Disclosure does not occur without concealment, manifestation without distortion, and so the path to the meaning that empowers humane living lies through a hermeneutic of suspicion. With this caveat Lonergan, for whom conversion is an ever-precarious emergence of authenticity from inauthenticity, would concur. Ultimately, perhaps, the reason for this state of affairs is what Christians call original sin. As Martin Luther would have it, we, and all our works – even those that God inspires – are simultaneously just and sinful. Be that as it may, Tracy's point receives abundant confirmation as feminist suspicion brings to light in a new way the ambiguity of the classics produced by a culture that feminists diagnose as patriarchal.

Only time will tell whether Bernard Lonergan's work will achieve classic status – time, and the hard work of those who, through his invitation to self-appropriation, have found themselves in possession of intellectual, moral, and religious foundations from which to respond to the cultural tasks of the present age. None the less, whatever the eventual impact of the Lonergan enterprise, certain facts must be reckoned with. Lonergan was a male, and white; he belonged to an exclusively male society, and he spent almost his entire career in exclusively male institutions. Furthermore, the intellectual tradition in which he stood drew its substance from the achievements of Aristotle, Augustine, and Aquinas. Notwithstanding their incomparable achievements, the writings of these giants of Western culture have also been the object of withering feminist criticism.

Thus the question arises: How likely is it that Lonergan's own writings will betray no trace of the androcentric world within whose confines he lived his life? Can he be expected to have imbibed no tinge of sexism from the tradition that nurtured him? More generally, if, as Tracy has it, one can expect to meet ambiguity in the encounter with any classic, is there reason to anticipate otherwise from the works of Bernard Lonergan? This is a question, not a charge, but it is a question that arises with some inevitability from the current cultural matrix. As such it deserves serious study of the sort represented by the essays in this volume. Surely no one was more insistent than Lonergan himself that questions are to be pursued and not, as he put it, burked.

Of course, the same line of questioning in its general form pertains to feminists as well. Feminisms are in fact many and diverse; while they may share a common starting-point in the negative experience from which they take their rise, diversity reigns even at the basic level of how that experience is described and explained, as well as in the dialectical analysis of the history from which it issues, and in the discernment of the values to be embodied in a remedy. Thus, one may anticipate that authenticity will be as precarious an achievement among feminists as among others, that the feminist movement and its tradition will be as fraught with ambiguity as any other.

The point of these brief remarks is to suggest that a common concern for freedom, authenticity, and genuine personhood constitutes a point at which the intellectual project of Bernard Lonergan and the burgeoning of contemporary feminist thought converge. The fact of that convergence will only make a difference, however, if it becomes concrete and actual through dialogue, a dialogue that will involve hard and critical questions. We have Cynthia Crysdale to thank for the perspicacity, initiative, and fortitude that she has exercised in making that dialogue a reality.

WILLIAM P. LOEWE

Acknowledgments

This book has been made possible by the hard work, patience, and collaboration of a great number of people. First and foremost I must thank the contributors, all of whom worked diligently to engage in the conversation between Lonergan's work and feminist critiques. They also willingly and patiently submitted themselves to often lengthy and detailed requests for revisions. Without the perseverance and scholarly acumen of the authors included in this text, the text would not exist.

Equally deserving of appreciation are the many persons who served graciously as reviewers of the various manuscripts that I received. The following persons served as an ad hoc editorial committee, providing astute and helpful editorial judgments and suggestions, enabling this book to exemplify high scholarly standards: Kenneth Melchin, Anne Dalton, Theresa Koernke, Michael Baur, Elizabeth Johnson, Phyllis Kaminski, Ann O'Hara Graff, Walter Conn, William Shea, Stephen Happel, James Price, Joann Wolski Conn, Chris Lind, Georgia Keightley, Margaret O'Gara, and Dave Hammond.

Two of my colleagues in the Department of Religion and Religious Education at the Catholic University of America were particularly available and patient with my many requests for advice: Sr Margaret Mary Kelleher and William Loewe. My friend and mentor, Michael Vertin, encouraged me in this project from its inception and consistently served as a wise adviser and consultant. Cora Twohig-Moengangongo carried on supportive conversations with me throughout the three years in which this 'bright idea' emerged and Fr Fred Crowe served as a supportive presence throughout. The Chair of my department, Sr Mary Collins, as well as the entire faculty and staff of the Department of Religion and Religious Education, showed continued interest and provided concrete support without which the project would have floundered. Finally, the publication of this volume was made possible by a Grant-in-Aid from the Catholic University of America, by the efficient editorial assistance of Patricia DeFerrari and Anna Minore, and by the diligent work of Ron Schoeffel and the staff at the University of Toronto Press.

Lonergan and Feminism

Introduction[1]

Over the last twenty-five years Bernard Lonergan's work in philosophy and theological method has attracted widespread interest, and no little acclaim. The first doctoral dissertation on Lonergan was written in 1967,[2] Lonergan's own *Method in Theology* came out in 1972,[3] and in the fall of 1984 Lonergan passed away. During this period, and since his death, the circle of those who study Lonergan's work and apply it to their own fields has widened steadily, from the first generation of students who studied under Lonergan to a second and third generation of scholars who are accepting Lonergan's invitation to self-appropriation.[4] Dissertations on Lonergan are now numerous and interest in his work spreads worldwide. Study centres devoted to the furthering of his thought exist around the globe, and the applicability of his transcendental method has been tested myriad times in relation to a wide range of issues and cultural settings.[5] Though Bernard Lonergan has not gained widespread popular acclaim, anyone doing theology in North America today, especially those engaged in Roman Catholic theology, must know something about him and his work. His work is pivotal in grasping the modern cultural shift from 'classicism' to 'historical consciousness,' a shift that has shaped the context of anyone attempting to mediate religion and culture today.[6]

In this same twenty-five-year period the voices of women decrying their invisibility in theology, philosophy, and religious practice have multiplied from a few lone soloists to a grand, though not always harmonious, choir. The women's liberation movement of the sixties found its way into the academy and the church in the early seventies. Women's studies programs proliferated and the critique of patriarchy in religion, human science, and philosophy began in force.[7] Since then attention has shifted from critique

of patriarchy, to retrieval of women's history and experience, to reconstructions of mutuality in theory and practice. The original hope of a unanimous
female voice has grown sober as feminists discover and admit their differences.[8] Nevertheless, to be a theologian or philosopher today and fail to be
aware of the radical challenge of feminism is to render oneself anachronistic
or irrelevant, or both. Daniel Maguire's bold claim about social ethics can
be applied equally to the academy in general: 'Anyone who plies the noble
art-science of social ethics (moral theology, Christian ethics), while taking
no account of the feminist turn of consciousness, is open to charges of
professional irresponsibility and incompetence.'[9]

Since what is often at issue in both of these movements is not the 'what'
but the 'how,' one might expect some interchange between the two over the
last twenty-five years. That is, questions concerning method seem to be at
the core of both the feminist turn and Lonergan's work. The connection is
made obvious when the fact that questions of knowing are central to Lonergan's thought is held alongside Maguire's claim that the feminist turn is an
epistemological one: 'Feminism is concerned with the shift in roles and the
question of the rights that have been unjustly denied women. But all of that,
however important and even essential, is secondary. The main event is
epistemological. Changes in *what* we know are normal; changes in *how* we
know are revolutionary. Feminism is a challenge to the way we have gone
about *knowing*. The epistemological *terra firma* of the recent past is rocking
and as the event develops, it promises to change the face of the earth.'[10]

Yet these two currents have followed largely separate courses. Feminists
have turned to various thinkers or schools of thought as methodological
resources for their work. In ethics they have used social analysis, Marxism,
and/or critical theory. Many feminist theologians see their work as an aspect
of liberation theology and consider the analysis of the roots of oppression
a central task.[11] Others appeal to the hermeneutical theories of Gadamer,
Habermas, Ricoeur, and Tillich as resources for their work.[12] But very few,
if any, rely on Lonergan's transcendental method to explain their endea-
vours. Lonergan's invitation to cognitive and deliberative self-appropriation
has not been accepted by feminists to any large degree.[13] The invitation has
not been accepted even in the negative fashion of criticizing his work from
a feminist perspective.

At the same time, the application and development of Lonergan's
method, while quite fruitful, has been dominated by male voices. In twelve
years of publication, the *Lonergan Studies Newsletter*, while listing over five
hundred references to works about Lonergan, cites only fifty-five publications by women.[14] Anthologies of articles in which scholars draw out the
implications of Lonergan's work abound, but the presence of female scholars is minimal.[15] While the relative paucity of female Lonergan scholars is

not necessarily to be equated with a lack of feminist awareness among Lonerganians, the virtual absence of feminism as a topic for discussion seems to be a significant gap in the application of Lonergan's thought.[16] It is the more astonishing when one tallies up the other kinds of applications that have been made. Robert Doran, Sebastian Moore, Walter Conn, and others have engaged in significant interchanges between Lonergan's work and the disciplines of psychology and spirituality.[17] Matthew Lamb and Frederick Lawrence have made connections between Lonergan's method, political theology, and liberation theology.[18] William Johnson has relied heavily on Lonergan in his Christian appropriation of Zen Buddhism.[19] Beyond this, Lonergan has been employed in constructing a Chinese contextual theology and has been related to Southeast Asian Shamanism. His thought has been developed in other cultural contexts such as the Philippines, Japan, Australia, and Africa,[20] and brought to bear on such ethical issues as the conception of human life and homosexual behaviour.[21] All this has occurred in conjunction with the 'Lonerganian' task of elucidating the foundations of theology and developing traditional theological topics such as Christology, ecclesiology, and soteriology.[22]

In light of this burgeoning material, the absence of women's voices and feminist questions becomes startlingly obvious. The purpose of this book is to begin a conversation, to initiate a dialogue among scholars interested in both Lonergan and feminist questions. As such this volume is merely a beginning, with the objective of becoming an incentive for further discussion. The articles do not address in any systematic way either the full range of feminist concerns or the many aspects of Lonergan's thought. Each author has chosen a topic that interests him or her within his or her field of specialization. The aim is to provide enough material to indicate that such a conversation is possible and to stimulate readers to pursue their own questions.

The book begins with an article by the 'grandfather' of Lonergan studies, Frederick Crowe, s.j. It is an apt beginning, since Father Crowe explains clearly and carefully just what is involved in the application of the thought of a generalist thinker, such as Lonergan, to a particular set of concerns, such as those of feminists. He uses examples from Lonergan's own writings of this transition from general to particular, indicating the difficulties of various tasks involved. Father Crowe suggests the kind of dialogue that must take place between genders, if cooperative understanding is to be gained, by examining Lonergan's concept of mutual self-mediation. His essay indicates in broad strokes the nature of the task undertaken in the remainder of the book.

The next three essays, written by philosophers, deal with questions of gender and epistemology. Paulette Kidder examines the 'third way' that feminist philosophers have advocated, between the objectivism that over-looks the 'situatedness' of the knower and the relativism of 'postmodernists.' Relying on the work of Sandra Harding and Lorraine Code, Kidder draws parallels between their approach and Lonergan's epistemology, at the same time suggesting that the feminist analysis of patriarchy provides a concrete account of the workings of bias. Michael Vertin takes on a similar task in relation to the work of the biophysicist Evelyn Fox Keller. He concludes that Lonergan's account of 'cognitional conversion' can both clarify and gener-alize Fox's 'dynamic objectivity,' while Keller's rejection of gender-bias as intrinsic to scientific knowing can elucidate the implications of cognitional conversion. Elizabeth Morelli examines the question of whether any cogni-tional operations are gender-specific, and in so doing gives an excellent review of the tradition in Western thought that assigns different types of rationality to men and women. She concludes with a phenomenological analysis of 'women's intuition' in light of Lonergan's cognitional theory.

The editor then takes up the question of the 'situatedness' of women's knowing, relying on a historical analysis given by Lorraine Code and the empirical work of Mary Belenky and her colleagues. Her point is to delineate the social conditions necessary for anyone to engage in the self-appropria-tion that is so central to Lonergan's method, and the particular obstacles that our culture places in the way of women attempting this task. Tad Dunne moves to an analysis of authenticity and power in trying to determine which feminist 'doctrines' or policies will indeed serve women's well-being. In particular, he discusses how Lonergan promotes a triple consciousness-raising that constitutes authenticity and that can cut through a feminism that is merely ideological. Denise Lardner Carmody, in a similar vein, expli-cates Lonergan's 'transcendental precepts' in reference to a feminist search for theoretical foundations. She stresses the transcendental nature of human consciousness itself, which ultimately provides a radical challenge to authenticity for both feminists and 'Lonerganians.'

The essays by Michael Shute and Mary Frohlich both focus on Lonergan's understanding of 'nature' and his theory about how human consciousness sublates a lower manifold of biological processes and animal sensitivity. Shute deals explicitly and thoroughly with the ecofeminist critique of the 'great chain of being' and the fact the Lonergan's analysis of world process (emergent probability) is hierarchical in structure. Frohlich deals with a very different context, that of the theological use of gender images. Criticizing the 'mystification' of sexuality in certain arguments against the ordination of women (and the gender-tied conceptions of grace and sacrament), she examines the psychoanalytic work of Jacques Lacan, Lonergan's under-standing of 'vertical finality,' and the relationship between mind and body, as well as feminist distinctions between 'sex' and 'gender'. She concludes with her own synthesis of how gender images might mediate grace without a sexist reductionism.

Frohlich's essay and the final one by Charles Hefling are the most explicitly theological chapters of this volume. While Frohlich tackles issues foundational for the use and understanding of gender in theology, Hefling takes on Lonergan's theology itself in light of feminist critiques. Thus, Hefling does not focus on Lonergan's epistemology, theory of world process, or methodology, but examines Lonergan's own attempt to explicate doctrine: his work in Christology. The question raised here regards, not gender in general, but the gender of Christ: to what degree is Christ's maleness intrinsic to his work as redeemer? Is Lonergan's own systematic theology subject to the critiques of sexist bias? Hefling concludes that while, according to Lonergan's position, Christ's 'assumption' of human nature is unrelated to Christ's maleness, Lonergan's emphasis on the 'Law of the Cross' may need further work and/or prove problematic for feminists.

Thus, the articles in this volume, while only the beginning of a conversation, engage several fields of enquiry: philosophy, natural science, human science, ethics, and theology. Several further observations can be made. First, while there is a diversity of fields and topics represented, and even a range of generations and geographical locations among the authors, most often the 'feminism' in play is white, middle-class, North American, and academic. This is a fact to be noted, not necessarily grounds for apology; after all, this volume is the *beginning* of a conversation. Second, all the authors herein are sympathetic to Lonergan's work and take the position that the *prospects* of an interchange between Lonerganians and feminists are greater than the *problems* involved. The fact that Lonergan was a celibate male cleric in a patriarchal church, who used gender-exclusive language, cannot be ignored or easily dismissed. That this makes his thought and work sexist is a thesis to be proven. Most of the authors in this book maintain that feminist problems with Lonergan either (1) can be resolved by a close and careful interpretation of Lonergan's intended meaning in light of his entire corpus or (2) can challenge Lonergan scholars to revise their work and themselves based on the imperatives to 'Be Attentive, Intelligent, Reasonable, and Responsible.' This latter possibility excludes an ideological use of Lonergan in future dialogue as it is excluded, the editor would maintain, in this current volume.

A final note, always important when dealing with Lonergan, is to point out that the basis of this book, the foundation on which it rests and its reception by readers rests, is not any dogma or ideology or fideism (on the Lonergan or the feminist side). Instead, as Lonergan invites his readers in *Insight* to engage in an experiment in self-appropriation, so too the foundation of this book is human subjects as attentive, intelligent, reasonable, and responsible. In the measure that authors and readers follow these most basic exigencies, this volume represents the beginning of a long and fruitful conversation.

CSWC

Notes

1 Sections of this introduction have appeared previously in an article entitled 'Lonergan and Feminism,' published in *Theological Studies* 53 (1992): 234–56. They are reprinted here with permission.
2 According to the Lonergan Research Institute in Toronto, the first dissertation that focuses fully on Lonergan's work is that of Joseph Flanagan: 'The Basic Patterns of Human Understanding According to Bernard Lonergan' (Fordham, 1967). There are several earlier dissertations that *use* Lonergan's thought (spanning 1957 to 1964), all written at the Gregorian University in Rome while Lonergan was teaching there. As a matter of academic policy, students at the Gregorian were not permitted to focus an entire dissertation on the work of a current professor at the Gregorian.
3 Bernard Lonergan, *Method in Theology* (New York: Seabury Press, 1972). Lonergan's earlier philosophical work (1957) is *Insight: A Study of Human Understanding*, vol 3. of *The Collected Works of Bernard Lonergan*, ed. F.E. Crowe and R.M. Doran (Toronto: University of Toronto Press, 1992).
4 In 1983 the *Lonergan Studies Newsletter* (vol. 4, pp. 28–30) included a reflection by Fred Lawrence on the Lonergan Workshop held in Boston that year – the tenth anniversary of this annual workshop. He mentions the invigorating atmosphere in which 'old-timers' who had studied with Lonergan himself (including Frederick Crowe, Matthew Lamb, Joseph Komonchak, David Burrell, David Tracy, and others) learned from the 'new generation' of Lonergan scholars (such as Patrick Byrne, Nancy Ring, William Loewe, Robert Doran, Michael Vertin, and Walter Conn). Ten years later this second generation has now mentored yet a third, whose names are too numerous to mention.
5 In 1987 the *Lonergan Studies Newsletter* listed the following Lonergan research centres around the world: two in Australia (Sydney, Melbourne), two in the U.S.A. (Boston, Santa Clara), two in Canada (Montreal, Toronto), one in Ireland (Dublin), two in Italy (Naples, Rome), and one in the Philippines (Manila). See *Lonergan Studies Newsletter* 8 (1987) 16.
6 For Lonergan's discussion of this shift, see 'The Transition from a Classicist World-View to Historical-Mindedness' and 'Theology in Its New Context,' in W.F.J. Ryan and B.J. Tyrrell, eds, *A Second Collection: Papers by Bernard J.F. Lonergan* (London: Darton, Longman, and Todd, 1974) 1–9 and 55–67.
7 For a review of gender studies and their emergence in university curricula,

see Anne Carr, *Transforming Grace: Christian Tradition and Women's Experience* (San Francisco: Harper and Row, 1988) 63–94. See also Anne E. Patrick, 'Women and Religion: A Survey of Significant Literature, 1964–1974,' *Theological Studies* 36 (1975) 737–65. Some basic early critiques include: Rosemary Radford Ruether, *Religion and Sexism: Images of Women in the Jewish and Christian Tradition* (New York: Simon and Schuster, 1974); Letty Russell, *Human Liberation in a Feminist Perspective* (Philadelphia: Westminster Press, 1974); and C. Christ and J. Plaskow, eds, *Womanspirit Rising* (San Francisco: Harper and Row, 1979).

8 For example, among feminist theologians there are those whose criticism of the Judaeo-Christian tradition leads them to reject it altogether and those who believe it can be reformed. The former group consider patriarchy to be at the very core of this tradition and therefore seek to create their own feminist spirituality. Feminists of this persuasion would include Mary Daly, Carol Christ, and Naomi Goldenberg. Others, such as Rosemary Ruether, Elizabeth Schussler-Fiorenza, and Phyllis Trible, believe that the Judaeo-Christian tradition can be reconstructed without its patriarchal bias. For Ruether's response to the radical feminists, see 'A Religion for Women: Sources and Strategies,' *Christianity and Crisis* (1979) 307–11. For other analyses of feminist diversity, see Joan L. Griscom, 'On Healing the Nature/History Split in Feminist Thought,' in B.H. Andolsen, C.E. Gudorf, and M.D. Pellauer, eds, *Women's Consciousness, Women's Conscience* (San Francisco: Harper and Row, 1985) 85–98; and Carol S. Robb, 'A Framework for Feminist Ethics,' in ibid. 211–34.

9 Daniel C. Maguire, 'The Feminist Turn in Ethics,' *Horizons* 10 (1983) 341.

10 Ibid. A similar claim is made by June O'Connor in 'On Doing Religious Ethics,' in Andolsen et al., *Women's Consciousness* 265–66.

11 For example, see E. Schussler-Fiorenza, 'Feminist Theology as a Critical Theology of Liberation,' *Theological Studies* 36 (1975) 605–26; R.R. Ruether, *Sexism and God-Talk: Toward a Feminist Theology* (Boston: Beacon Press, 1983); L.M. Russell, *Human Liberation*; and Carol Robb, 'Framework.'

12 See Anne Carr, *Transforming Grace*, chap. 5.

13 Exceptions include discussions of Lonergan and feminism in the following: Walter E. Conn, 'Two-Handed Theology,' *CTSA Proceedings* 38 (1983) 66–71; Denise Larnder Carmody, 'Feminist Redemption: Doris Lessing and Bernard Lonergan,' *Andover Newton Quarterly* 16 (1975) 119–30; Christina Allen, 'Emerging Religious Consciousness, Christianity, and the Female,' paper presented at the *Symposium on Contemporary Religious Consciousness*, Carleton University (Ottawa), October 1978; Nancy Ring, 'The Symbolic Function of Religious Doctrine as Revelatory of the Mind and Mystery of Christ: A Feminist Perspective,' paper presented at the *Lonergan Workshop*, Boston College, 1981, and 'Intentionality Analysis, the Church, and Wom-

en's Spirituality,' paper presented at the *Lonergan Workshop*, Boston College, 1988; Cora Twohig-Moengangongo, 'Bernard Lonergan and Feminism: A Conversation,' *Canadian Theological Society Newsletter* 10 (1991) 5–8; Paulette Kidder, 'The Feminine and Consciousness,' in *Presentations and Discussions from the VIIth Annual West Coast Eleanor Giuffre Memorial Lonergan Conference, March 22–24, 1991*, Timothy Fallon, ed., 16 May 1991; Sophie McGrath, 'Theology and Women's History, *Compass Theology Review* 25 (1991) 36–43; and Cynthia Crysdale, 'Lonergan and Feminism,' *Theological Studies* 53 (1992) 234–56.

14 This general figure includes the years 1980–92. The figure goes up if one includes doctoral dissertations (approximately twenty-three) and master's theses (approximately eight). At the same time, the history of Lonergan's thought reveals the important role of women in promoting and publicizing his ideas. The names of Cathleen Going and Charlotte Tansey stand out in reference to the Thomas More Institute in Montreal (where Lonergan first explored many of his ideas with Eric O'Connor and others), and Therese Mason was instrumental in bringing Lonergan to continuing education in Toronto, through Discovery Theater. Publications coming from the Thomas More Institute include: P. Lambert, C. Tansey, and C. Going, eds, *Caring About Meaning: Patterns in the Life of Bernard Lonergan* (TMI papers, 1982) [an autobiographical interview with Lonergan]; C. Going, ed., *Dialogues in Celebration* (TMI papers, 1980) [interviews with many Lonergan scholars and Lonergan himself]; and Elaine Cahn and C. Going, *The Question as Commitment* (TMI papers, 1979) [interviews with E. Voeglin, B. Lonergan, and others by E. Cahn and C. Tansey].

The 'next' generation of Lonergan scholars includes Nancy Ring, Denise Lardner Carmody, Eileen De Neeve, and Elizabeth Morelli. More recently, the number of women doing graduate work using Lonergan has burgeoned. Publications by 'third generation' women include works by Carla Mae Streeter, Margaret Mary Kelleher, Cynthia Crysdale, Carole Skrenes, and JoAnn Eigelsbach. Clearly, there has been no lack of interest in Lonergan among women and laypersons. However, the voices of these women are just beginning to be heard with regularity in public academic fora.

15 In the many anthologies of writings about Lonergan's method that have been published over the last twenty years women are very minimally represented. Most of these volumes are papers from workshops or symposia dedicated to Lonergan's thought, in which women likewise had little visibility. In a decade or more of publications of Lonergan Workshop volumes (vols. 1–8, 1978–90), only two women are included: Cathleen Going (vol. 3) and Nancy Ring (vol. 4). Other women contributors include Nancy Ring and Mary Gerhart in Matthew Lamb, ed., *Creativity and Method: Essays in Honor of Bernard Lonergan* (Milwaukee: Marquette University Press, 1981); Elizabeth

Morelli and Eileen De Neeve in T.P. Fallon and P.B. Riley, eds, *Religion and Culture: Essays in Honor of Bernard Lonergan, S.J.* (Albany: State University of New York, 1987); and Denise L. Carmody and Jean Higgins in Vernon Gregson, ed., *The Desires of the Human Heart: An Introduction to the Theology of Bernard Lonergan* (New York: Paulist Press, 1988). *Method: Journal of Lonergan Studies* has been published since 1983 and includes two book reviews by Eileen De Neeve (March 1985; March 1990) and an article by Elizabeth Morelli (vol. 6, 1988). Other exceptions would include the women involved in interviewing and in editing the papers published by the Thomas More Institute, cited in note 14 above.

16 Note the exceptions to this rule listed above, n. 13. I should also mention that, within my own experience, many Lonergan scholars are well aware of feminist critical thought and look to women's experience as a resource for theology. These would include (but would not be limited by) persons such as Walter Conn, Sebastian Moore, Robert Doran, Michael Vertin, and Frederick Crowe. I well remember a dinner party at which Fred Crowe surprised my husband by asking whether he had taken my surname or I had taken his; as the evening unfolded Father Crowe made his sympathies evident as he waxed eloquent about the need for female imagery to renew not only private prayer but the public prayer life of the Church as well.

17 See, for example, Walter E. Conn, *Christian Conversion: A Developmental Interpretation of Autonomy and Surrender* (New York: Paulist Press, 1986); Robert M. Doran, *Psychic Conversion and Theological Foundations: Toward a Reorientation of the Human Sciences* (Chico, CA: Scholars Press, 1981); Tad Dunne, *Lonergan and Spirituality: Towards a Spiritual Integration* (Chicago: Loyola University Press, 1985); Vernon Gregson, *Lonergan, Spirituality, and the Meeting of Religions* (Lanham, MD: University Press of America, 1985); and Sebastian Moore, *Jesus, the Liberator of Desire* (New York: Crossroad, 1989).

18 See, for example, Fred Lawrence, 'Transcendence as Interruption: Theology in a Political Mode,' in A.M. Olson and L.S. Rouner, eds, *Transcendence and the Sacred* (Notre Dame: University of Notre Dame Press, 1981). See also Lawrence, ed., *Communicating a Dangerous Memory: Soundings in Political Theology* (Atlanta: Scholars Press, 1987); and Matthew L. Lamb, *Solidarity with Victims: Toward a Theology of Social Transformation* (New York: Crossroad, 1982).

19 William Johnston, *The Inner Eye of Love: Mysticism and Religion* (San Francisco: Harper and Row, 1978).

20 For a sample of the application of Lonergan's thought to various cultures see: Hsien-Chih Wang, 'The Concept of Nature of Tao-Teh-Ching and Its Theological Meaning: A Search for a Methodology of a Chinese Contextual Theology,' *South East Asia Journal of Theology* 19 (1978) 118–31; Vicente Marasigan, 'Southeast Asian Shamanism: Liturgical Dramatization,' *East*

Asian Pastoral Review 20 (1983/84) 353–56, and *A Banahaw Guru: Symbolic Deeds of Agapito Illustrisimo* (Manila: Ateneo do Manila University Press, 1985); Walter L. Ysaac, ed., *The Third World and Bernard Lonergan: A Tribute to a Concerned Thinker* (Manila: Cardinal Bea Institute Press, 1986); J. Eduardo Perez Valera, 'The Flower from Lonergan's *Insight: Method*,' *Katorikku Kenkyu* [A Japanese journal of Catholic studies] 25 (1986) 121–55; Frank Fletcher, 'Gospel and Australian Culture: The Role of Personal Spiritual Experience and Praxis,' *Compass Theology Review* 21 (1987) 2–6; and Brian Cronin, 'Religious and Christian Conversion in an African Context,' *African Christian Studies* 3 (1987) 19–35.

21 Regarding homosexuality, Michael Vertin is currently working on the issue as part of a forthcoming book. See also Daniel A. Helminiak, 'The Trinitarian Vocation of the Gay Community,' *Pastoral Psychology* 36 (1987–88) 100–111. With reference to the conception of human life, Thomas Daly has done much work on this issue in Australia. See, for example, 'When Does Human Life Begin? The Search for a Marker Event,' in K. Dawson and J. Hudson, eds, *Proceedings of the Conference. IVF: The Current Debate* (Melbourne: Monash University Center for Human Bioethics, n.d.) 75–89. See also Frederick E. Crowe, 'The Life of the Unborn: Notions from Bernard Lonergan,' in Michael Vertin, ed., *Appropriating the Lonergan Idea* (Washington: Catholic University Press of America, 1989) 360–69.

22 See, for example, Lamb, ed., *Creativity and Method*.

The Genus 'Lonergan and ...' and Feminism

ABSTRACT   *The article starts from the genus 'Lonergan and ...,' examines what is involved in 'applying' the ideas of a generalist thinker like
Lonergan to a particular topic like feminism, and focuses on the need for
intelligent (fuller and more determinate understanding) rather than merely
logical mediation.*

*Samples of the fuller understanding needed in the transition from general
to particular are found in Lonergan's own writings: in the use of the classical laws of science, of Toynbee's ideal types in history, of the proverbial wisdom of common sense; in the mediation of the human sciences in a way of
life; and in moving from transcendental notions to determinate knowledge.
Some difficulties of the task are noted.*

*A second part brings these findings to the topic of this volume, acknowl-
edges the need for the human sciences, but suggests the possibility of a contribution from the personal experience of being male or female. Lonergan's
concept of mutual self-mediation is proposed as a useful category in understanding the experienced interrelationship of men and women.*

A book on 'Lonergan and Feminism' is an instance of a genus, 'Lonergan
and ...' The genus itself seems to merit some attention, especially since
instances of the present kind are multiplying (Lonergan and hermeneutics,
Lonergan and communications, and so on), and it occurred to me that
under that general heading I might make a contribution to this collection
of articles, though I hope to offer some suggestions on the particular application as well.

In general, if 'X and Y' is the title of a study, and both X and Y are writers
with something to say on a certain topic, the study may unfold quite simply.

Let us say that the doctrine on God of X and Y is to be compared and evaluated. We collect the data from both authors, interpret each in the appropriate context, set each in the ongoing discussion of the question, point out strengths and weaknesses, see them in a complementary, genetic, or dialectical relationship, and perhaps argue for the superiority of one over the other. The task is fairly straightforward.

The case could be somewhat different when X is an author and Y is a topic. Then it may still be, in some cases, a relatively simple matter: X has something to say on the question Y, and our task is still one of collecting and interpreting the data, locating X in the movements of the time, evaluating his or her contribution, and possibly taking a position in regard to it. But it may also happen that X is a thinker of the generalist type, whose ideas have applications in areas that X never personally studied, applications not only in Y but also in A, B, C, and so on without end; then we have the more difficult task of discovering the relevance of X's ideas to those new areas, and pursuing their 'application' (a tricky word, that) in ways X never attempted.

The latter is the particular subdivision of 'Lonergan and ...' that I wish to study. Lonergan certainly belongs to that class of thinkers (not very numerous) who have aimed at fundamental ideas, ideas of a type that should have wide-ranging implications, ramifications, applications, adaptations. It may indeed be possible to find in him explicit ideas on feminist questions, but I think that, independently of such good luck or careful research, we can still expect the fundamental character of his thinking to make it relevant to this volume. I will therefore first set forth the role of Lonergan as a generalist thinker, and ask what it means to 'apply' such a thinker to particular questions; then, in a second part, I will use these general ideas to suggest what might be a profitable approach to some of the questions raised by feminism.

1   General Thought and Its Application: 'Lonergan and ...'

The crux of the question is that Lonergan's thought is extremely general and fundamental (general because fundamental), that projects of the type 'Lonergan and ...' are to some degree particular, and that the transition from general to particular, if it is to advance our knowledge and understanding, requires further insights that will themselves be creative and hard won.

In other words, to 'apply' Lonergan to the particular case is not the simple and obvious matter of applying a yardstick to measure a new quantity.[1] It is not the automatic click of a logic-machine that, given a set of premises, adds the conclusion: all men are mortal, Peter is a man, therefore; or, all women are mortal, Portia is a woman, therefore. Such automatic results are most easily attained when the concepts used are hollow; but fill the concepts with meaningful content, and the matter is not so simple. For example, the mortality of Peter and Portia can be made the same only at the expense of hollowing out to some extent the concept of mortality. In the concrete, I would say, the two mortalities are significantly different: dying is a lifelong process, and the process goes forward differently in male and female. But let us take up these questions in proper order.

1.1 General and Particular

A word first, before we turn to the question of application, on the role Lonergan would assign to a generalist. A key passage is one where, in the context of the formation of philosophy teachers, he sets out the generalist ideal for philosophers: 'they must ... come to understand how arduous is their task. They are to be generalists.'[2] But that is only the beginning; in the turn to the particular (where all knowledge must in the last analysis find its referent) they cannot take the easy path of simply adding a conclusion to premises. Mediating this transition is a far more difficult matter.

> ... it cannot be stressed too strongly that the mediation of the gener-
> alists is intelligent rather than logical: by logical mediation I under-
> stand the process from universal concepts to particular instances as
> just instances; by intelligent mediation I understand the process
> from understanding the universal to understanding the particular.
> The difference between the two is a difference in understanding:
> in logical mediation one understands no more in the instance than
> one did in the universal; in intelligent mediation one adds to the un-
> derstanding of the universal a fuller and more determinate under-
> standing of the particular case. The generalist that is just a logical
> mediator turns out to be an obtuse intruder; the generalist that is an
> intelligent mediator speaks not only his own mind but also the lan-
> guage of his interlocutor.[3]

In other words – to come at once to the point – if Lonergan has something significant to say on the most general topic of the human, and we wish to 'apply' his general thought to the question of being female or male, we must achieve 'a fuller and more determinate understanding' of what it is to be female or male, and thus make the 'application' of the general to the particular – a process by no means simple.

1.2 'Application': Data Samples

There is no proper understanding without data; thus, when Lonergan aimed in *Insight* at understanding understanding, he provided sample after sample of understanding in operation. Can we find parallel samples for understanding his view of the process from general to particular? I believe we can, and will suggest four cases that seem to qualify, and a fifth that is rather special.

There is first the case of adding to the abstract science of 'classical' formulations the additional insights needed to make valid statements about the concrete. For example, you want to put an object into orbit around the earth; you can have all the science you want, in the classical sense of systematic laws, and you will not have enough for the task. 'To apply those laws to any concrete case one still has to have an insight into this concrete situation, an insight that enables one to select these laws rather than those, an insight that grasps what one has to measure in this situation to be able to apply the laws to it. One must have an understanding of the concrete situation to apply even perfect knowledge of physics to it.'[4]

For a second sample, somewhat akin to the first, there is the way Lonergan came to see Arnold Toynbee's contribution to history. From the first he was deeply impressed, but as his critical sense developed, he realized that Toynbee's work should be viewed 'not as an exercise in empirical method, but ... as a formulation of ideal types that would stand to broad historical investigations as mathematics stands to physics.'[5] You cannot create a physics out of a mathematics; you must add the insights of physics. Similarly, you cannot, from ideal types alone, write a history; you must add the insights needed for the particular case.

The procedure for using ideal types has some resemblance to the procedures of common sense, which is a third instance of transition from general to particular. Common sense understands in the same way as the scientific mind. It generalizes too, as science does, and with great abandon, but without the careful control that science exercises, and certainly without zeal for proper form. It 'applies' its general knowledge, but not by formal deduction. 'There is ... a flow of questions, and ... a clustering of insights ... but the cluster is not aimed at arriving at universal definitions and universal propositions that will bear the weight of systematic and rigorous deduction.'[6] 'It follows that where the scientist or the mathematician wants to lay down universal principles that hold in all applications, common sense deals with proverbs. What are proverbs? They are general rules that usually one will find worth while paying attention to. The truth of a proverb is not a premise from which you can deduce conclusions that are going to be found to be true in absolutely every case ... It is a piece of advice that is relevant to the processes of knowing.'[7]

A fourth instance is the role of the sciences, natural and especially human, and of human studies, in mediating theology and philosophy to give meaning and value to a way of life. This case differs somewhat from the previous three: not only does the concrete situation require further understanding, but the human sciences themselves have to be worked out to give that 'fuller and more determinate understanding' we need.

Three works of Lonergan illuminate this mediating process. First, there is his short essay 'The Example of Gibson Winter,' where the issue is the role of human sciences in developing a way of life, and in particular of inculturating the gospel.[8] A second essay is a paper he wrote for the International Theological Commission.[9] The issue is the same: the role of the human sciences in mediating a Christian way of life, specifically, a valid moral theology. The situation is analysed to the extent of considering three cases. There are cases where the science is sufficiently clear, and moral precepts can be laid down, as often happens in medical ethics. There are cases where the 'science is not sufficiently determinate to yield fully concrete applications,' and then Lonergan would advise 'a course of social experimentation'; sociology seems to be an example of a science in this state of uncertainty. And, finally, there are cases where the 'human science is itself open to suspicion. Its representatives are divided ideologically ... The notorious instance at the present time is economics.'[10] A third essay is his unpublished work in that very field of economics. So much did he feel this science to be in need of radical criticism that he devoted the last years of his life to its study.[11] I take that study as paradigmatic: besides the value it has in itself, whatever that may be, it also illustrates the effort we must make for a fuller and more determinate understanding of the human sciences in general if they are to mediate between a theology-philosophy and a way of life.

I have given four samples of moving from a universal to the particular, taking 'universal' in a broad sense that includes the laws of classical science, the ideal types of human action, the generalizations of familiar proverbs, the mediating role of the human sciences between theology and human living – there is a family resemblance in what is required in all these cases. What do you need to move from the abstract laws of science to a particular engineering project? To move from ideal cases of human activity to a particular chapter of history? To use the common sense of your proverbs when you find yourself in an unfamiliar situation? To apply your theology and philosophy to a way of life? Always one adds to the understanding of the universal a fuller and more determinate understanding of the particular.

There is a fifth instance of a transition from general to particular. It is the move from transcendental to categorial, and the transcendental character of Lonergan's thinking makes this, of course, an area of special interest in a volume of the type 'Lonergan and ...'[12]

It has some resemblance to the previous instances, but notable differences, most especially in the sense of 'general.' The other four all begin with determinate knowledge, the knowledge we have through classical science, the knowledge we have through common sense, the knowledge we have through ideal types, or through models, and the knowledge we have through human sciences and scholarship. The transcendental notions are not knowledge in that sense at all; rather, they are purely heuristic, like the notion of being in chapter 12 of *Insight*. Their application is not a matter of a determinate content becoming more determinate; it is a matter of a universal but indeterminate dynamism producing each and every determinate category. They are universal not in the way a universal concept is universal, but universal in the way a comprehensive intention is. To apply them is to move, not from object to object, but from subject to object, from the dynamic intentionality that is innate in the subject to the products and constructions that result from the free exercise of that intentionality.[13]

1.3 'Application': Difficulty of the Process

I have examined five samples of the move from generalist thought to particular cases. In the concrete the fourth comes closest, I think, to the topic of this volume; but the most wide-ranging, and the most powerful by reason of its comprehensive intentionality (not because of any alleged 'abstractness'), is the fifth. There is, however, the same requirement, and the same basic difficulty, in them all: the fuller understanding that must be added.

The difficulty in the first three is to add 'the fuller and more determinate understanding of the particular case' that we spoke of. The fourth has the further difficulty of elaborating the relevant human sciences. The fifth has both these sets of difficulties, along with its own special difficulty of moving from the innate intentionality of the subject to the objectified products and determinate knowledge of the things that are.

The question of that "fuller and more determinate understanding of the particular case' deserves more attention in studies of feminism, since it will remain a personal difficulty for each of us even after the intermediate human sciences have been worked out. I will return to it in the second part of my article. Meanwhile I would recommend that those working on the present question undertake this kind of personal study in some less sensitive area, and thus become acquainted with the process and what it involves.

May I illustrate this by two efforts of my own? Some years ago I was persuaded to speak and write in application of Lonergan's thought to education; lacking the specialization of educators, I still had long experience in being educated and contributed what I could from that personal experience.[14] More recently I felt compelled to write on Canadian identity and

Lonergan's thought on community; lacking again the demography, the political science, the critical history, and the other knowledge that a full treatment would require, I still had long experience in being Canadian, I asked myself what that meant to me, and contributed what I could from that perspective.[15] These two forays into 'fuller and more determinate understanding of the particular case' have helped to show me what is involved in the application of Lonergan to specific areas of thought and how handicapped one is without the human sciences, but also to offer hope of making a limited contribution from the side of experience, though, as I will presently remark, in the area of feminist questions each of us has only half the experience needed.

So much for these two little chapters of autobiography. So much also for the general case of the move from general to particular, or for generalities on the application of a generalist position to concrete instances.

2   '... and Feminism'

My division is indicated by the subtitles 'Lonergan and ...,' for the first part, and ' ... and Feminism,' for the second. That is, first the general pattern for application of a fundamental idea; then, its actual use in questions of feminism.

In this second part, the two steps would normally be: study of what it is to be human in general (or for present purposes, what Lonergan thought it is to be human), and study of what it is to be male or female in particular. But how to handle that first step without writing a treatise is a difficult question, which different contributors will answer in different ways. My own choice is to make certain assumptions, to describe them briefly (I will not say 'defend' them), and to proceed on that basis with my argument, leaving it to readers to determine how much the argument may suffer from a procedure they regard as faulty.[16]

My first assumption then is a traditionally Christian one: 'There is no longer Jew or Greek, there is no longer slave or free, there is no longer male and female; for all of you are one in Christ Jesus' (Galatians 3:28, as in the *New Revised Standard Version*). I take this passage to mean that in Paul's thought there is something, however one may define it, that makes us all one before God. If Paul himself is found to have relied on unexamined suppositions, I would fall back on a more general religious view of a loving God whose purpose it is to save the whole human race.

My other assumption is a more complex matter. I rely, as far as may be needed here, on Lonergan's position that we cannot revise his cognitional structure without using that very structure: 'revision cannot revise its own presuppositions. A reviser cannot appeal to data to deny data, to his new insights to deny insights, to his new formulation to deny formulation, to his reflective grasp to deny reflective grasp.'[17] I say 'as far as may be needed,' for my interest here is determined by the kind of discussion that this volume undertakes. There is an unmediated intersubjective immediacy (say, of parent to parent at the burial of their child) which may bypass the structure and certainly is unaware of it, but we could not discuss that intersubjectivity in the style proper to this volume without using the structure. Objections may certainly be raised at this point, but how to raise them without providing data, interpreting the data, and arguing the point – that is the question.

Still, this assumption needs more explanation, and the first thing needing explanation is the emotion with which men react to Lonergan's position. By 'men' I mean males; women may react to the position too for their own feminist reasons; but I have noticed that men with no feminist agenda can become quite emotional about it. I suspect that this is due to a sense that they are being manipulated from outside rather than being counselled and helped to exploit their own inner resources. It would be interesting, if we could recover the history, to learn how ancient sceptics reacted to the strategy that refuted them simply by getting them to talk, to say something; Lonergan's strategy is an elaboration of that.

But the major point in my explanation is to take a broader view and get Lonergan's position into perspective. We should not take it for granted that there is a one-to-one correspondence between the attention he gave to any one aspect of cognitional and intentionality theory and the importance he attached to that aspect in the integral whole. Certainly, the four-levelled structure of human intentionality, as it rises from experience through understanding and judgment to values and decision, received a great deal of attention from him; certainly, it is central to the picture. But it is not the whole picture; other very general and quite essential features have to be added, and in their context the seemingly rigid structure turns out to be a rather flexible instrument.

There is first the double movement along the structure: development from below upward, and development from above downward. Not only do we move up from experience to values, but we move in the other direction as well, and this movement is prior and more fundamental, for it begins at an early age in the affectivity of the infant.

> On affectivity rests the apprehension of values. On the apprehension of values rests belief. On belief follows the growth in understanding of one who has found a genuine teacher and has been initiated into the study of the masters of the past. Then to confirm one's growth in understanding comes experience made mature and perceptive by one's developed understanding. With experiential confirmation the

inverse process may set in. One now is on one's own. One can appropriate all that one has learnt by proceeding as does the original
thinker who moved from experience to understanding, to sound
judgment, to generous evaluation, to commitment in love, loyalty,
faith.[18]

I suggest that this prior and more fundamental form of development, from
affectivity through values, judgments, and understanding to richer and more
meaningful experience, puts a new light on what may seem a too cerebral
(and is certainly a one-sided) use of a structure beyond revision. But this is
an aspect of Lonergan's thought that we have hardly begun to study.

A second point, one that has received somewhat more attention but is
still far from being exhaustively studied and even more from being fully
exploited, is the role of feelings in being human, and indeed in knowing in
a human way. This role is implicit in that whole development from above
that begins in infancy, but there are also explicit statements that reveal the
wider importance of feelings, in development from below as well as from
above; one good example may suffice: 'Without feelings this experience,
understanding, judgment is paper-thin. The whole mass and momentum of
living is in feeling.'[19] We tend to associate this concern with the later Lonergan, but there is ample evidence for it in the earlier Lonergan too; many of
us were simply slow to notice the data.[20]

A third factor to broaden our perspective is the addition of what we may
call the historical side of consciousness in contrast with its ahistorical structure. The structure is a given that we all use, but the way we use it varies
with all the richness of human differences and human history. Everyone
operates at times in the commonsense pattern of consciousness, but besides
that some of us develop a theoretic pattern, others an artistic pattern, many
of us a religious pattern. Again, there are various conversions: many of us
are given a religious conversion, perhaps most of us achieve a moral and a
psychic conversion, and some few may become intellectually converted.
Further still, there are stages of meaning that successively characterize the
human race in its secular and in its religious development. All these variations can occur without prejudice to a given structure when that structure
is so flexible an instrument.[21]

If these three factors, to which others may be added,[22] dispose the reader
more favourably to the view that we can find a common basis for the discussions of this volume, it remains to note that the complexities that they
add to the discussion discourage any a priori or too hasty analysis of the
differences among tribes, classes, nations, cultures; so, likewise, they caution
great care in assigning causes for the differences between men and women.
It is conceivable that through natural disposition men and women are dif-

ferently involved in the upward or downward movements of development, differently disposed towards the active intentionality of the subject or the feelings of the subject, differently affected by the various conversions, differently situated in the stages of meaning. It is equally conceivable that, if these differences exist, many of them owe more to education and conditioning than they do to a natural disposition, conceivable too that individual men and women, as well as groups and societies, vary in the extent to which they have overcome or are overcoming that education and conditioning. Such matters are not to be settled without study.

So we come to the difficult question of moving from what it is to be human to what it is to be male or female, and we must return to the sciences and human studies, and their indispensable role of mediating between generalist notions and feminist questions. I do not mean that we need the sciences in *all* the everyday events of everyday life. To take a simple example, I do not need any human science to tell me what to do when I see a child running dangerously close to a cliff; spontaneous intersubjectivity acts without stopping to invoke systems of thought. But that is in the world of immediacy, of pure immediacy, and we live only a very small part of our lives there. That very day I may wish to buy grapes for the same child, and find myself in the world mediated by meaning and motivated by value. Where were these grapes grown? Were they harvested by oppressed migrant workers? What stand will I take on the boycott of the oppressors? Inevitably we are drawn into a world where the human sciences and studies play an essential role.

With adaptations the same is true of feminist questions, adaptations that are needed because any natural spontaneity there is between male and female was overlaid in former times by habits that were conditioned. Relationships between men and women that seemed natural then were actually natural only in the way the 'second nature' of a habit is, so that we really did not know what was natural and what was not. Today everything must be questioned. For example, I hesitate now to offer a courtesy that a few years ago would have been 'spontaneous.' Then there was no need for reflection to intervene; now I must reflect on the way my offer will be received. What will she think? What does she think I am thinking? We may soon get tied up in R.D. Laing's *Knots*, where human sciences could be rather helpful.

Leaving to others, however, the study of the relevant human sciences, I will concentrate on the further step that Lonergan introduced between 'classical' laws and concrete situations, one that I would introduce between the human sciences and concrete human situations. Just as classical laws need a fuller and more determinate understanding of the particular case, so also do the human sciences. Perhaps I can profit from my already mentioned forays into education and Canadian identity to say something on a parallel need and a parallel move for the present question. As we can accumulate years of experience as a pupil without ever reflecting on what it means to learn, as I can live all my life in a country without ever reflecting on what my country means to me, so also we can live all our lives as male or female without ever reflecting on what our experience is of being one or the other, without trying to determine what it means to us to be male or female. I wish to offer some suggestions on how to repair this neglect.

A useful context in which to consider the question is that of substance becoming subject. This awkward phrase is recurrent in Lonergan, it has a profound meaning, it is directly relevant to the present question, and so it is worth exploring. We are familiar with the shift in orientation of modern thought that is called the turn to the subject: from metaphysical categories like act and potency, form and matter, we have turned to meaning and value, consciousness and subjectivity, and the like. 'In contemporary philosophy there is a great emphasis on the subject, and this emphasis may easily be traced to the influence of Hegel, Kierkegaard, Nietzsche, Heidegger, Buber.'[23] Lonergan epitomizes this development as moving from substance to subject: 'by speaking of consciousness, we effected the transition from substance to subject. The subject is a substance that is present to itself, that is conscious.'[24]

What we have to note about this pair of words is that it does double duty: 'from substance to subject' can refer to a shift in philosophic *thinking*, but more properly it refers to the existential development in which a substance *becomes* a subject.[25] Thus, at the most elementary level there is 'the emergence of consciousness in the fragmentary form of the dream, where human substance yields place to the human subject.'[26] At the other end of the spectrum on the religious level the same phrase characterizes the difference between the newly baptized infant, who is in Christ Jesus with the being of substance, and one who is advanced in the spiritual life and is in Christ Jesus with the being of subject.[27]

Now these examples show that there is not only a development from substance to subject according to the levels of intentionality, so that we emerge as subjects according to *degrees* of consciousness, but a development also from substance to subject in the way we are human, that is, according to the *differentiations* of our consciousness; and this not only according to the major differentiations, so that we emerge as religious subjects, or artistic subjects, but also according to the minor differentiations of class or nation or whatever. Thus, to take a sample case already used, I was born a Canadian citizen without any experience whatever of what it means to be a Canadian; my being Canadian was a being of substance. But when circumstances led me to reflect on what this meant to me I began to transform this being of substance into a being of subject. And to come finally to the point: I believe a similar transformation is needed to pass from being male or female with the being of substance to being male or female with the being of subject: the difference again is in the conscious attention to what we are.

In mere animals this transition does not occur; there is physical development that breeders watch to determine when male and female characteristics have developed enough for their purposes, but the animal doesn't reflect on this, or consider the needs of its partner, or take any step towards transforming substance into subject. At the animal level in us a similar physical development occurs, and the question is whether it will occur with or without the transformation that turns substance into subject. No doubt a hundred influences are at work to promote or impede this transformation; no doubt, in stable times where the wisdom of a tradition operates in quasi spontaneity, the influence is on the whole beneficent; but if we are to live on the level of our times with the full realization of our potential, we are called to a more reflective appropriation of what we are, more especially in times that are as unstable as ours, with traditions that may be moribund and are in any case widely flouted.

There is, however, a very special difficulty for the human race when we come to reflect on our sexual nature: only half the experience of the race (roughly half – I simplify here the data of biology and psychology) is ours to reflect on. Men cannot reflect on the experience of being woman, nor women on the experience of being man. Fifty million French people can reflect on the experience of being French, but only twenty-five million of them can reflect on what their experience is of being male, and another twenty-five million on what their experience is of being female. This peculiarity, which seems to limit the value of the recommended reflection, can actually, however, be turned to advantage through Lonergan's little-known idea of mutual self-mediation.

In 1963 he did extensive study of the notion of mediation, first in a summer institute on 'Knowledge and Learning' at Gonzaga University, Spokane, and at the end of the summer in a lecture at Thomas More Institute, Montreal.[28] Mediation is a very general term, with applications in the mechanical, organic, psychic, logical, and other fields. Mutual mediation is illustrated mechanically in a watch: 'The function of movement is immediate in the mainspring ... The function of control ... is immediate in the balance wheel ... The two functions mediate each other. The balance wheel controls itself and the mainspring. The mainspring moves itself and the balance wheel.'[29] Self-mediation is illustrated in the growth of an organism, and one can find it in the species as well as in the individual organism.[30] A further grade is seen in the self-mediation of consciousness, and a further one still in the self-mediation of self-consciousness. 'The animal mediates itself not only organically but also intentionally,'[31] and the inward displacement to consciousness 'gives rise to the "we", the intersubjective community.'[32] Then in the area of self-consciousness, we have in human development 'the mediation of autonomy,'[33] reaching its climax in the existential moment 'when one finds out for oneself what one can make of oneself.'[34] 'Again, this disposing of oneself occurs within community and particularly within the three fundamental communities ... marriage ... state ... Church.'[35] 'Just as we extended the notion of mediation in the case of organisms to the perpetuation of the species, so we can say that the community mediates itself by its history.'[36]

I am afraid this is a rather hurried approach to the point I wish to make on the role of mutual self-mediation in human development. But the notion seems to me so significant not only for our common human development but also for our development as male or female that I could not omit it, yet I could include only in ruthlessly abbreviated form the broad context that gives it its full meaning. But we do what we can, and so with this abbreviated context I propose to set forth now what Lonergan means by mutual self-mediation. Perhaps it will be wisest to do so in his own words: 'we remarked of existential decision that it occurs in community, in love, in loyalty, in faith. Just as there is a self-mediation towards autonomy, so there is a mutual self-mediation and its occasion is the encounter in all its forms (meeting, regular meeting, living together).'[37] Various illustrations are given: 'Meeting, falling in love, getting married is a mutual self-mediation ... There is a mutual self-mediation in the education of the infant, the child, the boy or girl ... There is a mutual self-mediation in the relationships of mother and child, father and son, brothers and sisters. There is a mutual self-mediation between equals ... between superiors and inferiors.'[38]

The key word in these passages is 'encounter,' for this links mutual self-mediation at once with the dialectic that Lonergan worked out a few years later in *Method in Theology*, and makes of it, in fact, a very highly specialized case of dialectic. The functional specialties of research, interpretation, and history are concerned with the past but do not achieve an encounter with the past.

They make the data available, they clarify what was meant, they narrate what occurred. Encounter is more. It is meeting persons, appreciating the values they represent, criticizing their defects, and allowing one's living to be challenged at its very roots by their words and by their deeds. Moreover, such an encounter is not just an optional addition to interpretation and to history. Interpretation depends on one's self-understanding; the history one writes depends on one's horizon; and encounter is the one way in which self-understanding and horizon can be put to the test.[39]

We have only to substitute present living people for a word and message coming to us in documents from the past, to see mutual self-mediation as the dialectic of husband and wife, of teacher and pupil, of brother and sister, the dialectic that is operative in almost any meeting of persons, the dialectic that makes illusory the happy ending of a certain old-style novel and shows the authentic realism of the modern novel that stops in the midst of process and leaves ambivalent situations unresolved.[40]

So what does mutual self-mediation offer? I am not being facetious, though I make the point with a certain exaggeration, when I say that it offers what Churchill offered in the dark days of 1940: 'blood, toil, tears and sweat.' Mutual self-mediation is not an answer but the raising of a question. It is not a fact but an invitation. It is not an invitation to be but to become. If accepted it does not inaugurate a state but a process. It is not a sure-fire process but one fraught with uncertainty, ambivalence, false starts, repeated failures. It is an indefinitely ongoing process in which we are being continually challenged and continually responding or failing to respond, responding authentically or responding inauthentically. In brief, it has all the menace of the struggle for authenticity that dialectic is, and it offers no more guarantee of success than dialectic does.

> Human authenticity is not some pure quality, some serene freedom
> from all oversights, all misunderstanding, all mistakes, all sins.
> Rather it consists in a withdrawal from unauthenticity, and the with-
> drawal is never a permanent achievement. It is ever precarious, ever
> to be achieved afresh, ever in great part a matter of uncovering still
> more oversights, acknowledging still further failures to understand,
> correcting still more mistakes, repenting more and more deeply
> hidden sins. Human development, in brief, is largely through the
> resolution of conflicts.[41]

But if mutual self-mediation is fraught with menace it also has the silver lining of promise. It is a continual self-making. As Lonergan kept repeating, 'We are self-completing animals,'[42] and we complete ourselves in a never-ending process and in relation to one another. As method 'is not just a list of materials to be combined in a cake or a medicine' but 'regards recurrent operations, and ... yields ongoing and cumulative results,'[43] so living and meeting and growing in relation to one another is an ongoing series of attempts and successes and failures and renewed attempts.

If that is what mutual self-mediation is, we should not regard it suspiciously as simply a ploy to introduce a male fifth column into the meeting of men and women, or assume that it prejudices results by invoking a position worked out by male thinkers who were careful to exclude the possibility of revision. What it introduces is a method to uncover any fifth column there is and banish it from the scene. What it invokes is an open mind and a ready will. For the key word is encounter, and a chief positive supposition of encounter is that I may be wrong, that I have much to learn, that meeting others will challenge my self-understanding, that it opens up the possibility of growing together, that while failure is always possible so too are repentance after failure, fresh resolve, and renewed efforts.

All this, I venture to suggest, has a direct relevance to the kind of effort this volume makes. For it would add to the list of encounters that Lonergan uses in illustration (husband and wife, brother and sister, and so on) not just another instance but another kind of encounter; in inviting several men and several women to contribute it looks beyond individual persons to a wider collaboration. Besides the mutual self-mediation that two persons may experience as a pair, it envisages the mutual self-mediation that each half of our human race may experience as a unit in relation to the other half. It is a symbol of encounter not only between nations, between churches, between university faculties and between groups of every kind, but of encounter on a global scale between the race of men and the race of women. While it will not achieve the intimate partnership of husband and wife, that model can serve to inspire the partnership of the two halves of God's creation working out our human destiny, not in the parliament of a nation but in the worldwide parliament of men and women – Tennyson's 'Parliament of Man' transposed to the realities of a hundred years later.

In the measure that such attempts succeed, they will, it seems to me, add a new dimension to the Pauline vision in which we grow to the fulness of the body of Christ where there is neither male nor female. For all the emphasis on growing and becoming in relation to others does not alter the fact that what we ultimately become is ourselves, our authentic selves, to be sure, but nevertheless ourselves. That means becoming our authentic male selves and our authentic female selves, and enriching the unity of spiritual fulness that Paul proclaims with the diversity of a material human fulness – the human fulness, that grows with human history, of being men and women. In any case, while we are on the way, our study must surely be, not of feminism, and equally not of masculinism, but of both, and of each in relation to the other. Neither will it be just a study *of*, or a learning *about*, but an *encounter* in mutual self-mediation.[44]

Notes

1 Without venturing into etymology, I suggest that the simplest illustration of 'ply' for present purposes is 'plywood': one layer 'applied' to another. From that we could move to a yardstick being 'applied' to measure a length, then

to standards in general being applied, and so to our usage in the present study.

2   *Method: Journal of Lonergan Studies* 2:2 (October 1984) 32. It was an ideal that Lonergan himself regularly aimed at. For example, at the end of his long exposition in *Insight* of organic, psychic, and human development, he wrote, 'It has all been ... very general. It is meant to be so' (*Insight: A Study of Human Understanding* [London: Longmans, Green and Co., 1957, 478; Toronto: University of Toronto Press, 1992, 503]). There is a short note on his usage of 'general' and 'universal' in *Collection* (*Collected Works of Bernard Lonergan*, vol. 4; Toronto: University of Toronto Press, 1988) 272 (note *d* to chap. 6).

3   *Method: Journal of Lonergan Studies* 2:2 (October 1984) 32–33.

4   *Understanding and Being* (*Collected Works of Bernard Lonergan*, vol. 5; Toronto; University of Toronto Press, 1990) 70; see also 353: there is 'a step between a scientific system and the solution of a concrete scientific problem. That step is the occurrence of an insight that selects which laws are relevant to this concrete situation, which elements in this concrete situation have to be measured, and with what degree of accuracy the laws are to be applied to these elements when we work out a solution, and so on. There's that mediating insight.'

The case of abstract science and the concrete is worked out more fully in *Insight* (1957, 46–53; 1992, 70–76). For present purposes, I note the statement that 'concrete inferences from classical laws suppose not only knowledge of laws and information on some basic situation but also an insight that mediates between the situation and general knowledge' (1957, 51; 1992, 75).

5   *A Third Collection* (New York: Paulist Press, 1985) 178. Again, 'Toynbee thought he was contributing to empirical science. Since then, however, he has recanted. But, I believe, his work remains a contribution not to knowledge of reality, not to hypotheses about reality, but to the ideal types that are intelligible sets of concepts and often prove useful to have to hand when it comes to describing reality or to forming hypotheses about it' (ibid. 10).

In the well-known scissors action of empirical method, ideal types give no more than the upper blade of theory meeting the lower blade of data; it's a case again of the move from general to particular, with the qualification that we may have to add to or revise theory to get the scissors working. We could, I think, associate the role of models to that of ideal types; but there is some discussion of Lonergan's use of the term, models, and I don't wish to get sidetracked into that.

6   *Understanding and Being* 88–89.

7   Ibid. 92. Lonergan continues with a proverb that illustrates this very principle: 'For example, "Look before you leap" is the proverb that governs the point that usually you have to complete your habitual nucleus of insights if

you want to deal in exactly the right fashion with a situation that is a bit
novel, a bit strange, not the sort of thing to which you are accustomed. And
it is a good bit of advice: it hits off exactly the point that the nucleus has to
be completed as soon as the situation ceases to be within the ordinary rou-
tine.'

The ascetical advice to do as Jesus would do provides a simple but classic
instance of the way 'application' of common sense works. Jesus acted in a
different way with Herod, Pilate, the Pharisees, Judas, Peter – the list goes
on and on, and each case has the role of a virtual universal as soon as I
consider it as model. But which of these 'universals' comes nearest to my
present situation? How apply it, with what modification, etc.? Only a further
insight into the concrete present situation will tell me that.

  8 *A Second Collection* (London: Darton, Longman and Todd, 1974; Philadel-
     phia: Westminster, 1975) 189–92. This essay is especially useful for the stra-
     tegy and tactics employed; that is, Lonergan does not feel responsibility here
     for creating the sciences needed; he simply goes to those who are already
     expert in them.

  9 'Moral Theology and the Human Sciences,' File 105.31 of the Lonergan
     papers, Archives, Lonergan Research Institute, Toronto. The covering letter
     to Cardinal Seper is dated 28 February 1974.

 10 'Moral Theology' 1.

 11 Lonergan's work in economics is extant in manuscript under the title 'Essay
     in Circulation Analysis'; it will be vol. 15 in the *Collected Works of Bernard
     Lonergan* (University of Toronto Press). He had given special attention to
     economics in 'Moral Theology'; speaking of the radical critique from an
     independent base needed by some sciences, and illustrating it by Ricoeur's
     critique of Freud, he continued: 'the human science, economics, is in need
     of similar radical criticism.' In economic theory the main variants ('the tradi-
     tional market economy, the Marxist-inspired socialist economy, and the new
     transactional economy constituted by the giant corporations') are all under
     the influence of an ideology, and what is needed in the first place 'is a pure
     economic analysis of the exchange process untainted by any ideology' (p. 16,
     with correction of a misprint). In this case there did not seem to be a Gibson
     Winter to provide guidance, and Lonergan felt compelled to enter the field
     of economics himself.

 12 It is here that the difference between 'Lonergan on ...' and 'Lonergan and
     ...' comes to light. A study of 'Lonergan *on* the Community of the Swiss'
     might result in a single line, 'Lonergan has nothing on the community of the
     Swiss'; but a study with the title 'Lonergan *and* the Community of the Swiss'
     could exploit ('apply') for that instance all his rich thought on community.
     This difference illustrates the difference between mediating and mediated
     functions; in the first we are much more limited by what we find in research,

in the second we can be more creative. This remark, of course, and similar
remarks throughout this essay are true not only of Lonergan, but of other
thinkers of his type.

13 It is this property of the transcendentals, a property shared in due measure
by the functional specialties of *Method in Theology*, that has led some friendly
readers to ask whether the transcendental notions are not a bit thin. They
are thin in determinate content; but, like the intellectual light of Thomas
Aquinas, they have the whole of knowledge in their range of power: 'in
lumine intellectus agentis nobis est quodammodo omnis scientia originaliter
indita' (*De veritate*, q. 10, a. 6: 'in the light of agent intellect all knowledge is,
in some way, originally given to us'). Light, perhaps, might be called thin;
but to those who live in darkness, it is extraordinarily rich in what it enables
them to see, in its potential content.

14 F.E. Crowe, *Old Things and New: A Strategy for Education* (Atlanta: Scholars
Press, 1985).

15 Crowe, *Bernard Lonergan and the Community of Canadians: An Essay in Aid of
Canadian Identity* (Toronto: Lonergan Research Institute, 1992). For this
foray I blame no one. There were no invitations to lecture on the topic.
There was only my conscience prodding me. My country was being torn
apart, Lonergan had a great deal to say on what unites a community and
what tears it apart, I had had more opportunity to study Lonergan's thought
than most Canadians had, and it was on my conscience to bring that thought
to bear on our national identity.
    The role of the sciences, and the complementarity of sciences and per-
sonal experience came home to me in a new light in a third exercise in *docta
ignorantia* when I attempted to write on Lonergan and the life of the
unborn; here I could draw on neither sciences nor experience, but could
only set out what seemed to be relevant ideas from Lonergan and ask others
to determine their usefulness; see 'The Life of the Unborn: Notions from
Bernard Lonergan,' in F.E. Crowe, *Appropriating the Lonergan Idea*, ed.
Michael Vertin (Washington: Catholic University of America Press, 1989)
360–69.

16 I am grateful to the editor of this volume for a careful critical reading of my
article and in particular for alerting me to some objections feminist writers
would have to my procedure; working under some pressure I cannot at the
moment undertake a study of those objections, but I hope to make it possible at least to discern more clearly the differences in our views.

17 *Insight*, 1957, 336; 1992, 360.

18 *A Third Collection* 181.

19 *A Second Collection* 221.

20 It is quite instructive from this point of view to compare the index to 'feel-

ings' in the first edition of *Insight* with the index in the fifth and observe how many entries have been added in the latter.

21 Another instructive exercise is to examine the six canons of empirical method (chap. 3 of *Insight*) and ask whether they pertain to the historical aspect of consciousness or the structural. The first canon is obviously related to the structure, but the second is obviously related to the ongoing history of science, to what happens within the structure.

22 For example, the communal context of individual learning. The contribution of C. Crysdale to this volume corrects a common misapprehension on this point; I am grateful to her for allowing me to read her article in manuscript.

23 *A Second Collection* 69–70. In a note to this passage Lonergan writes as follows: 'One should, perhaps, start from Kant's Copernican revolution, which brought the subject into technical prominence while making only minimal concessions to its reality. The subsequent movement then appears as a series of attempts to win for the subject acknowledgement of its full reality and its functions.'

24 *Topics in Education* chap. 4, #1.3 – lectures Lonergan gave at Xavier University, Cincinnati, in 1959; they have now appeared as vol. 10 of the *Collected Works of Bernard Lonergan* (Toronto: University of Toronto Press, 1993); the quoted passage is on p. 83.

25 There is a helpful parallel in *Insight* between cognitional process and the 'reciprocal notion' of world process: 'For it is not only our notion of being that is heuristic, that heads for an objective that can be defined only in terms of the process of knowing it, but also the reality of proportionate being itself exhibits a similar incompleteness and a similar dynamic orientation towards a completeness that becomes determinate only in the process of completion' (1958, 444; 1992, 470). The 'reciprocal' pair in question here are the turn from substance to subject in *thought*, and the development from substance to subject in our existential *becoming*.

26 *A Third Collection* 208.

27 *Collection* 231.

28 'The Mediation of Christ in Prayer,' *Method: Journal of Lonergan Studies* 2:1 (March 1984) 1–20. In the first seven sections the editor, Mark Morelli, has 'integrated the two sources' (the Gonzaga University notes, and the Thomas More Institute tape-recording); the last section (on prayer) is from the tape alone (p. 19, n. 1).

29 Ibid. 4.

30 Ibid. 6–7.

31 Ibid. 8.

32 Ibid. 9.

33 Ibid.

34 Ibid. 10.

35 Ibid.

36 Ibid. 11.

37 Ibid. 13.

38 Ibid.

39 *Method in Theology* 247.

40 In his lectures on mutual self-mediation Lonergan makes a remark that I find highly suggestive for further study: 'The exploration of the field of mutual self-mediation is perhaps the work of the novelist'; he returns to the point a moment later: 'Mutual self-mediation proves the inexhaustible theme of dramatists and novelists.' I believe there is no better way to obtain a real apprehension of his meaning than to examine novels and plays under this heading of mutual self-mediation, but to illustrate this is perhaps a separate task.

41 *Method in Theology* 252.

42 *A Third Collection* 127, 141, 154, 207, and passim elsewhere.

43 *A Third Collection* 140.

44 I wish to thank Robert Croken for reading this article in typescript and helping me to clarify a number of points.

Woman of Reason: Lonergan and Feminist Epistemology[1]

ABSTRACT *This paper proposes that Lonergan's account of human knowing can complement feminist insights and illuminate problems in contemporary feminist epistemology. Many feminists have criticized the objectivist strains in the philosophical tradition, arguing that objectivism has failed to attend to the 'situatedness' of knowers, has excluded both women and typically feminine ways of thinking, and has served as a mask for men's power over women. Feminists have turned to 'postmodern' philosophers such as Richard Rorty for an alternative. Yet such feminists as Lorraine Code and Sandra Harding have argued that, because of its epistemological relativism, postmodernism is incompatible both with feminists' political goals and with women's belief that their experiences, as well as their knowledge, have some kind of objective validity.*

Lonergan offers an alternative to both objectivism and relativism. While he would agree with postmodernists (and feminists) that all judgments are made by 'situated' knowers, he avoids the relativistic implications and the endless play of possibility often associated with anti-objectivist thought. Moreover, Lonergan offers precise ways of articulating both women's contribution to knowledge and the workings of patriarchal bias. In turn, feminism offers to Lonergan scholars a rich account of the workings of bias in thought, culture, and society.

To those who have heard of feminism casually, but who have not taken the time to study it in any depth, the word 'feminism' conjures up a predictable set of images and associations. Those associations range from the cultural caricature of the feminist as a humourless, hostile ideologue, to the image of the feminist as heroine of women's political struggle. Someone with a superficial acquaintance with feminist thought could offer a few phrases that go beyond these cultural images, phrases such as 'women's experience,' 'the critique of patriarchy,' and 'women's ways of knowing.' To be superficially acquainted with feminism is to see it as a single movement that can be summarized in such images and catch-phrases. Examined more closely, however, feminism begins to fragment, the way a mosaic, which at a distance looks like a seamless picture, breaks up into multiple patches of colour when approached more closely. Thinkers who identify themselves as feminists can and do disagree profoundly over such basic issues as what feminism is, what its goals should be, what it should have to say about gender difference, and – the topic of this paper – what kind of epistemology is properly 'feminist.'[2]

It is in these cracks in the feminist mosaic that I find hope of a dialogue between feminism and students of Lonergan. If feminism as a movement is not a seamless picture, if there is room for disagreement and for dialogue about even very basic issues, then perhaps even a Thomist might find a place in the feminist conversation. On the face of things, certainly, a dialogue between feminists and Lonergan on epistemology seems wildly improbable. For one of the dominant motifs of contemporary feminism has been its critique of traditional epistemologies. Feminists appear to have much more in common with 'postmodern' philosophical critics of foundationalism and objectivism than they do with someone like Lonergan, whose thought is deeply rooted in Platonic, Aristotelian, Thomist, and modern scientific thinking.[3] However improbable, I would like to open up such a dialogue, and to claim in its course that Lonergan's epistemology is *more* potentially empowering to feminists than is the 'postmodern' epistemology currently predominant in feminist circles.

1   Feminism and the Critique of Epistemology

Although feminists have explored or embraced a variety of epistemological positions, most agree about what they are *against*: feminists oppose the positivist and objectivist strains within the philosophical tradition.[4] Along with many others, feminists have rejected the notion that knowledge is a 'view from nowhere,' in Thomas Nagel's evocative phrase, that is, that to know something is to purge one's mind of prejudice, to encounter objects in a way that is uncorrupted by the peculiarities of one's language, one's education, one's desires, one's feelings, or one's values.[5] Scientific method, in this view, enables the 'man of reason' to overcome subjective influences in order to encounter the natural or the social world in its purity and independence.[6]

Despite its former power, such an objectivistic account of reason is in our day almost too feeble to fight back against the many attacks it has endured.

It is enough to recite the names 'Marx, Nietzsche, and Freud' in order to call up the most devastating objections against reason's claims to be free from irrational influences. Phenomenologists, pragmatists, critical theorists, hermeneuticists, and social constructionists, for all their philosophical differences, have in common their critiques of the Cartesian and positivist ideals of science, which are now widely believed to rest on an exaggerated estimation of the human ability to step outside our own finite perspectives.[7]

Feminists have deepened the critique of objectivist epistemology by exploring the ways that this epistemology is oppressive to women.[8] It is not news that most of the great philosophers in the Western tradition have explicitly denied that women possess the same rational capacities as men. In the realm of ethical reasoning, in particular, women have often been said to lack men's superior ability to think in universal and impartial terms.[9] But feminists have gone beyond stating this obvious (and, it might appear, easily correctable) fact. In works such as Susan Bordo's *The Flight to Objectivity*, Genevieve Lloyd's *The Man of Reason*, and Nancy Tuana's *Woman and the History of Philosophy*, feminist authors have argued that the epistemological reflections of Plato, Aristotle, Augustine, Descartes, Rousseau, Hume, Kant, and Hegel not only explicitly exclude *women* from full rationality, but that the ideals of rationality that they celebrate are often inextricably connected to habits of mind and traits of character that are culturally defined as masculine. To take Descartes as an example, Susan Bordo argues that his epistemological project rejects the maternal, 'organic universe' of the Middle Ages with its (more feminine) 'participating consciousness,' and replaces it with a masculine ideal of reason as detached, distantiated, and autonomous.[10] Genevieve Lloyd points out that the Cartesian ideal of reason implicitly excludes women, who 'have been assigned responsibility for that realm of the sensuous which the Cartesian Man of Reason must transcend, if he is to have true knowledge of things.' Women, she argues, are expected to keep intact for men the realm of the 'intermingling of mind and body.'[11] Nancy Tuana argues that a woman who wished to pursue Cartesian rationality

> would have to deny all that is seen as female – attachment to individuals, private interests, maternal feelings. She would have to learn to be cool, dispassionate, impersonal, distant, detached. She would have to deny the many voices of her upbringing and culture whose definition of her would preclude her success in the arduous training required for the life of reason, for all the traits needed for this life are stereotypically masculine. Even the positive characteristics associated with the feminine, such as empathy, nurturance, and imagina-

tion, would have to be rejected, for they are relegated to the irrational in the Cartesian system.[12]

Feminist critics of natural and social science, too, have complained that purportedly objective and value-free research has often served to reinforce the oppression of women. In *Whose Science? Whose Rationality?* Sandra Harding cites, as examples of such critics, Ruth Hubbard and Carol Gilligan. In 'Have Only Men Evolved?' Hubbard uncovers the ways in which females have been omitted from the history of human evolution. Similarly, Gilligan's *In a Different Voice* exposes the fallacy of 'failing to question why women's responses to moral dilemmas do not comfortably fit categories designed to receive men's responses.'[13]

By highlighting the ways in which objectivist epistemology excludes both women and feminine traits, as well as the way it often serves to put a respectable face upon power masquerading as unbiased knowledge, feminists have added a fascinating dimension to the contemporary critique of objectivism. But raising such issues has left feminists with the further, thorny question of whether there is a properly 'feminist' alternative to objectivism, and if so, what that alternative is.

2   Epistemological Options: Objectivism and Relativism

In constructing an alternative to objectivism, what options do feminists have? One possible feminist epistemology is what Sandra Harding calls 'feminist empiricism.'[14] As Harding points out, feminist empiricism is not an alternative to objectivism so much as a critique of the ways that scientists in particular have failed to live up to their own ideals. In writings such as those of Hubbard and Gilligan mentioned above, feminists have criticized scientists for 'androcentric bias,' in the design and execution of their research. The feminist empiricist would like to see scientific research maintain its goal of unbiased knowledge, but clean up its act by no longer excluding women or defining them as defective men.[15]

Simply to criticize scientists for failing to live up to their own ideals of unprejudiced methodical inquiry, however, is a problematic strategy for feminists, for it fails to take into account both the widespread criticisms of those ideals and the way that the ideals themselves exclude 'feminine' qualities. If, then, objectivist epistemology is to be rejected, in part because it ignores the ineradicable bias of all knowers, feminists have a second option: to adopt a radically relativistic epistemology (which is sometimes termed 'postmodern').

This second option has been described in detail in an essay by Kenneth Gergen. Drawing upon the work of Wittgenstein, J.L. Austin, and Richard

Rorty, Gergen has described four theses of a postmodern epistemology: first, 'knowledge claims may properly be viewed as forms of discourse.'[16] That is, because the mind is not a mirror representing the world, knowledge claims do not refer to the world but to 'the process of discourse.' Indeed, to speak of 'mind' at all is for Gergen to invoke an untenable dualism between mind and speech. Second, postmodern epistemology, as Gergen uses the term, claims that 'what there is does not in itself dictate the properties of the discourse by which intelligibility is rendered.' Gergen argues that, because all data are 'interpreted,' there are no independent or objective data that can be used to validate or invalidate any interpretation. Third, 'because discourse is inherently social we may look to social process for an understanding of how knowledge claims are justified.' On this account, scientific discovery is a matter of interactions between scientists rather than between scientists and a world represented in scientific theory. Finally, postmodernism claims that 'because knowledge claims are constitutive of social life they should properly be opened to evaluation by the full range of discursive communities.' Feminists, he argues, as well as anyone else affected by science, should be allowed to criticize the ways in which science is biased against females or other particular groups.[17]

Gergen offers the foregoing position as a properly feminist epistemology. Clearly, such an epistemology is compatible with feminists' belief that all human knowledge is inevitably affected by the subjectivity of the knower, that no one, as the metaphor goes, can step over his (or her) own shadow. Gergen urges feminists to accept that if they assert that every claim to knowledge is biased they must admit that their own position is as biased and impossible to validate as anyone else's. He proposes that, in view of this implication of the feminist critique of objectivism, feminists should learn to see the feminist project as a dialogue about 'social practices' rather than a struggle over true or false versions of reality.[18]

Should feminists be satisfied with the postmodernist option? Perhaps they should not accept it without examining the matter further. First, let me point out that Gergen's defence of postmodernism rests, like Rorty's, on an assumption that he shares with objectivist epistemology, to wit: to know the real world is to know the world as independent of human subjective bias. To know the real world, according to both objectivists and postmodernists, would be to experience a 'raw feel,' that is, to have unmediated contact with reality, to reflect reality like a flawless mirror that neither adds to nor subtracts from that which it reflects. Rorty shares with objectivism the further assumption that, if such pure reflection is impossible, knowledge of the real world is impossible. Where he parts company with objectivism is in saying that such pure knowledge cannot exist.[19]

But what if the choice between objectivism and the epistemological relativism of postmodernism rests upon a false dilemma? That is, what if there is a third possibility: that knowledge might be both 'subjective' and 'objective,' that the knower might be both 'situated' and self-transcendent? It is this third possibility that many feminists, uneasy with the prospective marriage between feminism and postmodernism, have called for. Sandra Harding, for one, rejects 'the fruitless and depressing choice between value-neutral objectivity and judgmental relativism,'[20] and complains that 'the Postmodernist critics of feminist science, like the most positivist of modernity's thinkers, appear to assume that if one gives up the goal of telling one true story about reality, one must also give up trying to tell less false stories.'[21] Lorraine Code, too, in her recent *What Can She Know?* criticizes philosophers for seeing only the two alternatives of relativism and objectivism: 'Philosophers tend to argue that if knowledge is less than purely objective, then it must follow that reality itself is socially constructed: there are *no* facts of the matter and hence there is no point in trying to discover how things "really" are.'[22]

Feminists' desire to find a third alternative to objectivism and relativism arises in part from the suspicion that postmodernist assumptions are incompatible with feminist goals. Sondra Farganis asserts that feminist social science, 'in its commitment to feminism, is imbued with a moral dimension; thus, it runs counter to the relativism and the ethical neutrality held to govern both contemporary philosophy and science.' Rather than embrace epistemological relativism, she argues, 'feminism as a political movement must try to create the conditions whereby we can intelligently and reasonably agree upon substantive values.'[23] Code points out that the feminist projects of investigating 'sexism, class and racial injustices, women's oppressions, or women's biological experiences' are rendered meaningless by an epistemological position that says, in effect, that such things are 'all in [women's] minds.' According to Code, 'a contention that there are *no* objective social realities would obliterate the purpose of feminist political projects.'[24] These feminists are not ready to accept that feminist claims concerning oppression, or their attempts to show the value of qualities historically labelled as feminine, are only moves within a closed universe of discourse. Sandra Harding echoes such concerns when she argues that, despite the fact that the notion of objectivity has often been used to oppress and marginalize women, nevertheless the only alternative to having some standards of objectivity is that 'might makes right in knowledge-seeking just as it tends to do in morals and politics.'[25] Indeed, she argues, appeals to objectivity have often served oppressed groups in their struggles against entrenched beliefs.[26]

In spite of sharing the postmodern criticisms of objectivism, then, Code, Harding, and other feminists see the epistemological relativism of postmodernism as unable to account for the differences between valid and invalid claims to possess knowledge. They also see epistemological relativism as incompatible with the feminist goal of taking women's experience, and the kinds of understanding that can arise from it, seriously. Clearly, there is a way in which epistemological relativism, for all its celebration of difference, remains indifferent to anyone's claim to be 'right' about anything, and thus takes the urgency out of debates that many feminists find important. That indifference has fuelled feminists' search for another epistemological option.

3   A Feminist Third Alternative

What might a feminist third alternative look like? Both Sandra Harding and Lorraine Code propose that, while a feminist epistemology must acknowledge the role of prejudice in shaping knowledge, feminists should distinguish between those prejudices (or presuppositions) that are legitimate and those that are illegitimate. In calling for such a distinction, Code and Harding take a leaf from Hans-Georg Gadamer's *Truth and Method*.[27] Gadamer has argued that part of the legacy of the Enlightenment is a 'prejudice against prejudice.' As I pointed out above, modern objectivists have followed Descartes in idealizing the autonomous knower and assigning dubious epistemological status to beliefs that are influenced by education, upbringing, language, and so forth. Only 'unprejudiced' or presuppositionless knowledge is reliable, on the objectivist view. Gadamer argues that there is no such thing as an unprejudiced knower. Understanding always occurs within a 'horizon,' of language, culture, education, and history, within which certain questions – and thus certain answers – occur (and others do not). But for Gadamer the fact that all understanding is 'prejudiced' in this sense does not mean that there are no correct or incorrect answers to questions. Through a process of question and answer that takes its inspiration from Platonic dialogue, one attempts, for Gadamer, to acknowledge one's situatedness and to reinforce legitimate prejudices while undermining illegitimate ones.[28]

Code and Harding agree that the search for knowledge never occurs in a vacuum; all questions arise from some kind of presupposed background of ideas. Code proposes that, in contrast to the objectivist ideal of the autonomous knower, knowledge should rather be sought using an 'ecological' model. This model begins from the premise that all knowing occurs within an environment in which knowers depend on one another for their information and beliefs. The goal of 'ecological' epistemology, for Code, is not to do away with the interdependence of knowers but to restructure the social environment in such a way as to promote a kind of political friendship, allowing dialogue to occur and undermining the epistemological distortions that are said to arise from differences in power and authority.[29] Code envisions a situation in which people who are usually not considered to be 'knowers' or 'experts' are acknowledged for the expertise they have concerning their own (oppressive) circumstances.

However, despite her belief that the experiences of socially and politically oppressed people, including women, have a kind of authority, Code is cautious about uncritically celebrating traditionally 'feminine' traits such as emotion and maternal care. While she sees the value in feminists' appreciation of such traits, she also fears the damage that can be done to both women and men by stereotyping. Code's 'ecological' epistemology is feminist, then, not primarily in celebrating 'feminine' values of interdependence (although it does that), but rather in its goal of listening both respectfully and critically to women's experiences.

Although Code prefers to call her third alternative 'mitigated relativism,' rather than 'mitigated objectivism,' she strongly rejects unmitigated epistemological relativism.'[30] And, while she shares the overall feminist goal of respecting women's experiences, she particularly objects to the kind of relativism that celebrates *anyone's* experience without any critical assessment of what 'experience' really means, that is, what kind of 'knowing' one can claim to have on the basis of one's experience.[31]

As noted above, Harding agrees with Code that all knowers are 'situated,' and that knowers' situations give rise to both legitimate and illegitimate presuppositions. She defends 'feminist standpoint theory,' an account of epistemology that developed out of Marxism, which argues that dominant groups within a society know the world in a more distorted and partial fashion than do dominated groups.[32] According to feminist standpoint theory, women bring a valuable 'outsider's' or 'stranger's' perspective to the understanding of societies ruled by men; women have less interest in maintaining the status quo than men do and so are more free to question it; women see the oppressive effects of sexist social practices more easily than men do because they experience those effects personally; women who do 'women's work' are less likely than men to allow the everyday tasks of living to become invisible to social theory.[33]

Like Code, then, Harding believes that any social scientist's claim to possess knowledge must take women's experiences into account. Like Code, too, Harding does not think that women's experiences or women's perspectives *by themselves* constitute knowledge. Rather, she calls for the development of theories that take women's experiences as a starting-point and that move on to make general explanatory claims.[34]

Feminists such as Code and Harding seek, then, to show that objectivism and postmodern relativism are not the only two epistemological alternatives for feminists. They propose that there exists a third option: a mitigated relativism or a standpoint theory that acknowledges that, although no one possesses absolute truth, nevertheless not all claims to knowledge are equally valid. For these feminists, unless such a third alternative exists, women have no grounds for saying that our experience is uniquely valuable or that our lives have in the past been falsely characterized by mainstream natural and social science.

4   Lonergan and Feminism

What does Lonergan have to offer to feminists seeking to articulate such an alternative epistemology?[35] Let me begin by recalling some basics of Lonergan's cognitional theory. For Lonergan, human knowing is a recurrent pattern of operations, consisting most basically of experience, understanding, and judgment, and leading finally to an act of decision. Sensory experience (as well as experience of the data of consciousness) gives rise to the question 'What is it?', which in turn gives rise, if one is lucky, to insights, and then to the further question 'Is it so?, that is, 'Is my insight correct?' One can make a *judgment* to the effect that one's insight is correct or incorrect once all further relevant questions have been answered. Finally, having made a judgment of fact, one responds by asking, and then deciding, what one should do in response to that judgment.

In working out the implications of this cognitional theory, Lonergan foreshadowed many of the contemporary criticisms of what is now called objectivism. First, he insists, contrary to the empiricist strain of objectivism, that knowledge is not like 'taking a look' at what Lonergan calls the 'already out there now real.'[36] For Lonergan, knowers move from the infant's world of immediate experience to a world 'mediated by meaning,' and although unmediated experience of objects does occur, such experience is only a preliminary to knowledge; it is not the goal of scientific or any other method of acquiring knowledge. Acts of seeing, hearing, and touching are of limited epistemological significance unless there unfolds out of them a process of questioning that leads to understanding, judgment, and decision. These latter three 'mediating' acts are related directly to words, images, and symbols and only indirectly to objects. Yet it is in these mediating activities, particularly in the act of judgment, that objectivity is found.

Unlike thinkers of the postmodern movement, Lonergan does *not* say that knowing, if we were capable of it, *would be* like taking a good look at things (or reflecting them, like a mirror), or that it would consist in an immediate experience of objects. Immediate experience of objects is not objectivity but a preliminary step towards the objectivity that is the culmination of a whole process of asking and answering questions. For Lonergan, then, we do know the real world but not in the immediate way that both objectivists and postmodernists believe it must be known. Human knowledge is *both* objective and mediate. Thus Lonergan takes up a third alternative, like those of Harding and Code that I discussed earlier. Lonergan's version of the 'third alternative' is, paradoxically, both traditionalist and revolutionary. It is traditional insofar as he traces the key elements of his cognitional theory to St Thomas Aquinas; it is revolutionary in that Lonergan questions the very starting-point of modern epistemology: the subject standing over against objects, attempting to build a bridge to them, to know them as they are independent of human subjectivity. Lonergan's knowing subject is immediately directed to the real through his or her *questions*. The questioning process is the unfolding of human nature in its desire to know what is true and to appreciate what is good. Judgments of fact and of value are the culmination of that process.

Like Code and Harding, then, Lonergan rejects the objectivist ideal of the knower as having a perfect view of everything that exists. With them, he accepts that all knowers are 'situated,' that one who seeks knowledge never begins from scratch. According to Lonergan, in the formation and pursuit of questions people draw upon the common meanings that have come to them through what is variously called education, acculturation, and socialization.[37] Most of what anyone claims to know has not been verified by that person independently. Rather, each of us is part of a web of belief, like the person reading a map, who depends not only on the mapmaker but on every source the mapmaker used. Lonergan argues that even the scientist, thought to be the paradigm of the independent knower, personally verifies very little of what he or she claims to know.

In acknowledging that people depend on others for most of what they know, Lonergan suggests neither that we should believe only what we can confirm individually nor that we should believe everything that is part of the common fund of information. Rather, like Code and Harding, he sees belief as both a gift and a possible trap. Without the beliefs inherited from ancestors, each successive generation would have to begin from scratch, and human progress would be impossible.[38] Thus, Lonergan rejects the positivist vision in which the ideal knower begins with an 'empty head,' leaving all his prejudices aside.[39] Still, Lonergan also admits that the common fund of information, attitudes, and values from which each of us draws 'may suffer from blindspots, oversights, errors, bias.'[40] Instead of eliminating their beliefs, he argues, people should be attentive to possible errors that have become part of the common fund.[41] Rather than disbelieving in authorities, texts, and traditions, one should determine which ones are worthy of one's belief.

How is one to discover errors in one's common sense, or determine which experts deserve to be believed? For Lonergan, it is through the faithful raising and answering of questions – what he has called fidelity to the pure and unrestricted desire to know. Such fidelity requires that one apply what Lonergan calls the 'transcendental precepts,' to 'Be attentive, Be intelligent, Be reasonable, Be responsible.'[42] One should, in other words, pay attention to one's experiences, allow questions to arise and pursue them avidly, inquire whether one's hypotheses are actually the case, make judgments that are neither hasty nor infinitely delayed, and follow up one's judgment of fact with a decision to take action.

Doing all this is more difficult than it may sound, for we must constantly struggle to overcome, both at the personal and the cultural levels, various forms of bias.[43] Lonergan defines bias as 'a block or distortion of intellectual development,' which may have its source in the unconscious depths of the individual psyche, the egoism of an individual, the identification with a group, or in the resistance of persons of common sense to theory.[44] Bias can interfere with the process of knowing by undermining any or all of the transcendental precepts: instead of attentiveness, intelligence, reasonableness, and responsibility, bias substitutes blindness, dullness, rationalization, and inaction. It suppresses questions and blocks images and insights. Because of bias, individuals, groups, and whole cultures can build up self-serving fictions in place of potentially painful realities, or in place of realities that demand self-transformation.

5   Lonergan as Feminist Resource

We have seen above that Lorraine Code and Sandra Harding are concerned, like Lonergan, to uncover and overcome the errors that have become part of our webs of belief. If Harding and Code were to propose their own 'transcendental precepts,' they would certainly include the commands to 'Respect women's experiences (and the experiences of all disadvantaged persons),' and to 'Overcome the distortions brought about through differences of power (particularly differences between the power of men and women).' It is possible now to see that these feminist precepts are compatible with Lonergan's account of bias and of the human struggle to overcome it through fidelity to the pure desire to know. I would contend that the patriarchal bias towards women and the feminine can be easily added to the examples of what Lonergan calls the bias of the group.[45] If this is so, then we may extend Lonergan's analysis of bias to the case of 'androcentrism.' Using his analysis, one would expect to find inattention to women's experiences, devaluation of images associated with the feminine, and suppression of questions raised by women or arising from typically feminine experiences. One would expect to find, further, the loss of the further insights, questions of fact, and decisions that might have occurred had women's experiences and questions not been suppressed. And, indeed, there are feminist scholars who have identified bias in each of these forms (although without articulating them within Lonergan's overall framework).

The 'precepts' of Code and Harding and the transcendental precepts of Lonergan thus overlap and complement one another. The work of Harding and Code adds to that of Lonergan a concern to identify the way bias has worked to suppress women and feminine experiences. Lonergan's work, in turn, adds to that of Code and Harding a greater precision concerning the way bias works (by inhibiting experience, understanding, judgment, and decision) and the way it may be overcome (through fidelity to the transcendental precepts).[46] Rather than speaking simply of 'women's experience,' feminists could use Lonergan's terminology in order to distinguish a whole range of feminine contributions to knowledge (that is, not only our experience but our images, questions, insights, and judgments).

Lonergan makes clearer than either Harding or Code (or, for that matter, Gadamer) that within the dialogical play of question and answer, or the conversation among those from differing standpoints, there is a moment of closure. For Lonergan, this moment of closure is the act of judgment, the moment at which one has answered all further relevant questions and can affirm that something is or is not the case.[47] Distinguishing such a moment of closure is important if one wishes to affirm something other than an infinitely open play of arguments and counter-arguments – and especially if one wishes to move to a moment of decision. For this reason, too, Lonergan's cognitional theory may be a helpful resource for feminists.

There are other reasons that feminists might be interested in Lonergan's 'third alternative.' For one, Lonergan, unlike Harding and Code, addresses directly questions of metaphysics. Where they remain vague concerning the nature of the reality revealed by human questioning, Lonergan develops an account of being as having a structure (of potency, form, and act) that is formally identical with the structure of the human mind.[48] For another, Lonergan does more than simply affirm that there is an alternative to objectivism and relativism. He returns, in his writings, to the Humean, Kantian, and other philosophical roots of the present-day debate and questions the assumptions that led past thinkers to deny that an analysis of human subjectivity could lead to any true account of objectivity.[49]

In raising so many issues I have already, perhaps, said too much, since the scope of this paper does not allow me to do justice to them all. My purpose is only to suggest that despite Lonergan's appearance as a thoroughly 'masculist' thinker, his work may provide precisely the resources that feminists such as Code and Harding have been looking for. Appropriating Lonerganian ideas could help feminists to articulate what is wrong with both the objectivist and the postmodern epistemological options and to formulate an alternative to them; it could help them to say precisely how male bias against women has operated in the past and how it may be overcome in the future, and it could add some precision to discussions of 'women's experience.' Thus, in a variety of ways, Lonergan's explanatory account of knowing could further empower feminists.

In turn, Lonerganians have much to learn from feminists. Feminists have quite convincingly shown the presence of anti-feminine bias where Lonergan (and everyone else) had overlooked it.[50] Lonergan scholars who have heretofore ignored or dismissed feminism could greatly deepen their understanding of bias, as well as their self-understanding, by attending to what feminists are saying. My proposal that Lonergan be allowed into the feminist dialogue, then, is not a proposal that he be invited to transform it into a monologue. As Plato knew, in a real conversation, no one escapes without being transformed.

Notes

1 The author would like to thank Cynthia Crysdale, Michael Vertin, Paul Kidder, and an anonymous reviewer for their helpful comments on an earlier draft.

2 For an account of the different feminist schools of thought, see Rosemarie Tong, *Feminist Thought: A Comprehensive Introduction* (Boulder and San Francisco: Westview Press, 1989).

3 The most influential spokesman for the 'postmodern' position I have in mind is Richard Rorty. See especially his *Philosophy and the Mirror of Nature* (Princeton: Princeton University Press, 1979).

4 In order to avoid undue complexity, I will not be discussing the themes of French feminism in this essay. For a comparison between the epistemological themes of French and American feminism, see Arleen B. Dallery, 'The Politics of Writing (the) Body: *Écriture Féminine*,' in Alison M. Jaggar and Susan R. Bordo, eds, *Gender/Body/Knowledge: Feminist Reconstructions of Being and Knowing* (New Brunswick and London: Rutgers University Press, 1989) 52–67.

5 See Thomas Nagel, *The View from Nowhere* (Oxford: Oxford University Press, 1986).

6 See Jaggar and Bordo, eds, *Gender/Body/Knowledge* 2–4.

7 Readers looking for discussions of these issues could turn, for example, to Richard Bernstein, *Beyond Objectivism and Relativism* (Philadelphia: University of Pennsylvania Press, 1983), or to G.B. Madison, *The Hermeneutics of Postmodernity: Figures and Themes* (Bloomington and Indianapolis: Indiana University Press, 1988).

8 Jaggar and Bordo, eds, *Gender/Body/Knowledge* 4.

9 See Rosemary Agonito, *History of Ideas on Woman, a Source Book* (New York: G.P. Putnam's Sons, 1977), especially the selections from Kant, Hegel, Freud, and de Beauvoir.

10 See Susan R. Bordo, *The Flight to Objectivity: Essays on Cartesianism and Culture* (New York: State University of New York Press, 1987).

11 Genevieve Lloyd, *The Man of Reason: 'Male' and 'Female' in Western Philosophy* (Minneapolis: University of Minnesota Press, 1984) 50.

12 Nancy Tuana, *Woman and the History of Philosophy* (New York: Paragon House, 1992) 41.

13 Sandra Harding, *Whose Science? Whose Rationality? Thinking from Women's Lives* (Ithaca: Cornell University Press, 1991) 39 and 57. See Ruth Hubbard, 'Have Only Men Evolved?' in S. Harding and M.B. Hintikka, *Discovering Reality: Feminist Perspectives on Epistemology, Metaphysics, Methodology, and Philosophy of Science* (Dordrecht, Holland: D. Reidel Publishing Co., 1983) 45–69, and Carol Gilligan, *In a Different Voice: Psychological Theory and Women's Development* (Cambridge: Harvard University Press, 1982).

14 See Harding, *Whose Science?* esp. pp. 111–18.

15 Whereas Harding focuses on the natural sciences, the issues she raises in her work have implications for epistemology as a whole.

16 Kenneth Gergen, 'Feminist Critique of Science and the Challenge of Social Epistemology,' in Mary McCanney Gergen, ed., *Feminist Thought and the Structure of Knowledge* (New York and London: New York University Press, 1988) 27–48. See esp. p. 36.

17 Ibid. 37–42.

18 Ibid. 43.

19 See Rorty, *Philosophy and the Mirror of Nature*.

20 Harding, *Whose Science?* 142.

21 Ibid. 187.

22 Lorraine Code, *What Can She Know? Feminist Theory and the Construction of Knowledge* (Ithaca and London: Cornell University Press, 1991) 43.

23 Sondra Farganis, 'Feminism and the Reconstruction of Social Science,' in Jaggar and Bordo, eds, *Gender/Body/Knowledge* 207–23. See p. 217.

24 Code, *What Can She Know?* 44–45. Compare the feminists' reservations about postmodernism quoted in Harding, *Whose Science?* 182–83.

25 Harding, *Whose Science?* 160.

26 Harding argues that a third reason that feminists need an account of objectivity is in order to mediate among the conflicting claims of various feminisms. See *Whose Science?* 160.

27 Code explicitly credits Gadamer for this suggestion, in *What Can She Know?* 200. See Hans-Georg Gadamer, *Truth and Method*, 2nd rev. ed., trans. revised by Joel Weinsheimer and Donald G. Marshall (New York: Crossroad,

1990) 265–306. Harding traces the idea to the 'strong programme' in the sociology of knowledge. See *Whose Science?* 149.

28 See Gadamer, *Truth and Method* 362–79.

29 See Code, *What Can She Know?* chap. 7.

30 Ibid. 320.

31 Ibid. 255.

32 For a list of authors and texts representing feminist standpoint theory, see Harding, *Whose Science?* 119ff.

33 Harding, *Whose Science?* 121–33.

34 Ibid. 124.

35 Cynthia Crysdale has asked why Lonergan's thought initially appears to be incompatible with feminism, discussing the themes of universalism, individualism, intellectualism, and lack of appreciation of pluralism. See her 'Lonergan and Feminism: Problems and Prospects,' in *Theological Studies* 53 (1992) 234–56.

36 See Bernard Lonergan, *Method in Theology* (New York: Herder and Herder, 1972) 262–63.

37 Lonergan, *Method in Theology* 79. See also the discussion of belief in *Insight* (New York: Philosophical Library, 1957) 703–18.

38 Lonergan, *Method* 43.

39 Ibid. 223.

40 Ibid. 43.

41 Ibid. 41–47.

42 Ibid. 231.

43 As Lonergan puts it, 'all men are subject to bias' (*Method in Theology* 231). Feminists might be inclined to agree!

44 Lonergan, *Method in Theology* 231. See also *Insight* 191–206 and 218–44.

45 See *Insight* 222–25.

46 Ultimately, for Lonergan, human fidelity to the transcendental precepts is impossible without divine grace. See, for example, his discussion of the solution to the problem of evil in *Insight*, chap. 20.

47 See *Insight* chaps 9 and 10.

48 Ibid. chap. 15.

49 See, for example, *Insight* 339–42.

50 Above I discussed three ways in which feminists have argued that objectivist epistemology is biased: it excludes women, it excludes 'feminine' ways of thinking, and it serves as a mask for male domination of women. It is worth asking whether any of these forms of masculine bias is intrinsic to Lonergan's cognitional theory. First, does Lonergan's cognitional theory exclude women? It is true that Lonergan's language is by no means gender-inclusive. But unlike many of his philosophical predecessors, he never explicitly says

that women are less likely than men to raise questions, to have insights, and so on. Indeed, among the thinkers that Lonergan publicly admired most were several women, including Jane Jacobs, Rosemary Haughton, and Suzanne Langer. Second, if a woman wishes to pursue Lonergan's method of understanding, must she deny all the qualities that are culturally defined as feminine? Certainly any answer would have to recognize that the culturally 'feminine' quality of *emotion* plays a crucial role in Lonergan's account of the human apprehension of value, and that the interdependence so fundamental to Lonergan's account of belief is reminiscent of the 'feminine' sense of connectedness so often mentioned in feminist literature. Finally, might Lonergan's notion of objectivity serve as a mask for men's domination of women? It seems to me that *any* account of objectivity could be abused; one who wished to use 'truth' as a weapon could make use of Lonerganian categories as well as objectivist ones. But, as Sandra Harding has said, the relativist alternative can also become a weapon, depriving people of recourse to reasonable arguments and leaving them only with the principle that 'might makes right.' There is at least, in Lonergan's work, a principle undermining the human tendency to turn truth, or method, or science into a weapon against other people, for as we have seen, one who takes Lonergan seriously can scarcely avoid asking about the sources of bias within his (or her) own life.

Gender, Science, and Cognitional Conversion

ABSTRACT *In 1985, Evelyn Fox Keller, a biophysicist by training and a feminist by recent conviction, published a collection of nine essays entitled* Reflections on Gender and Science. *My reading of this book suggests that in key respects Keller's feminist discussion of present-day science can both complement and be complemented by Bernard Lonergan's philosophical discussion of cognitional method. My essay has four main parts. I begin by sketching (1) Keller's feminist analysis and critique of what she takes to be the reigning account of scientific knowing, and (2) Bernard Lonergan's transcendental or heuristic methodology of human knowing in general and scientific knowing in particular. Next, (3) I propose that Lonergan's portrayal of 'cognitional conversion' can both clarify and generalize the 'dynamic objectivity' that in Keller's view distinguishes the correct account of scientific knowing and the 'static objectivity' that distinguishes incorrect accounts. Finally, (4) I propose that Keller's rejection of gender-bias as intrinsic to scientific knowing in turn can highlight gender-neutrality as part of what, according to Lonergan, cognitionally converted scientific and general cognitional methodologists affirm and gender-bias as part of what they deny.*

In 1985, Evelyn Fox Keller published a collection of nine essays entitled *Reflections on Gender and Science.*[1] In the introduction, Keller indicates her own background and the underlying motivation of her essays: 'A decade ago, I was deeply engaged (if not quite fully content) in my work as a mathematical biophysicist. I believed wholeheartedly in the laws of physics, and in their place at the apex of knowledge. Sometime in the mid-1970s –

overnight, as it were – another kind of question took precedence, upsetting my entire intellectual hierarchy: How much of the nature of science is bound up with the idea of masculinity, and what would it mean for science if it were otherwise? A lifelong training had labeled that question patently absurd; but once I actually heard it, I could not, either as a woman or as a scientist, any longer avoid it.'[2]

One conclusion to which Keller's ensuing exploration led her, a conclusion that is the central theme of her book, is that there is a correlation between the way a society thinks of gender and gender-differences and the way it conceives the scientific enterprise. The book itself is devoted to explicating and criticizing various historical, psychological, and philosophical aspects of that correlation. The author's contentions are receiving a good deal of attention in both scholarly and popular circles. Her book was widely reviewed; it has become a regular entry on bibliographies in social studies of science and women's studies; and in 1990 the author herself was the subject of an hour-long interview by Bill Moyers in his 'World of Ideas' series on U.S. public television. The same year, she collaborated in editing two additional volumes that extend the feminist dimension of her exploration.[3]

My own reading of Keller suggests that in key respects her critique of present-day science can both complement and be complemented by Bernard Lonergan's philosophical discussion of cognitional method. In what follows, I will first sketch (1) Keller's analysis and critique of the dominant scientific cognitive paradigm and (2) Lonergan's transcendental cognitional methodology, and then propose ways in which (3) Lonergan's work can complement Keller's and (4) Keller's work can complement Lonergan's.[4]

1   Evelyn Fox Keller's Feminist Analysis and Critique of the Reigning Scientific Cognitive Paradigm

1.1   The Background

Two relatively new scholarly enterprises constitute the immediate background of Keller's analysis and critique of current science: social studies of science, and feminist studies.[5] Most working scientists, not to mention the public at large, are prone to regard successive scientific conclusions as wholly unaffected by 'extra-scientific' presuppositions of the investigators, and as directly and ever more amply expressing a reality that stands over against the investigators themselves. Since the early 1960s, however, the historiography and sociology of science have been undercutting this popular notion. They show that the conclusions flowing from actual scientific practice invariably are conditioned both extrinsically and intrinsically by the expectations, interests, and commitments of the scientists themselves and the greater society in which they function. These presuppositions influence which data are adverted to, which questions are asked about the data, which hypotheses are likely to emerge, which standards of verification are invoked, and, consequently, which conclusions are deemed acceptable.[6]

While social studies of science manifest the way that extra-scientific presuppositions in general affect science in particular, feminist analyses reveal how presuppositions about gender-differences in particular affect society in general. Coming into full bloom in the 1970s, feminist scholarship has investigated, among other things, the social process of labelling certain human traits 'masculine' and others 'feminine' and treating them differently as a result. It has uncovered the key role in this process played by sexist assumptions – views that esteem the 'masculine' traits more highly than the 'feminine' ones, but that stem from antecedent desires and fears, hopes and convictions, rather than from investigation of the facts. Feminist studies have illuminated and critiqued the negative influence of sexist assumptions on the self-understanding and self-valuing of women in our society as a whole. Much work also has been done on the influence of sexist presuppositions in the humanities and the social sciences. Notably less attention, however, has been given in this regard to the natural sciences.[7]

1.2 The Foreground

Profiting from the studies of society and science and, again, of gender and society, Keller focuses her own scholarly concern on gender and science. Through her detailed studies of the history of both modern scientific practice and the theories of that practice, she aims to analyse and critique the role of gender-presuppositions in the scientific enterprise.[8] As it turns out, some of her most important conclusions in this connection are about the model or paradigm of scientific knowing, and the 'objectivity' that allegedly is the hallmark of scientific method.

The first of Keller's three central analytical findings is that a particular cognitive paradigm continues to dominate the thinking of most current theorists of science and most working scientists alike. This 'objectivist' paradigm construes objectivity as the result of successfully negotiating the supposedly radical disjunction between oneself as investigator and the reality one is striving to know. To be objective is cognitively to bridge the gap between subject and object while simultaneously maintaining recognition of that gap. Her second finding is that this dominant paradigm regularly identifies the propensity to be objective in just this sense – and, correlatively, to think in abstract and general terms, and to be rational and impersonal in one's approach – as a masculine trait. By the same token, it identifies the propensity to be merely subjective – and, correlatively, to think in concrete and particular terms, and to be emotional and personal in one's approach – as a feminine trait. Keller's third finding, already implicit in the conjunction of the first two, is that the dominant paradigm envisions the scientific enterprise as essentially masculine. Women may indeed occasionally become successful scientists, but only if they overcome their feminine proclivities; for science, not just in its ambient culture but more importantly in its intrinsic method, is masculine through and through.

Keller's analytical conclusion that the reigning scientific cognitive paradigm envisages scientific knowing as intrinsically masculine is followed by her critical response to that conclusion. She elaborates this response partly through contrasting it with three others.[9] A first response, that of 'traditional' theorists and practitioners of science, is one of unqualified approbation. It could be paraphrased as follows: 'The dominant paradigm correctly attributes the undeniable achievements of science to the objectivity of scientific knowing, and correctly interprets that objectivity in masculine terms. As such, the dominant paradigm accurately expresses both what science has been and what it ought to be.'[10] Keller lauds this response for clearly recognizing the genuine effectiveness of science and for correlating that effectiveness with the objectivity of its method. On the other hand, she argues that interpreting that objectivity as masculine derives from extra-scientific presuppositions, not from something essential to science; and in overlooking this fact the 'traditionalist' response is unreflective and naïve.

A second response, which Keller names 'liberal,' partly agrees with the first and partly disagrees. 'It is correct to correlate the splendor of scientific achievements with the objectivity of scientific knowing; but it is biased to conceive the latter as masculine. Rather, a distinction should be drawn. Scientific objectivity should indeed be conceived as objectivist, but not as masculine; for women are just as capable of meeting the demands of the objectivist model as men are. Consequently, both the dominant paradigm and the practice that it accurately expresses need to be reformed in this respect, purged of their masculine bias.' In Keller's view, this response is an improvement over the first, for it discerns the reigning paradigm's masculine bias. None the less it remains unsophisticated in thinking that this masculine bias is separable from the objectivist model itself, wrongly taking the objectivist model to be essentially gender-neutral rather than recognizing its intrinsic androcentrism.

A third response, which Keller calls 'radical,' differs quite dramatically from the second. 'The objectivist model of scientific objectivity is indeed intrinsically androcentric, but it also expresses the very nature of scientific knowing. Consequently, the scientific project is inescapably androcentric at its very core, and the only alternative for self-respecting women is to reject science completely – or at least to replace it with something totally different.' Keller approves of this response for unequivocally avoiding the most obvious defect of the second. None the less, now speaking explicitly as a scientist, she argues that it would be 'suicidal' for women to reject science altogether, for such a move would be tantamount to fleeing modern culture, putting women beyond the pale and leaving them powerless to combat the culture's oppressive androcentrism. Alternatively, to claim that science can and should be supplanted by something wholly different is mistakenly to suggest that science is nothing but the product of arbitrary presuppositions and to overlook its genuine contributions to the human community.

Keller applies the label 'radical' not just to the third response but to her own as well because, like the third, her response recognizes that the objectivist model of scientific knowing is essentially male-biased. Unlike the third, however, her response does not envision the objectivist model either as reflecting the actual optimum practice of scientific knowing (by contrast with many practitioners' muddled thoughts about their own practice) or as part of the correct theory of scientific knowing (by contrast with the currently reigning paradigm). Objectivity does not imply objectivism, either in concrete practice or in proper theory. To be objective is not somehow to negotiate an allegedly primitive disjunction of object from subject. On the contrary, the commonality of subject and object is primitive and basic, the subject-object distinction is secondary and derivative, and to be objective is to become aware of the distinction precisely as grounded in the commonality. Careful study of real-life scientific inquiry shows that developing such awareness is a matter of both feeling and reasoning, both thinking concretely and thinking abstractly, and in general employing both stereotypically 'feminine' skills and stereotypically 'masculine' ones.[11] Calling objectivity conceived in disjunctive, masculinist terms 'static,' and objectivity conceived in conjunctive, humanist terms 'dynamic,' Keller expresses the core of her position as follows:

> I define objectivity as the pursuit of a maximally authentic, and
> hence maximally reliable, understanding of the world around one-
> self. Such a pursuit is dynamic to the extent that it actively draws on
> the commonality between mind and nature as a resource for under-
> standing. Dynamic objectivity aims at a form of knowledge that
> grants to the world around us its independent integrity but does so
> in a way that remains cognizant of, indeed relies on, our connectivity
> with that world. In this, dynamic objectivity is not unlike empathy,-

a form of knowledge of other persons that draws explicitly on the commonality of feelings and experience in order to enrich one's understanding of another in his or her own right. By contrast, I call static objectivity the pursuit of knowledge that begins with the severance of subject from object rather than aiming at the disentanglement of one from the other. For both static and dynamic objectivity, the ambition appears the same, but the starting assumptions one makes about the nature of the pursuit bear critically on the outcome.[12]

2   Bernard Lonergan's Transcendental Cognitional Methodology

Turning now to our second principal thinker, we may begin by noting that Lonergan's cognitional methodology comprises his answers to three basic questions.[13] The first he calls the basic question of *cognitional theory*: What am I doing when I am knowing? More precisely, what acts do I experience myself performing when I am doing what I label 'knowing'? What are the characteristic features of my 'noetic' operations? The second is the basic question of *epistemology*: Why is doing that knowing? That is to say, why (if at all) is my aforementioned performance distinguished by the objectivity proper to 'cognitional' acts that are indeed cognitional, namely, noetic objectivity, or truth? In my concrete 'noetic' operations, what is the criterion of noetic objectivity that I presuppose, and how (if at all) do my operations satisfy that criterion? The third is the basic question of *metaphysics*: What do I know when I do it? What are the characteristic features of the known? If what I 'know' is distinguished by the objectivity proper to 'cognitional' contents that are indeed cognitional, namely, noematic objectivity, or reality, then what is the make-up of that real content?[14]

In Lonergan's view, exhaustive answers to these three questions are partly *empirical*, in the sense that some features of the acts and contents they regard are proper to this or that individual act or content, and are manifested only by my actually considering that individual element. However, exhaustive answers are partly *philosophical* or *transcendental* or *heuristic* as well, in the sense that some features they regard are proper to groups of acts and contents, and are prefigured by the very structure of my questions about those groups.[15] Moreover, philosophical or transcendental or heuristic answers subdivide into *special*, those regarding some groups of elements but not others, and *general*, those regarding every group. Consequently, cognitional methodology may be either empirical or heuristic, and the latter may be either special or general.[16] In the present essay, our particular concern is with Lonergan's general heuristic methodology of human knowing, and his special heuristic methodology of scientific knowing. Let us consider each in turn.

2.1 Lonergan's Heuristic Account of Human Knowing in General

Lonergan's own heuristic answer to the basic question of cognitional theory in general is that a complete instance of my 'knowing' properly so called is never a single act. Rather, it is always a complex of acts on four successive levels. My acts on these levels are simultaneously *intentional,* oriented towards contents distinct as such from the acts themselves, and *conscious,* non-reflexively present to themselves and, more fundamentally, to me as actor. The four successive levels of 'cognitional' conscious intentionality are designated summarily by Lonergan as the levels of *experiencing, understanding, judging,* and *evaluating.*[17] First, I experience. I am aware of data, the merely given – data that subsequently I may distinguish as data of *sense* (shapes, colours, sounds, smells, and so on) and data of *consciousness* (my conscious-intentional acts of sensing, and all my further conscious-intentional acts as well). Second, I understand. Motivated by my desire to know, I form some hypothesis about how the data hang together intelligibly, how they embody the intelligible identity of some 'thing' or the intelligible similarity of some 'property.' Third, I judge. Pushed further by my curiosity, I verify or falsify my hypothesis, I determine whether or not my bright idea is also a right idea. Fourth, I evaluate. Driven still further by cognitional eagerness, I assess the worth of the intelligible identity or similarity I have verified in the data I have experienced, I attribute value or disvalue to the thing or property I have discovered.

Moreover, Lonergan continues, at best I carry out this four-level 'cognitional' performance in a way that is *authentic.* That is to say, I proceed in a manner that makes maximum possible use of my apprehensive and appreciative abilities, both native and acquired. My performance as a 'noetic' subject is authentic insofar as my experiencing is *attentive,* my understanding is *intelligent,* my judging is *reasonable,* and my evaluating is *responsible.* To the objector who protests that the meanings of such words are either hopelessly vague or hopelessly controverted, Lonergan replies with a modern version of an ancient exhortation: Know thyself. Advert to your own concrete 'cognitional' performances, successful and failed alike. Can you recall some instance where your experiencing was neglectful, by contrast with another where you were more alert? Have you ever been simple-minded in forming a hypothesis, even if you are usually quite shrewd? Have you ever made a mistake when checking something and later corrected it? Have you ever made a value-judgment about something or someone but later felt obliged to change your mind? If you can answer these questions affirmatively, then you possess concrete personal examples of the meanings of 'attentive,' 'intelligent,' 'reasonable,' 'responsible,' and their opposites. If you cannot answer these questions affirmatively, then perhaps – as you contend – you have no inkling of what those words mean. But in that case you effectively concede the essential vacuousness of everything you say – including your very objection!

Lonergan's heuristic answer to the basic question of epistemology in general is that my 'knowing' is genuinely cognitional exactly insofar as it is authentic. Noetic objectivity is functionally identical with authentic 'noetic' subjectivity. My 'cognitional' performance is true precisely to the extent that my experiencing is attentive, my understanding is intelligent, my judging is reasonable, and my evaluating is responsible. Although the matter is often overlooked or distorted by inadequate theories, at the level of my actual practice the very meaning of 'objective knowing' or 'true knowing' is nothing other than 'authentic "knowing."' ' If this seems implausible, let me observe how my every effort to deny it self-destructs. Careful concrete self-study manifests that whenever I reject 'cognitional' authenticity verbally as the ultimate functional criterion of noetic objectivity, I invariably affirm it operationally by appealing to it in my attempt to substantiate what I am saying.

Finally, Lonergan's heuristic answer to the basic question of metaphysics in general is that *noematic* objectivity is what follows from *noetic* objectivity. But, as we have seen earlier, noetic *objectivity* is functionally identical with authentic 'noetic' *subjectivity*. Consequently, noematic objectivity is nothing other than what results from authentic 'noetic' subjectivity. Reality is what authentically I 'know,' and its characteristic features are prefigured by the characteristic features of authentic 'knowing.' Or, again, reality is the composite content of my attentive experiencing, intelligent understanding, reasonable judging, and responsible evaluating. Whenever I attempt to deny this, a contradiction arises between what I say and what inevitably I presuppose and invoke in trying to justify my saying it.[18]

Lonergan's general heuristic methodology of human knowing has a negative moment as well as an affirmative one. Besides recounting what he deems the correct heuristic answers to his three basic questions, answers that collectively determine the outlook he calls *critical realist*, Lonergan discusses answers he deems mistaken. In his judgment, the mistaken answers that are the most fundamental, as well as the most common, all are variants of the view that valid knowing is essentially a matter of the would-be knower's overcoming an allegedly primitive gap between herself and an object-to-be-known. For example, the *naïve realist* argues that noematic objectivity is fundamentally the result of 'noetic' non-subjectivity. Valid knowing is either identical with or at least very much like seeing the real objects that stand over against oneself as subject, and one's effort to do this is sometimes successful. The *critical idealist* agrees with the principle but adds that the requisite seeing never occurs. Valid knowing, consequently, is but a futile aspiration. Going to the opposite extreme, the *absolute idealist* claims that noematic objectivity is ultimately identical with 'noetic' subjectivity. Valid knowing is merely an aspect of creative constituting: one overcomes the subject-object gap by recognizing objects as radically the products of one's own subjectivity.[19]

How do mistaken general heuristic cognitional methodologies arise? In Lonergan's judgment, there may be as many as three joint grounds. The first is simple failure adequately to reflect upon my own optimum practice. From my earliest years my efforts to know things are marked by increasing skill and success. But it is one thing to perform successfully as a knower, and quite another to give an accurate and ample account of that performance. Reflexively to objectify the recurrent features of my 'noetic' activities, the functional criteria of noetic and noematic objectivity that I invariably invoke, and the implications of the foregoing – this is a tedious and difficult task, and most people do not undertake it. The second ground is my grasp of the partial truth embodied in the mistaken outlook. For basic outlooks are mistaken not because they are totally incorrect but rather because they are unwarranted generalizations of partial truths (for instance, that my knowing is sensory intuiting, or that it is not intellectual intuiting, or that it is cognitive self-constituting). The third ground is my dim but real anticipation of the practical consequences of adopting the correct outlook. For my general cognitional methodology has implications for my special cognitional methodologies and my moral methodology and, in turn, for the specialized cognitional practices and moral living whose optimum features these supposedly reflect. I may obscurely grasp that changing my general cognitional methodology would require, on pain of explicit inconsistency, that I also rewrite my dissertation and reform my life; and I may deem it easier to rationalize than to rewrite and reform.

How are mistaken general heuristic cognitional methodologies to be rectified? The Lonerganian reply to this question obviously is that the deficient grounds of the mistaken accounts must be redressed, a move so crucial and yet so difficult that it is labelled 'cognitional conversion.'[20] First, I must appropriate and objectify my own concrete cognitional practice. This cognitional self-appropriation and self-objectification will manifest explicitly (a) that my authentic 'noetic' subjectivity is nothing other than my attentive experiencing, intelligent understanding, reasonable judging, and responsible evaluating; (b) that noematic objectivity is exactly what follows from the authentic 'noetic' subjectivity; and (c) that a full-fledged cognitional distinction between myself-as-knower and other-things-I-know emerges only when I begin noting diversities *within* the field of what I have *already* come to know, and thus my knowledge of the so-called subject-object difference is secondary and derivative rather than primitive and basic.[21] Second, rectifying my previous oversight-of-self will facilitate my discernment of the dogmatic claims and/or merely ideological commitments that at least to some degree usurp the place of critical evidence behind every mistaken account. Third, I must commit myself to accepting and implementing the practical implications, moral and specialized cognitional alike, of the correct account.[22]

2.2 Lonergan's Heuristic Account of Scientific Knowing

If Lonergan's heuristic account of human knowing in general regards the features proper to *all* cognitional acts and contents insofar as those features are prefigured by the very structure of my questions about them, his heuristic account of scientific knowing regards the additional features proper to *specifically scientific* cognitional acts and contents insofar as those features are prefigured by the very structure of my questions about them.[23] Thus, like every special heuristic account, the heuristic account of scientific knowing presupposes the general heuristic account and adds determinations to it. It comprises heuristic answers to the three basic questions as extended into the special realm of science, it has a negative moment as well as an affirmative one, and it envisions its correct answers as arising from an extension of cognitional conversion.

Lonergan's heuristic conclusions about science are extensive and detailed, but for present purposes four in particular are important to highlight.[24] The first simply extends the general perspective elaborated earlier. One cannot properly characterize science without characterizing scientists. For scientific knowing, like all human knowing, is not first and foremost a matter of escaping one's subjectivity in order to grasp contents that are *distinct from oneself*. On the contrary, it is first and foremost a matter of employing one's subjectivity authentically in order to grasp contents that are *noematically objective*, regardless of any subsequent distinction one may draw within the latter between what is distinct from oneself and what is identical with oneself.[25] Hence an adequate account of the scientific cognitional enterprise requires that one treat not just what scientists investigate but also the presuppositions and procedures of authentic scientific investigators. Second, like all other authentic investigators, authentic scientific investigators are committed in advance to experiencing attentively, understanding intelligently, judging reasonably, and evaluating responsibly. Third, the presuppositions and procedures of specifically *scientific* investigators (in the modern sense of the word) orient them towards discovering universally valid conclusions, conclusions whose validity is independent of any particular place or time. The work of scientists thus may be contrasted usefully with that of *scholarly* investigators, who are concerned to discover what is distinctive of particular places and/or times.[26] Fourth, there remains an important distinction within the field of contents investigated by scientists. Commonly expressed as the distinction between the human world and the natural world, it may be put more precisely as the distinction between contents constituted partly by acts of meaning and contents not so constituted.[27] In terms of this distinction the work of *human* scientists may be contrasted usefully with that of *natural* scientists.[28] It is crucial to remember, however, that this useful contrast does not characterize natural science adequately. For although what natural scientists investigate is not constituted partly by acts of meaning, their investigative work – like that of human scientists and all other investigators alike – certainly is thus constituted.

3   How Lonergan's Work Can Complement Keller's

Thus far in this essay I have briefly outlined Evelyn Fox Keller's feminist analysis and critique of what she finds to be the currently prevailing conception of scientific knowing, and Bernard Lonergan's philosophical or transcendental or heuristic methodology of human knowing in general and of scientific knowing in particular. For the remainder of the essay I wish to consider the relations between the two studies. Beginning this consideration from Lonergan's side, I suggest that his work can complement Keller's in at least two main ways.

3.1 Lonergan Can Clarify the Heuristic Aspect of Keller's Critique

In my judgment, the first main way Lonergan's work can complement Keller's is that it can clarify the heuristic aspect of her critique. Let me expand this claim in two steps. First, there is a dimension of Keller's critique in which her affirmations and denials bear a striking substantive resemblance, in both their evidential basis and their content, to Lonergan's affirmations and denials. For although she does not perhaps expressly grasp it as such, one dimension of Keller's critique is radically philosophical in exactly the transcendental or heuristic sense of that word. That is to say, in her reflections on scientific knowing, the ultimate evidence to which she appeals is nothing other than the operationally incontrovertible features of optimum concrete scientific investigative practice – in the limit, her own.[29] Moreover, although she has not yet moved fully beyond the equation of *knowing the real* with *knowing an object*, her affirmation (under the label 'dynamic objectivity') of a cognitional pursuit that 'actively draws on the commonality between mind and nature' and her denial (under the label 'static objectivity') of a cognitional pursuit that 'begins with the severance of subject from object' clearly orient her in that direction.[30] In reality, she is not far from

Lonergan's account of what cognitional conversion (as extended into the realm of scientific cognitional methodology) moves one to accept and to reject.

Second, if Keller's heuristic critique of scientific knowing is substantively similar to Lonergan's outlook, it remains that the considerable strength of that critique can be manifested more fully by utilizing the conceptual and terminological clarifications available within the Lonerganian framework. In the first place, the distinction between empirical and transcendental or heuristic cognitional methodology can be more clearly and precisely drawn. In the second place, the heuristic dimension of Keller's reflections can be specified more crisply as scientific rather than scholarly, and natural scientific more than human scientific. In the third place, key elements of what Keller affirms as 'dynamic objectivity' can be summarized more lucidly in terms of the view Lonergan envisions the cognitionally converted scientific cognitional methodologist *embracing*, namely, (1)(a) noematic objectivity in science is the result of one's authentic 'noetic' subjectivity, and (b) the latter is one's attentive experiencing, intelligent understanding, reasonable judging, and responsible evaluating; and (2)(a) noematic subjectivity in science is the result of one's inauthentic 'noetic' subjectivity, and (b) the latter is one's inattentive experiencing, unintelligent understanding, unreasonable judging, and/or irresponsible evaluating.[31] In the fourth place, key elements of what Keller rejects as 'static objectivity' can likewise be summarized more lucidly in terms of the view Lonergan envisions the cognitionally converted scientific cognitional methodologist *renouncing*, namely, (1)(a) noematic objectivity in science is the result of one's 'noetic' non-subjectivity (namely, preventing oneself-as-knower from obscuring the object-to-be-known), or at least (b) one's authentic 'noetic' subjectivity is something other than one's attentive experiencing, intelligent understanding, reasonable judging, and responsible evaluating; and (2)(a) noematic subjectivity in science is the result of one's 'noetic' subjectivity (namely, allowing oneself-as-knower to obscure the object-to-be-known), or at least (b) one's inauthentic 'noetic' subjectivity is something other than one's inattentive experiencing, unintelligent understanding, unreasonable judging, and/or irresponsible evaluating.

Among other things, the foregoing clarifications delineate more exactly certain basic differences between Keller and those whom, as we have seen earlier, she calls 'traditional,' 'liberal feminist,' and (in one sense of the expression) 'radical feminist' theorists of science. In Lonerganian terms, whereas Keller herself is (at least virtually) cognitionally converted, each of those three groups lacks cognitional conversion. That is to say, the members of each group deny either (a) that noematic objectivity in science is the result of one's authentic scientific 'noetic' subjectivity, or at least (b) that the latter is properly identified as one's attentive experiencing, intelligent understanding, reasonable judging, and responsible evaluating in the scientific context. (In fact, the first point is usually the one denied.)

3.2 Lonergan Can Generalize the Heuristic Aspect of Keller's Critique

The second main way I propose that Lonergan's work can complement Keller's is that it can generalize the heuristic aspect of her critique. The focus of Keller's concern is knowing in science, especially natural science; and the explicit aim of her critique is to challenge what she deems an incorrect account of scientific knowing and to replace it with a correct account. In fact, however, the import of that critique in its heuristic dimension is not limited to accounts of *scientific* knowing. It extends potentially to accounts of *any* knowing.[32] And that very important latent potential can readily be actualized when the critique is recast within the Lonerganian framework.[33] In the first place, the distinction between special scientific and general heuristic cognitional methodology can be drawn with clarity and precision. In the second place, what I presented above as summarizing key elements of Keller's 'dynamic objectivity' in Lonerganian terms can now be fruitfully generalized, taken as expressing what not only the cognitionally converted *scientific* cognitional methodologist but also the cognitionally converted *general* cognitional methodologist adopts. And, in the third place, what I presented above as summarizing key elements of Keller's 'static objectivity' in Lonerganian terms can similarly be generalized with profit, taken as expressing what not just the cognitionally converted *scientific* cognitional methodologist but also the cognitionally converted *general* cognitional methodologist dismisses.

4   How Keller's Work Can Complement Lonergan's

In my view, just as Lonergan's work can complement Keller's in at least two main ways, the converse is also true.

4.1 Keller Can Augment Lonergan's Heuristic Account of
Scientific Knowing

The first main way I propose that Keller's work can complement Lonergan's is that it can augment Lonergan's heuristic account of scientific knowing. For Lonergan, as we have seen, noematic objectivity in science is the result of one's authentic 'noetic' subjectivity, where the latter is identified as one's attentive experiencing, intelligent understanding, reasonable judging, and responsible evaluating; and I have argued that Keller is in virtual agreement with Lonergan's view here as far as it goes. I now suggest that Keller provides an important *additional* specification of authentic scientific 'noetic' subjectivity, namely, that it is gender-neutral. First, as we have seen above in sketching her critique, Keller maintains that in correct theory as in optimum practice, scientific knowing is a matter of both feeling and reasoning, both thinking concretely and thinking abstractly, and in general employing both the cognitional skills our society associates with women and those it associates with men. But in being intrinsically characterized by both stereotypically 'feminine' and stereotypically 'masculine' skills, scientific knowing is adequately characterized by neither; and in just that sense it is gender-free, gender-neutral. Essentially it is neither male-biased, androcentric, nor female-biased, gynocentric; rather, it is properly humanist, anthropocentric.[34] Second, Keller on my reading takes gender-neutrality to be a part of scientific knowing as conceived in terms of what she calls 'dynamic objectivity,' just as she takes gender-bias, gender-specificity – the absence of gender-neutrality – to be a part of scientific knowing as conceived in terms of what she calls 'static objectivity.'[35] But if I am correct in my earlier Lonerganian clarification of her 'dynamic objectivity' and 'static objectivity' respectively in terms of cognitional conversion and its absence, then her gender-neutrality and gender-specificity can be understood in conversional terms as well. In those terms, my scientific knowing will be authentic only if it is gender-neutral, neither stereotypically 'feminine' alone nor stereotypically 'masculine' alone.[36] I will be an authentic scientific knower only if I experience, understand, judge, and evaluate in a way that gives short shrift to neither feelings nor percepts, neither concrete insights nor abstract concepts, neither values nor facts.[37]

On my interpretation of gender-neutrality as an additional key element of what Keller affirms as 'dynamic objectivity,' one arrives at the following augmented characterization of the view Lonergan envisages the cognitionally converted scientific cognitional methodologist *endorsing*: (1)(a) noematic objectivity in science is the result of one's authentic 'noetic' subjectivity, (b) the latter is one's attentive experiencing, intelligent understanding, reasonable judging, and responsible evaluating, and (c) 'gender-neutral' is part of what is meant by 'attentive,' 'intelligent,' 'reasonable,' and 'responsible'; and (2)(a) noematic subjectivity in science is the result of one's inauthentic 'noetic' subjectivity, (b) the latter is one's inattentive experiencing, unintelligent understanding, unreasonable judging, and/or irresponsible evaluating, and (c) 'gender-specific' is part of what is meant by 'inattentive,' 'unintelligent,' 'unreasonable,' and/or 'irresponsible.' Correlatively, on my interpretation of gender-specificity as an additional key element of what Keller rejects as 'static objectivity,' one arrives at the following expanded characterization of the view Lonergan envisages the cognitionally converted scientific cognitional methodologist *disputing*: (1)(a) noematic objectivity in science is the result of one's 'noetic' non-subjectivity (namely, preventing oneself-as-knower from obscuring the object-to-be-known), or at least (b) one's authentic 'noetic' subjectivity is something other than one's attentive experiencing, intelligent understanding, reasonable judging, and responsible evaluating, or at least (c) 'gender-neutral' is not part of what is meant by 'attentive,' 'intelligent,' 'reasonable,' and 'responsible'; and (2)(a) noematic subjectivity in science is the result of one's 'noetic' subjectivity (namely, allowing oneself-as-knower to obscure the object-to-be-known), or at least (b) one's inauthentic 'noetic' subjectivity is something other than one's inattentive experiencing, unintelligent understanding, unreasonable judging, and/or irresponsible evaluating, or at least (c) 'gender-specific' is not part of what is meant by 'inattentive,' 'unintelligent,' 'unreasonable,' and/or 'irresponsible.'[38]

The foregoing characterizations illuminate still more fully the range of basic differences between Keller and 'traditional,' 'liberal feminist,' and certain 'radical feminist' theorists of science. In our augmented Lonerganian terms, Keller herself is (at least virtually) cognitionally converted. By contrast, each of those three groups lacks cognitional conversion in one way or another. That is to say, the members of each group deny either (a) that noematic objectivity in science is the result of one's authentic scientific 'noetic' subjectivity, or at least (b) that the latter is properly identified as one's attentive experiencing, intelligent understanding, reasonable judging, and responsible evaluating in the scientific context, or at least (c) that 'gender-neutral' is part of what is meant by 'attentive, 'intelligent,' 'reasonable,' and 'responsible' in the scientific context.[39]

4.2 Keller Potentially Can Augment Lonergan's Heuristic Account of Human Knowing in General

The second main way I suggest that Keller's work can complement Lonergan's is that potentially it can augment Lonergan's heuristic account of human knowing in general. Just now I contended that Keller's heuristic critique of science can bring to light additional elements of what Lonergan envisions the cognitionally converted *scientific* cognitional methodologist affirming and denying. The additional element envisioned as affirmed is that scientific knowing is intrinsically gender-free, gender-neutral; as denied, that it is intrinsically gender-biased, gender-specific. But earlier I also contended that Lonergan's general cognitional methodology can generalize the heuristic aspect of Keller's critique. I now bring together these two contentions and propose that Keller potentially can contribute to that generalized account. That is to say, Keller potentially can bring to light additional elements of what Lonergan envisages the cognitionally converted *general* cognitional methodologist affirming and denying. The additional element envisaged as affirmed is that human knowing as such is intrinsically gender-neutral, neither stereotypically 'masculine' alone nor stereotypically 'feminine' alone. The additional element envisaged as denied is that human knowing as such is intrinsically gender-specific. Not just in science but right across the board, I attain noematic objectivity only if I experience, understand, judge, and evaluate in a way that does justice to both percepts and feelings, both abstract concepts and concrete insights, both facts and values; and I risk reaching only noematic subjectivity if I do not.[40]

It is of course important to recognize that to affirm gender-neutrality and deny gender-specificity as intrinsic features of human knowing is not to dispute that women, by virtue of their distinctive physical awareness of certain ranges of data, may be better situated than men to achieve noematic objectivity on those ranges. (Presumably the same would be true for men in relation to certain other ranges of data.) Nor is it to dispute that differences in the ways men and women are socialized can lead to significant differences in how their awareness of all data is patterned, in the specific cognitive skills they cultivate, and even in their conceptions of themselves as knowers. But these points are *empirical* ones. By contrast, the contention I am attributing to Keller and Lonergan is a *heuristic* one.[41] It is not that human knowing is *totally* gender-indifferent. Rather, it is that human knowing is *radically* gender-indifferent. Whatever the range of data with which one begins, and however one is socialized, the most fundamental features of the procedure for attaining noematic objectivity do not depend upon whether one is a man or a woman. Attentiveness, intelligence, reasonableness, and responsibility at root are distinctively neither masculine nor feminine skills; rather, they are distinctively just human skills.

To be sure, the foregoing contention is disputed by some radical feminist theorists (for instance, the third group of theorists, above, with whom Keller disagrees). Their assertion that men and women have radically different ways of knowing is reminiscent of the assertion by some biblical exegetes in the 1960s of radically different 'Jewish' and 'Greek' ways of knowing. In an essay first published in 1965, Frederick Crowe offers an explicitly Lonerganian rejection of the latter assertion.[42] I am claiming that Keller offers elements of an implicitly Lonerganian rejection of the former assertion.[43]

5   Conclusion

I have sketched Evelyn Fox Keller's feminist analysis and critique of what she takes to be the reigning account of scientific knowing, and Bernard Lonergan's transcendental or heuristic methodology of human knowing in general and scientific knowing in particular. I have proposed that Lonergan's portrayal of 'cognitional conversion' can both clarify and generalize the 'dynamic objectivity' that in Keller's view distinguishes the correct account of scientific knowing and the 'static objectivity' that distinguishes incorrect accounts. And I have proposed that Keller's rejection of gender-bias as intrinsic to scientific knowing in turn can highlight gender-neutrality as part of what, according to Lonergan, cognitionally converted scientific and general cognitional methodologists affirm and gender-bias as part of what they deny. These proposals may be of interest both to persons attracted by Keller's work and to persons attracted by Lonergan's.

Notes

1   Evelyn Fox Keller, *Reflections on Gender and Science* (New Haven: Yale University Press, 1985). Four of the nine essays had been published previously. I should note that I worked out an early version of the present essay's main themes in preparation for serving as a panellist in a workshop entitled 'Theology, Science, and Gender: Advances in Feminist Consciousness,' at the 1991 Annual Convention of the Catholic Theological Society of America. I am grateful to Professor Mary Gerhart, chair of the workshop, for inviting me to participate. I also wish to thank Professor Paulette Kidder and Professor Cynthia Crysdale for their helpful comments on my penultimate draft.
2   *Reflections* 3.
3   Marianne Hirsch and Evelyn Fox Keller, eds, *Conflicts in Feminism* (New York: Routledge, 1990); and Mary Jacobus, Evelyn Fox Keller, and Sally Shuttleworth, eds, *Body/Politics: Women and the Discourses of Science* (New York: Routledge, 1990).
4   To underline what will be obvious to most readers, the relations of complementarity I am suggesting between Keller and Lonergan are simply systematic possibilities, not necessarily historical possibilities and certainly not historical actualities. I know of no evidence that Lonergan ever read Keller: indeed, his scholarly career had largely ended by the time Keller's most distinctive work began to appear. And, in the other direction, I have no reason to think that Keller thus far has been influenced in any way by Lonergan.
5   The résumé in this paragraph and the next is based on Keller, *Reflections* 4–9.
6   Thomas Kuhn, *The Structure of Scientific Revolutions* (Chicago: University of Chicago Press, 1962), is perhaps the best known and most influential of these social studies of science.
7   On the difficulties and present state of feminist studies of science – which here means especially natural science – see Anne Fausto-Sterling's review of Keller's book in *Signs: Journal of Women in Culture and Society* 11 (1986) 780–83.

8 Like many commentators, Keller normally speaks simply of 'science,' without sharply distinguishing natural science and human science. While the
importance of this distinction for what Keller says should not be overesti-
mated, it is worth noting that most of her concerns are framed in terms of
natural science, and most of her examples are drawn from it. We shall
return to this issue below, in this essay's third main section.

9 *Reflections* passim, but esp. 4–12, 177–79. Characterizations of what in fact
are these three responses appear in Sandra Harding, 'The Instability of the
Analytical Categories of Feminist Theory,' *Signs: Journal of Women in Culture
and Society* 11 (1986) 645–64, esp. 650–60. Harding herself maintains a
highly nuanced version of the third response. By contrast, for a detailed
account not simply of scientific knowing but of human knowing in general
that is akin to Keller's own view, see Lorraine Code, *What Can She Know?
Feminist Theory and the Construction of Knowledge* (Ithaca: Cornell University
Press, 1991), esp. 'Knowledge and Subjectivity' 27–70.

10 The formulation of the first response as a little speech by a supposed respon-
dent is my own, though based on my reading of Keller. The same is true for
the second and third responses, shortly to follow.

11 Representative of Keller's own careful study of real-life scientific inquiry is
her work on the 'maverick' and 'visionary' geneticist Barbara McClintock
(1902–92). The final essay of Keller's present collection offers a detailed
account of McClintock's scientific style. Keller earlier published a book that
covers the same ground in even greater detail: *A Feeling for the Organism: The
Life and Work of Barbara McClintock* (New York: Freeman, 1983).

12 *Reflections* 116–17.

13 Lonergan provides many articulations of his cognitional methodology, but
the most detailed and perhaps the best-known of these articulations appear
in *Insight: A Study of Human Understanding* (New York: Philosophical Library,
1957; rev. and augmented ed., Toronto: University of Toronto Press, 1992)
and *Method in Theology* (New York: Herder and Herder, 1972). On the
emergence of the three basic questions as such, see Michael Vertin, ' "Knowing," "Objectivity," and "Reality": *Insight* and Beyond,' *Lonergan Workshop* 8
(1990) 249–63. Cf. Vertin, 'Lonergan's "Three Basic Questions" and a Philosophy of Philosophies,' ibid. 213–48.

14 The first form of each of these three questions is Lonergan's own, while the
second and third forms of each are mine. In the latter regard, I should point
out two things. First, here and throughout this essay I regularly put quotation marks around such words as 'knowing,' 'cognitional,' and 'noetic' when
those words designate operations (or contents) within the context of the first
basic question – i.e., operations (or contents) about which the question of

whether they are genuinely cognitional or not has yet to be raised. This practice can be semantically clarifying, even though it is not stylistically neat. Second, I regularly distinguish *noetic objectivity*, or *truth*, as the characteristic of genuinely cognitional *acts*, and *noematic objectivity*, or *reality*, as the characteristic of genuinely cognitional *contents*. This use of the word 'objectivity' is broader than Lonergan's, but I would argue that it is consistent with Lonergan's underlying intentions and also recognizes important senses the word is apt to have in present-day scholarly discussions. (Also see n. 21, below, and the references provided there.)

15 On this very specific sense of the word 'philosophical' as correlated with 'transcendental' and 'heuristic,' see *Method* 20–25; cf. 83, 85, 94–95, 141.

16 While the substance of these distinctions appears throughout Lonergan's writings, a useful summary may be found in *Method* 281–93. I should add, however, that by 'empirical' and 'philosophical' or 'transcendental' or 'heuristic' I mean *a posteriori* and *a priori* respectively. These senses of the words are slightly different from the senses Lonergan typically gives them. For the latter, see *Method* 6–20, esp. n. 4. Cf. Lonergan, *A Second Collection* (Philadelphia: Westminster, 1974) 207, n. 1. Also see Vertin, 'Lonergan's "Three Basic Questions" ' 226 and n. 10.

17 According to Lonergan, although all my 'cognitional' acts are both conscious and intentional, not all my conscious intentional acts are 'cognitional.' Specifically, my acts of deciding and executing decisions, acts that presuppose but go beyond the strictly 'cognitional,' are located (along with 'cognitional' acts of evaluating) on the fourth level of conscious intentionality. See, e.g., *Method* 6–20; cf. 120–22.

18 On the impossibility of remaining consistent while rejecting Lonergan's answers to the basic questions of cognitional theory, epistemology, and metaphysics in general, see esp. *Insight*, 1992, 352–62, 372–76 [= 1957, 328–39, 348–52]; and *Method* 13–25, 265, 292, 338.

19 Lonergan does not of course envision naïve realism, critical idealism, and absolute idealism as exhausting the specific ways in which ordinary folk and professional investigators alike can be mistaken in their basic outlooks. See, e.g., *Method* 76, 238–40, 262–65. Cf. Vertin, 'Lonergan's "Three Basic Questions" ' 217–19. I should also note that, besides his own schematic delineation of what he deems correct and mistaken accounts, Lonergan provides an extensive interpretation of the history of explicit philosophy in this regard. On his interpretation, such 'traditional' thinkers as Aristotle and Aquinas (by contrast with, say, Plato and Augustine) stand firmly in the trajectory of critical realism. See, e.g., *Verbum: Word and Idea in Aquinas* (Notre Dame: University of Notre Dame Press, 1967).

20 Lonergan's own preferred expression is 'intellectual conversion.' I use the expression 'cognitional conversion' in an effort to highlight that the shift in

question affects one's account of *all* one's knowing, knowing not only of facts but also of values. For more on this issue, see Michael Vertin, 'Dialectically-Opposed Phenomenologies of Knowing: A Pedagogical Elaboration of Basic Ideal-Types,' *Lonergan Workshop* 4 (1983) 1–26, esp. 17. Cf. Walter Conn, 'Moral Conversion: Development Toward Critical Self-Posession,' *Thought* 58 (1983) 170–87, esp. 176–81 and n. 14.

21 Notice: the latter point is *not* a denial that sometimes what I know is distinct from myself. Rather, it is that *knowing the real* is not properly equated with *knowing an object* (in the sense of knowing what is distinct from myself). Nor, of course, is it properly equated with *knowing the subject* (in the sense of knowing myself). On the contrary, *knowing the real* is fundamentally a matter of grasping the composite content of authentic experiencing, understanding, judging, and evaluating. Grasping the distinction between subject and object (in the aforementioned senses of those words) is a subsequent achievement. More amply, knowing the real is primarily a matter of authentically experiencing the *experienceable*, understanding the *intelligible*, judging the *judicable*, and evaluating the *evaluable*. Only secondarily is it a matter of grasping the distinction within this composite content between (a) what is *merely* experienceable, *merely* intelligible, *merely* judicable, and *merely* evaluable, on the one hand, and (b) the *conscious* experienceable, *intelligent* intelligible, *reasonable* judicable, and *responsible* evaluable, on the other hand. For more on this issue, see *Insight*, 1992, 399–409, esp. 401–402 [= 1957, 375–84, esp. 377]; and *Method* 262–65. Cf. *A Second Collection* 121–24; and *Insight*, 1992, 346–48, 538–44, 575–76, 639–42 [= 1957, 322–24, 514–20, 552–53, 616–19].

22 In fact, Lonergan argues that typically (though not necessarily) what he terms *intellectual conversion* is preceded by *moral conversion,* and both these are preceded by *religious conversion* (where the latter is unrestricted being-in-love, not yet any confessional commitment). See, e.g., *Method* 238–44, esp. 243. Cf. 'Bernard Lonergan Responds,' in P. McShane, ed., *Foundations of Theology* (Notre Dame: University of Notre Dame Press, 1972) 233–34.

23 For more on the precise character of heuristic as distinct from empirical accounts, recall above, nn. 15–16.

24 Careful consideration of the scientific enterprise has marked Lonergan's writings from their beginning, albeit generally in function of broader philosophical and theological concerns. For the single most sustained discussion, see *Insight*, esp. chaps 2–5.

25 Recall above, n. 21.

26 More exactly, scholars are concerned with the *meanings* distinctive of particular places and/or times – acts of understanding, judging, evaluating, deciding, and their expressions and implementations. See *Method* 233–34. Cf. pp. 179–80, 219, 229, 364–65.

27 See *Method* 179–80, 219. Cf. pp. 135, 201–203, 212, 247–49, 325. Notice, of course, that this distinction is not identical with the distinction between myself and what is distinct from myself. I do indeed *directly* know myself as partly constituted by acts of understanding, judging, evaluating, and deciding. But, starting from a very early age, I also come *inferentially* to know words, deeds, and artefacts as expressing and resulting from others' acts of meaning. Hence, sometimes contents distinct from myself are contents constituted partly by acts of meaning.

28 Taking these two distinctions together, Lonergan divides specialized researchers into three broad groups: natural scientists, human scientists, and scholars, with their corresponding enterprises of natural science, human science, and scholarship. See the references in nn. 26–27, above.

29 Recall above, n. 11.

30 See *Reflections* 116–17 and, more broadly, 115–38. Cf. pp. 69–114.

31 Just as *noematic objectivity*, or *reality*, is the characteristic of contents that are genuinely cognitional, so *noematic subjectivity*, or *unreality*, is the characteristic of contents that are not genuinely cognitional. Cf. above, n. 14.

32 While I have no reason to think that Keller would deny this, it remains that she does not expressly affirm it.

33 The importance of that latent potential is signalled by the fact that, among other things, the issues addressed by a generalized version of Keller's heuristic critique are central to some of the most important controversies in the history of explicit philosophy. See, e.g., *Insight*, 1992, 388–98, 410–15, 426–55 [= 1957, 364–74, 385–90, 401–30]. Cf. n. 19, above.

34 It may be useful to clarify three features of Keller's claim here, as I am interpreting it. First, her claim expresses what in her view are certain skills intrinsic to successful scientific practice as such, whatever the practitioner's gender. Successful scientific practice includes both feeling and reasoning, both concrete thinking and abstract thinking, concern for both values and facts, and so on. Second, at one level this claim is simply *empirical* and thus highly probable at best, resting on the evidence provided to Keller by her historical studies of science past and present. At a deeper level, however, the claim is *philosophical* (or, more precisely, *heuristic*) and thus certain at best, resting ultimately on evidence constituted for Keller by operationally incontrovertible features of her own optimum concrete scientific practice. Third, to speak of the set of these characteristic scientific cognitional skills as 'both stereotypically feminine and stereotypically masculine' is accurate but also potentially misleading. It is accurate, for society does indeed tend to correlate some of these skills with women and others with men. But such language (which, in fact, Keller herself does not use much) is also potentially misleading. It can suggest – wrongly – that the most basic and secure account of the characteristic skills is no more than an *empirical* characteriza-

tion of certain cognitional abilities possessed by women *as women* and men *as men* respectively. On the contrary, however, the most basic and secure account of the characteristic scientific cognitional skills is a *heuristic* characterization of certain cognitional abilities possessed by both women and men *as authentic humans.* The heuristic characterization of authentic scientific knowers is *methodologically prior to* the further differentiation of such knowers into women and men. Hence in the dimension of precisely such a heuristic characterization, a dimension in which I am suggesting that Keller's work complements Lonergan's, one speaks properly of successful scientific knowing not as gender-inclusive or gender-integrative but rather as gender-free or gender-neutral. (See also n. 43, below.)

35 See *Reflections* 116–17 and, more broadly, 115–38. Cf. pp. 69–114, 117–79. As those pages indicate, it is of course primarily *male*, not *female*, gender-bias that Keller sees as historically implicated in distorted accounts of scientific knowing. But it is clear as well, if less drawn out, that she also views female gender-bias as inimical to a veritable account.

36 On this view, gender-neutrality of course is only a *necessary*, not a *sufficient*, condition of authentic scientific knowing.

37 For a brief but suggestive use of Lonerganian conversional categories to articulate gender-neutral knowing in a context somewhat different from the one we are considering here, see Walter Conn, 'Two-Handed Theology,' *Catholic Theological Society of America Proceedings* 38 (1983) 66–71, esp. 67–68.

38 Students of Lonergan in particular may find it helpful to recognize that *every* erroneous assertion about what is intrinsic to scientific knowing – or, indeed, human knowing as such – provides an opportunity for making explicit some element of what cognitional conversion is *from* – and, correlatively, what it is *to*.

39 In my augmented characterization of cognitional conversion as extended into the realm of scientific cognitional methodology, importance attaches not just to the characterization's elements but also to their sequence, a sequence running from more basic to less basic. This is worth noting, since it affects the specific way the scheme helps one interpret theorists who disagree with Keller. Three persons, for example, might all disagree with Keller that scientific knowing is intrinsically gender-neutral. But for one that disagreement might rest on nothing more than a rejection of 'gender-neutral' as part of what is meant by 'attentive,' 'intelligent,' 'reasonable,' and 'responsible' in the scientific context. For the second, the disagreement might stem partly from something more basic, namely, a denial that authentic scientific 'noetic' subjectivity is properly identified as one's attentive experiencing, intelligent understanding, reasonable judging, and responsible evaluating in the scientific context. For the third, the disagreement might stem partly from something still more basic, namely, a denial that noematic objectivity

in science is the result of one's authentic scientific 'noetic' subjectivity.

40 Just as before, of course, gender-neutrality is only a *necessary*, not a *sufficient*, condition. Recall above, n. 36.

41 On the distinction between empirical and heuristic claims about human knowing, recall above, n. 34.

42 Frederick E. Crowe, 'Neither Jew nor Greek, but One Human Nature and Operation in All,' in Crowe, *Appropriating the Lonergan Idea* (Washington: Catholic University of America Press, 1989) 31–50.

43 My colleague, Professor Margaret O'Gara, has suggested that one could imagine an essay inspired by Keller's work and playing – like Crowe's essay – on Galatians 3:28, entitled 'Neither Male nor Female, but One Human Nature and Operation in All.'

Women's Intuition:
A Lonerganian Analysis[1]

ABSTRACT *In this paper distinctions afforded by Lonergan's intention-ality analysis are employed to critique the notion of women's intuition. The broader question of whether any cognitive acts constituting the process of knowing are gender-specific is discussed first. Two reasons for the emergence of this question are sketched: the tradition in Western thought which attri-butes rationality specifically to men, and the relativism of contemporary feminist epistemological theory.*

A phenomenological analysis of what has been called 'women's intuition' follows, which focuses on the issues of the appropriation and objectification of conscious acts. The paper concludes with a brief reflection on a comment on women and intersubjectivity made by Lonergan in Insight.

How do women know? Is this question the same as the question 'What is knowing?' When I studied Lonergan's *Insight* as a student, my initial con-versional insight was that 'the subject' referred to throughout the book was in fact *me*. As I went on to examine the history of philosophy and studied consciousness in Sartre and in Husserl, rational self-consciousness in Hegel, rationality in Kant, the cogito in Descartes, the intellect in St Thomas and in Aristotle, I never doubted that the mind being investigated was mine, even when the accounts given were inadequate in numerous ways. I persisted in this conviction in the face of explicit statements to the contrary by some of these very same thinkers. Today, in our post-Enlightenment, postmodern context the question of whether there is a distinctive, gender-specific way of knowing has been raised anew, and answered affirmatively by such fem-inist theorists as McFague, Gilligan, and Jaggar.

In this essay I propose to tackle the question of whether women know differently than men by employing certain distinctions made possible by Lonergan's intentionality analysis.[2] First of all, it should be acknowledged that the term 'knowing' is ambiguous, and the question is muddied by this ambiguity. 'Knowing' in ordinary language, and in theory uncritical of ordinary usage, can mean anything from sensing or perceiving to rational judgment or even decision. Further, knowing is sometimes equated with experience, and the term 'experience' is also ambiguous; referring either to the sensory and non-intelligent or to the whole field of consciousness. Finally, 'knowing' used strictly refers to cognitive operations, but it may also be used to refer to the affective, as in 'He knew in his heart that ...' In light of this ambiguity, I will reformulate the question: Is there a conscious operation or set of operations (cognitive and/or affective) that is specific to women?

It should be noted that my question regards the *noetic* rather than the *noematic* correlates of consciousness, the conscious operations or acts rather than the conscious contents or objects of these acts. Some contemporary feminist critiques of traditional accounts of women's knowledge examine the *noematic*. McFague, for example, explores feminine and masculine models, images, or symbols of the divine. Her investigation takes place at the level of the religious and theological imagination, on which she uncovers the metaphors and models underlying theological conceptual systems.[3] Her focus is on the conscious content, the images themselves, rather than on the conscious operations that give rise to such images. Similarly, feminist analyses of the language employed in religious texts and liturgies are concerned with the *noematic*, specifically with names given to God.[4] The religious words formulated, the images and models elaborated, all are contents of the conscious operations that are the focus of this inquiry. My question regards the operations that give rise to such formulations, metaphors, concepts.

Also, my question regards 'women's knowing.' While this phrase is admittedly awkward, 'feminine knowing' is misleading. A woman or a man may engage in acts or pursuits considered to be feminine or masculine. Accordingly, the phrases 'a very feminine woman' or 'a rather masculine woman' have commonly understood meanings. The designations 'feminine' and 'masculine' are derivative terms. They get their meanings from the historically and culturally conditioned body of common wisdom and common nonsense concerning the differences between women and men. We can avoid any unintentional connotations the term 'feminine' may carry by asking whether there is a gender-specific knowing.[5] Does woman qua woman have a unique way of knowing?

Having clarified the meaning of our question, let us now turn to the historical reasons for its emergence. I can discern at least two reasons why this question has arisen. The first and, perhaps, the most prominent reason is a tradition of Western thought stretching back as far as the sixth century BC. The second is a contemporary reason, the relativism of postmodern epistemological reflection.

First, there is a long-standing tradition that attributes rationality exclusively to men. The notion of a set of opposites, such as Hot-Cold or Wet-Dry, played an important role in the cosmologies of the pre-Socratics from the time of Anaximander. In his *Metaphysics*, Aristotle refers to a standard table of ten pairs of opposites, which he attributes to the Pythagoreans. In this table the opposite Female was listed in the column characterized generally by lack and disorder. Female was on the negative side along with the opposites Unlimited, Evenness (as the opposite of the more perfect unity of Oddness), Many, Left, Motion, Darkness, Badness, Curved, Oblong.[6] While Female as an opposite was itself a form or a universal, it was one of the forms characterized by a lack of definition, order, perfection. In addition, Aristotle defined man (humanity as distinct from plants and merely sentient animals) as a rational animal, an animal possessing intellect. There were, then, two basic tenets that could be combined: (1) Female is the opposite of Male, or woman is not man; and (2) Man is rational. Unfortunately, these two propositions can be combined as the premises of an invalid argument: Man is rational; woman is not man; therefore, woman is not rational. This argument is invalid whether the ambiguous term 'man' in the first premise is taken to mean humanity or men. If we mean by 'man' humanity, then the second premise is false, and the argument is invalid. If we mean by 'man' men, then the argument is an example of a standard fallacy. 'All A's are B's' does not entail that 'All not-A's are not-B's.' I am not attributing this actual argument to anyone, but only illustrating the kind of faulty reasoning that has served to bulwark centuries of misogyny. Because man is defined as rational, and woman clearly is not man, then woman must be in some sense non-rational.[7]

The attribution of an essential, defining characteristic of humanity to only one of its sexes, has serious metaphysical implications. If woman is non-rational and rationality is essential to being human, then woman must be, in Sayers's words, 'not quite human.'[8] We can read the most brilliant and ambitious accounts of the human spirit, and find at the back of the weighty tome a small section entitled 'On Women' or 'The Woman Question.' It is disheartening, at least, for the serious student of philosophy reaching up to the mind of a great thinker to come upon a remark such as the following by Hegel: 'Women are capable of education, but they are not made for activities which demand a universal faculty such as more advanced sciences, philosophy, and certain forms of artistic production.'[9] After having wrestled more or less successfully with the intricacies of dialectical method, the student discovers that, after all, she does not have the faculty to comprehend herself as rationally self-conscious. The same opinion of woman was expressed by

Schopenhauer: 'For women, only what is intuitive, present and immediately real truly exists; what is knowable only by means of concepts, what is remote, absent, past, or future cannot really be grasped by them.'[10] Woman is understood to be bereft of the wherewithall, lacking the universalizing faculty, to engage in abstract reasoning. (If one should happen to encounter an 'analytic' woman, her possession of this masculine trait is typically considered to be an aberration.)

Returning to the same passage in Hegel's *Philosophy of Right*, we read further: 'The difference between men and women is like that between animals and plants. Men correspond to animals, while women correspond to plants because their development is more placid and the principle that underlies it is the rather vague unity of feeling.'[11] Kierkegaard, who differed so radically on major points with Hegel, reiterates fundamentally the same metaphysical view of woman: 'This being of woman (for the word existence is too rich in meaning, since woman does not persist in and through herself) is rightly described as charm, an expression which suggests plant life ... She is wholly subject to nature and hence only aesthetically free.'[12] As non-rational, or more precisely pre-rational, woman has a different being than man, and this metaphysical difference grounds an ethical difference. Woman is not free, not autonomous, and, thus, she is rightly subject to authority. Insofar as woman is incapable of grasping and applying the categorical imperative, she cannot conduct her life according to the law of reason, except indirectly by obeying one who does.

A litany of similar opinions on the nature of woman, expressed over the centuries by representatives of various disciplines, could easily be recited. I have quoted these few remarks in order to illustrate that the attribution of rationality to men exclusively has grave ramifications for epistemological, metaphysical, and ethical accounts of woman. It is well known that similar presuppositions concerning the nature of woman persisted well into this century. The traditional belief in woman's passive, non-rational nature underpins the theories and methodologies of the pioneers of otherwise new fields of thought (Freud, Scheler, Wilson, Kohlberg, to name a few). In addition, even some feminists critical of the patriarchal tradition of male domination, from the time of Wollstonecraft in the late eighteenth century to the present, have nevertheless adopted this presupposition of female non-rationality.[13]

Historically, the non-rationality ascribed to woman has taken three forms: pre-rationality, extra-rationality, and supra-rationality. First, Enlightenment thinkers and many post-Kantians characterize woman as pre-rational, as adept at intuitive, pre-conceptual knowing. As such, she is likened to the animals (or as we have seen, to plants) and to children. The main difference between the woman and the child, however, is that the child (boy) has the potential to become fully rational, autonomous, and free; whereas the woman is thought to live her life as a perennial child (girl). The primary cognitive ability characteristic of woman, according to this view, is the intuitive. As Hegel remarks: 'Women are educated – who knows how? – as it were by breathing in ideas, by living rather than acquiring knowledge.'[14]

Second, non-rationality can also mean that which is extra-rational or complementary to rationality; namely, the volitional and the affective. The volitional, insofar as it is grounded in rationality, was not associated with woman. She was thought by Kant to be heteronymous, lacking the moral authority of the rational moral agent.[15] Her wilfulness was considered to be a function of childish arbitrariness or animal stubbornness, rather than the exercise of a free will grounded in the law of reason. The proper domain of woman was considered to be the heart, the emotional or affective.

The affective as non-rational is not necessarily sub-rational. Phenomenologists of the heart have shown that the range of human emotion extends spiritually at least as high or as deep as reason. Scheler and Strasser, for example, have uncovered complex hierarchies of affectivity, from the simplest sensations to the most profound passions.[16] If woman is associated exclusively with the heart, this does not, then, impose a limitation on her potential spirituality. Unfortunately, even Scheler, who embraces affectivity as a more significant field for a priori investigation than rationality, does not redeem woman as man's spiritual equal. On the contrary, while woman's domain may be the heart, she is relegated to its basement. Scheler characterizes woman as essentially prone to negative emotions, such as envy, jealousy, spite, and, particularly, *ressentiment*. In addition, owing to her ontological inferiority, woman is associated with feelings of the lower ranks – sensory and vital feelings and desires.[17]

Scheler explains how *ressentiment*, which is a complex condition of self-poisoning of the heart, originates in individuals or groups on the basis of social conditions or hereditary factors. He considers women to be a preeminent example of such a group. While not every woman will fall victim to *ressentiment*, woman's essential nature makes her especially prone to this condition. In his analysis of this susceptibility, Scheler characterizes the domain of woman's most vital interest to be the erotic. He writes: 'She is always forced to compete for man's favor, and this competition centers precisely on her personal and unchangeable qualities.' Woman is vulnerable to *ressentiment*, because 'feelings of revenge born from rejection in the erotic sphere are always particularly subject to repression.'[18] We can gather from these remarks that woman's primary interest is the erotic on the sensitive and vital levels. The higher levels of affectivity, the feelings and interests corresponding to the cultural values of beauty, justice, and wisdom, require the intelligence and self-reflection of spirit. Owing to her nature, and not only to social conditioning, woman is not motivated by the higher spiritual affects. So, we find that even in her own special domain of the emotions woman is relegated to an inferior status. The key differentiating factor in the affective potential of women and men is the ability to be articulate, and self-reflective; in short, the capacity to be spiritual (rational).

Third, the non-rational can mean not that which is inferior to reason or that which is complementary to reason, but that which transcends reason. The non-rational in the sense of the supra-rational is the transcendent realm of the mysterious and the holy. In experiencing the mystical, one moves beyond the mediation and articulation of intelligence and reason to the silence of mystery. One moves beyond the experience of any sensory or imaginatively based affect to an experience of the sublime, the *mysterium tremendum*. One moves beyond acts of will, to self-surrender to God's will. Has woman, historically, been specifically associated with the non-rational in this sense?

The mystical is understood to correspond to the highest potential of the human as person. Insofar as women have not been considered persons, mystical experience, the experience of the holy, has not been attributed to them. In those cultures and times in which women have been considered to be family property or things, they have not been considered to be persons.[19] The Christian tradition does recognize a religious personal nature in woman and, with this, a capacity to experience the mystical. Women, such as St Teresa, have been ranked among the greatest mystics. But this gift of mystical union with God seems to transcend all specific differences of age, education, social status, education, and gender. The non-rational in this sense has not been specially attributed to woman, although it has, in some cultures, been specially denied her.

Besides the mystical as ultimately self-transcending, there is also a romantic sense of the spiritual, which has been specifically associated with woman. This spirituality is non-rational, not as having transcended reason, but once again as lacking rationality. It is a 'spirituality' defined by a lack of *Geist*, a romantic notion of the spiritual grounded in the imagination. Woman as not transcending materiality is thought to be somehow aligned with the dark forces of nature. As 'earth mother' she possesses a mysterious power, described by Hein in her critique of woman's spirituality: 'But it is not an individuating, intellectualizing, or morally elevating property. It is rather an elemental and undifferentiated force that 'passes through' and occupies a woman ... Woman's spirituality is in no way incompatible with her passivity or with her lack of moral authority.'[20] Possessing mysterious power and yet not capable of rational, personal autonomy, woman was logically linked to another source of supernatural power – the devil. Traditional practices of enrobing women, foot-binding, and other forms of physical mutilation, and the excesses of witch burning, have been attributed to the powerful psychological need to control the dark forces women represent.[21]

In summary, the non-rational can be understood in at least three ways – as pre-rational, as extra-rational, or as supra-rational. The supra-rational, as ultimately transcending reason, as the highest, most profound human experience, is not, at least in the Christian tradition, considered to be gender-specific. However, woman has been specifically associated with the mystical in the romantic sense. The extra-rational, as affective, is also associated specifically with woman, but only in the limited sense of the erotic. The extra-rational as volitional has not been associated with woman, because she is thought to lack or to fail to exercise the rationality that grounds free self-determination or autonomy. Finally, the pre-rational, the realm of the inarticulate and the intuitive, has been most consistently attributed to woman.

The second reason for the emergence of the question of women's knowing is the contemporary relativistic trend in epistemology. The question of how women know is not essentially different from the question of how any distinct human group knows. Contemporary epistemologists and cognitive sociologists seek to determine how differences in knowing are a function of an individual's age, ethnicity, gender, sexual orientation, nationality, economic class, or education. 'Radical feminists,' according to Jaggar, are so called insofar as they accept the Marxist argument that 'there is no epistemological standpoint "outside" social reality and that all knowledge is shaped by its social origins.' She adds: 'Claims that knowledge is objective in the sense of being uninfluenced by class interests are themselves ideological myths.'[22] Other feminists have found class distinctions alone to be too impoverished to adequately account for the cognitive differences in groups, particularly in groups of women. Stimpson, for example, calls for a greater recognition of national characteristics: 'To understand an Israeli woman, one would have to understand the power of the religious courts; to understand an Australian woman, the presence of an overwhelming, empty landscape ...'[23] Women as a group are thought to know differently than other groups, and sub-groups of women are thought to know differently than each other. Thus, a young, black, lesbian professional from Paris is going to experience or know differently than a white, middle-aged, heterosexual, working-class female from Milwaukee; and they are both going to think differently than their male counterparts.

The discovery and affirmation of pluralism in historical viewpoints, cultural mores, socio-economic classes, religious beliefs, scientific frameworks, philosophic methodologies, and so on has led to a despair of the universal. The postmodern suspicion and denigration of the a priori or transcendental was originally expressed in Nietzsche's eloquent and reflective critique of the will to truth.[24] Henceforth, to seek a universal ground for objectivity, a way of knowing that is trans-cultural, has been considered to be ideologically recalcitrant or, at best, naïve. There is not one, universal way that human beings experience, think, or reason. MacIntyre has shown that the very meaning of reason itself, of what it means to be rational as we have been discussing it so far, is historically conditioned.[25] It follows that if one is to attempt to do epistemology at all, one must study the ways of reasoning or thinking or believing of various, distinct groups. The question of whether woman has a unique way of knowing, then, arises in the contemporary context, regardless of any traditional differentiation of rationality in terms of gender.

I referred above to a 'despair of the universal' because of certain nihilistic undercurrents in the postmodern wave. Rather than a celebration of the fact of pluralism, one detects a sense of loss, a loss of the surety that attended the classical notion of necessary truth. But the recognition of pluralism in all its forms does not preclude the possibility of a universal core of human knowing, feeling, and willing. Lonergan with his transcendental structure of conscious intentionality, as well as Scheler with his a priori structure of the heart, have shown that thorough study of historical and cultural differences only provides further evidence for the affirmation of a universal ground of objectivity.

The non-rational as outlined above has three senses and each is associated with woman, but of the three the pre-rational or intuitive is most uniformly associated with woman. While feelings and desires may be considered to be woman's domain, still it is the sensitive and pre-rational affects with which she is especially associated. Similarly, woman has been considered uniquely gifted with spiritual powers, but only insofar as those powers are understood to be natural or material – again, intuitive. Let us examine, then, whether or not intuition is a unique *noetic* constituent of woman's consciousness. In other words, to rephrase one of Heidegger's questions, What is called 'women's intuition'?

First, I would like to eliminate what is not meant by 'women's intuition.' I am not referring to the sensitive intuition of Kant's 'Aesthetic,' which is no more than sensory experience; nor do I mean the eidetic intuition of Husserl's phenomenology. The latter is not fundamentally different from the intelligent abstraction of the intelligible form found in the Aristotelean tradition. The intuition attributed to women is not mere sense experience nor is it an act of intelligence, an insight, although both of these *noetic* correlates are pre-rational. The former is pre-rational as merely empirical; the latter, as pre-conceptual, though intelligent. When a woman says, 'I just know. Don't ask me how,' she is not claiming greater perceptual acuity – sharper vision or a stronger sense of smell. She is also not claiming greater capacity for abstracting the universal. The content of such 'intuition' is not the provisional supposition of theoretical operations. It is, rather, pronounced as a judgment, as knowledge that has been attained. This intuitive knowledge is not thought to be reached through the mediation of intelligent grasp, conceptual formulation, and rational verification; but immediately and wholly. Such a claim to 'just know' something directly without or apart from the mediation of abstraction and formulation would be considered preposterous, as indeed Kant considered all speculative claims of intellectual intuition. Yet, the myth that there is such a thing as women's intuition has persisted, even when its possibility in general has been radically critiqued.

What accounts for the persistence of the myth of women's intuition? We are predisposed to accept this myth, as we have seen, because of the historical association of woman with the pre-rational. There is also the inescapable fact that the claims made on the basis of women's intuition often times turn out to be confirmed. What is pronounced, independently, has in fact taken place or does actually transpire. The not uncommon confirmation of women's intuition is met by the bemused shrug of the rational agent. Further, women themselves have been known to take pride in this unique, incomprehensible power. If one is deprived of other socially acceptable exercises of power, it is understandable that what is thought to be a unique source of female power would be cherished. As McMillan points out, some feminists have even begun to argue that women ought to embrace this identification of women with the intuitive. The feminists' appropriation of women's intuition is lauded as part of a therapeutic move away from the excessive abstractness of rationalism.[26]

As I think the attribution of the non-rational specifically to woman is fallacious, so I think the notion of women's intuition is also ungrounded. The nature of the mistake in this instance is not so much the fruit of biased reasoning as it is the result of incorrect objectification. I contend that something is going on in woman's consciousness, and that she can arrive at the truth, but that it is inaccurate to refer to this process as 'intuition.'

Conscious acts, the *noetic* elements of consciousness, are essentially intentional, that is, directed towards objects. A conscious act invariably makes us aware of its content. The act itself qua conscious is also self-present. However, the fact that both content and act are conscious does not mean that the subject is reflecting on either. For example, at the movies, while engrossed in a film, you may be tasting buttered popcorn, feeling irritated with the person kicking the back of your seat, recalling a similar scene in a previous film, questioning the coherence of the plot, and so on. These and any number of similar conscious operations are not taking place unconsciously. If someone were to ask you how the popcorn is, you would be able to answer coherently, yet you were not 'thinking' about it previously. Your attention was on the film. Conscious acts and contents that are not attended to or reflected upon constitute unobjectified consciousness. In reference to feelings Lonergan writes: 'not to take cognizance of them is to leave them in the twilight of what is conscious but not objectified.'[27] He adds in a note that this 'twilight' is what seems to be meant by the psychiatric notion of the unconscious.[28] In fact, Freud's 'unconscious' is effectively undermined by acknowledgment of unobjectified consciousness.[29] Conscious acts, including affective, volitional, and cognitive acts, and their contents can occur without being reflected upon. The acts, while themselves conscious and intentional, need not be the object of intention.

What is called 'women's intuition' is, I think, a matter of pre-reflective or unobjectified conscious acts of perception, intelligence, affectivity, and reason. In pronouncing what she 'just knows,' a woman is simply objectifying the end-product of a series of conscious and intentional, but pre-reflective, operations. When a mother 'just knew,' for example, that her daughter was going to be involved in a car accident, she may have been drawing upon a more attuned sensitivity to her daughter's mood, the manner of her date, the sound of his car's engine, recollections of previous misadventures. Into this data, which might not be available to a less concerned individual, she may have gotten a practical insight regarding what was likely to happen, and this insight may have been reinforced by further worried attention to detail, until, finally, it is confirmed as a fact by the police officer at the door. Through sensory, affective, imaginative, intelligent, and rational activity, she arrived at a judgment of probability. Her conscious acts were not reflected upon, not objectified, all her attention being directed towards the object of her concern. So, when she is asked later how she knew the accident was going to happen, she answers simply, 'Women's intuition.' With this illustration I do not mean to imply that women claim to be intuitive only because they are not often phenomenologists. Yet, as long as one's conscious and intentional operations remain unobjectified, one will tend to fall back upon the most readily available account of cognition. So, someone who may be just as perceptive, intelligent, and rational as any man, but who has already identified being a woman with not being rational, will not surprisingly cite women's intuition.

It could be argued, especially in an instance like the one described in the preceding example, when a woman claims to know what has not yet happened, or what happens at a distance, that there is an extrasensory dimension to be considered. I do not mean to rule out the possibility of extrasensory data, but as mere data it is not knowledge, any more than ordinary sensation is. If a woman is to employ such data in order to arrive

at knowledge, intelligent and rational acts are still required. The pronounce-
ment, at least, must be formulated, and this requires insight and conception.

The only difference between a cognitive claim, such as 'It's a simple matter
of deduction, my dear Watson,' and the claim 'I just know it – women's
intuition' is a habit of objectifying and appropriating conscious operations
traditionally accepted as gender-specific. The process of knowing in any case
involves the same basic pattern of conscious and intentional operations,
more or less attended to or objectified. As Lonergan has shown, there is a
universal, transcultural, and, I would add, gender-transcendent, structure
of conscious intentionality.[30] This is not to say, of course, that the *noematic*
correlates are the same. Different sensations, interests, images, expectations, and desires do give rise to different affects and questions, and in turn
these occasion different insights and formulations. So, to return to the
example of the worried mother, what she noticed, which gave rise to her
prediction, would vary according to her interests, preoccupations, and training, and may very well differ from what another woman or her husband
might notice. Yet, the process of arriving at her conclusion involves the same
set of conscious and intentional operations, which anyone employs to know
anything.

'Women's intuition' is an imprecise and abstract term for a set of conscious and intentional operations that is neither distinctly intuitive nor specifically female. The a priori set of acts constitutive of the process of knowing
consists of both logical, rational acts, and so-called intuitive, pre-conceptual
or non-conceptual, acts. Even the act of insight, which I believe Schopenhauer was approaching when he referred to the universalizing faculty, is
pre-conceptual.[31] Just as there is no such thing as women's intuition, so there
is no universalizing faculty attributable only to men.

If, as I have argued, intelligence and rationality are not uniquely male
achievements, what are we to make of Lonergan's reference to women in
chapter 7 of *Insight*? In 'Common Sense as Object,' Lonergan sets up the
basic principles of the dialectic of community, spontaneous intersubjectivity
and practical common sense, by describing a basic duality to be found in
the human subject. The human person is not only the intelligent sponsor
of the good of order, but also a member of an intersubjective community.
Lonergan describes intersubjectivity as follows: 'Even after civilization is
attained, intersubjective community survives in the family with its circle of
relatives and its accretion of friends, in customs and folkways, in basic arts
and crafts and skills, in language and song and dance, and most concretely
of all in the inner psychology and radiating influence of women.'[32] This
attribution of intersubjective radiance to women may sound complimentary,
but does it not also echo the traditional view that associates the non-rational
with women? If it is women somehow who most especially exemplify this

intersubjective side of human nature, does it not follow that it is men who most especially exemplify the drive of pure intelligence and reason?

What is meant by women's 'radiating influence'? Is it the warmth of a well-tended hearth, the aroma of bread baking, ironed curtains on the windows, flowers on the tables, and a smiling face and loving arms to return to? If this kind of ambience has been traditionally provided by the woman of the household, I do not think it is a function of her being a women, but rather of her traditional relegation to and mastery in the domestic sphere. The ambience of any home is created by the dominant figures who spend time in it, and its smooth functioning is a result not only of intersubjective feeling but also, as Lonergan would attest, of practical intelligence. Perhaps what is meant by this radiating influence is the erotic effect a woman can have on those around her. If so, this pertains more to the desires and responses of those affected by a woman than to her own feelings.

The radiating influence of women, finally, can be interpreted to mean the *Befindlichkeit* that creates the atmosphere of intersubjectivity. One's *Befindlichkeit* is the fundamental state-of-mind, disposition, or mood that underlies and permeates all of one's conscious intentionality. Examples of *Befindlichkeit* are boredom and joy.[33] Just as I have not found intellectual and rational acts to be specific to men, I do not think that the empathetic communication of one's *Befindlichkeit* is unique to women. The black mood, for example, of an angry or grieving father can cast a pall over a family, as the optimistic courage of a general can cheer his troops, as the paranoia of a chief executive can infect members of his administration with suspicion. In these cases the communication of one's mood seems to be a function of one's centrality to the situation. It is also possible, I suppose, for one's *Befindlichkeit* to radiate an influence because of its own strength. In any case, it seems clear that both men and women have a radiating influence on those around them.

Lonergan's specific mention of the intersubjective radiating influence of women could be interpreted as another instance of the traditional tendency to identify women with the affective, or non-rational. However, Lonergan attributes a basic duality to the human subject, both male and female. Men too are involved in familial bonds, feelings of kinship and sympathy, and the elementary schemes of recurrence constitutive of the mundane.[34] And, Lonergan clearly did not mean to deny the other half of the human duality to women, for he elsewhere refers to women of intelligence.[35] Finally, the question of whether the 'inner psychology' of women, which Lonergan mentions in the above passage, most concretely exemplifies intersubjective community remains open, but it lies beyond the scope of this paper.

I believe that Lonergan has provided in his account of the transcendental structure of conscious intentionality a foundation from which we can methodically dismantle sexist theory and in particular the myth of women's intuition, whether from non-feminist or feminist sources.

Notes

1 This essay is a substantially revised version of one entitled 'The Question of Woman's Experience of God,' which originally appeared in Alvin F. Kimel, Jr, ed., *Speaking the Christian God: The Holy Trinity and the Challenge of Feminism* (copyright © 1992 by William B. Eerdmans Publishing Co. All rights reserved. Used by permission).

2 For an account of Lonergan's generalized empirical method of intentionality analysis, see Elizabeth A. Morelli, *Anxiety: A Study of the Affectivity of Moral Consciousness* (Lanham, MD: University Press of America, 1985) 5–11.

3 Sallie McFague, *Models of God: Theology for an Ecological Nuclear Age* (Philadelphia: Fortress Press, 1987) x–xi.

4 Daphne Hampson, *Theology and Feminism* (Cambridge, MA: Basil Blackwell, 1990) 156–61.

5 I do not think it is necessary to introduce into this inquiry the controversy concerning the distinction between sex differences and gender differences. For an introduction to this area of analysis, see Deborah L. Rhode, ed., *Theoretical Perspectives on Sexual Differences* (New Haven and London: Yale University Press, 1990).

6 Kathleen Freeman, *Companion to the Pre-Socratic Philosophers* (Oxford: Basil Blackwell, 1966) 248.

7 Actually, Aristotle fares better in this regard than thinkers of the Enlightenment. He, at least, characterized woman as essentially rational, as possessing intellect; however, he understood woman to possess an inferior rationality to that of man. This inferiority was a function of woman's limited sphere of the exercise of her reason. Woman was not allowed to participate in the public, political arena, but was capable of exercising reason in the domestic sphere. See Hannah Arendt's *The Human Condition* (Chicago: University of Chicago Press, 1974).

8 Dorothy L. Sayers, 'Human-Not-Quite-Human,' in Richard L. Purtill, ed., *Moral Dilemmas* (Belmont, CA: Wadsworth Publishing Co., 1985) 236–40.

9 G.W.F. Hegel, *Philosophy of Right*, trans. T.M. Knox (New York: Oxford University Press, 1973) 263–64; cited in Carol McMillan, *Women, Reason, and Nature* (Princeton, NJ: Princeton University Press, 1982) 8.

10 Arthur Schopenhauer, *On the Basis of Morality* (Indianapolis: Bobbs-Merrill, 1965) 151; cited in McMillan, p. 11.

11 Hegel, *Philosophy of Right* 263–64.

12 Søren Kierkegaard, *Either/Or*, vol. 1, trans. David F. Swenson and Lillian Marvin Swenson (Princeton, NJ: Princeton University Press, 1944) 426. Kier-

kegaard speaks pseudonymously in this passage, as the master aesthete Johannes the Seducer. This accounts for the haughty tone of the remarks, but not, I think, for the essential message, because as far as I know Kierkegaard does not disavow this opinion elsewhere.

13 Mary Wollstonecraft in her *Vindication of the Rights of Woman* (1792) celebrated the 'manly virtues,' and urged women to 'every day grow more and more masculine.' Jean Bethke Elshtain, *Mediations on Modern Political Thought: Masculine/ Feminine Themes from Luther to Arendt* (New York: Praeger Special Studies, 1986) 27.

For a contemporary example, Carol Gilligan in her critique of Kohlberg's methodology, does not critique his Kantian-Rawlsian presupposition of male rationality. She rather pursues the question of whether or not women develop morally as far as men, but along different lines, along the lines of greater interpersonal sensitivity as distinct from legalistic negotiating. Carol Gilligan, *In a Different Voice* (Cambridge, MA: Harvard University Press, 1982).

14 Hegel, *Philosophy of Right* 263–64.

15 In describing the process of attaining enlightenment, the difficult appropriation of one's own autonomy, Kant remarks: 'That the step to competence is held to be very dangerous by the far greater portion of mankind (and by the entire fair sex) – quite apart from its being arduous – is seen to by those guardians who have so kindly assumed superintendence over them.' *Foundations of the Metaphysics of Morals*, trans. Lewis White Beck (Indianapolis: Bobbs-Merrill Co., 1959) 85.

16 Max Scheler, *Formalism in Ethics and Non-Formal Ethics of Value*, trans. Manfred S. Frings and Roger L. Funk (Evanston: Northwestern University Press, 1973); Stephen Strasser, *Phenomenology of Feeling: An Essay on the Phenomena of the Heart*, trans. Robert E. Wood (Pittsburgh: Duquesne University Press, 1977). For a summary account of their affective typologies, see Elizabeth A. Morelli, *Anxiety* chap. 2.

17 Max Scheler, *Ressentiment*, trans. Lewis Coser (New York: Schocken Books, 1961) 60–62.

18 Ibid. 61.

19 Scheler, *Formalism* 481–82.

20 Hilda Hein, 'Liberating Philosophy: An End to the Dichotomy of Spirit and Matter,' in Ann Garry and Marilyn Pearsall, eds, *Women, Knowledge, and Reality* (Boston: Unwin Hyman, 1989) 299.

21 Ibid. 300. See also Simone de Beauvoir's account of how woman becomes the wielder of black magic in the imagination of threatened man in *The Second Sex*, trans. H.M. Parshley (New York: Bantam Books, 1953) chap. 9.

22 Alison M. Jaggar, *Feminist Politics and Human Nature* (Sussex: Harvester Press, 1983) 378.

23 Catharine Stimpson, 'Women as Knowers,' in Diane L. Fowlkes and Char-
    lotte S. McClure, eds, *Feminist Visions: Toward A Transformation of the Liberal
    Arts Curriculum* (Tuscaloosa: University of Alabama Press, 1984) 21.

24 Friedrich Nietzsche, *The Genealogy of Morals*, trans. Horace B. Samuel (New
    York: Modern Library, 1927) III.24, p. 782. For an analysis of Nietzsche's
    critique in juxtaposition to the notion of an a priori desire to know, see
    Elizabeth A. Morelli, 'A Reflection on Lonergan's Notion of the Pure Desire
    to Know,' *Ultimate Reality and Meaning* 13 (1990) 50–60.

25 Alasdair MacIntyre, *Whose Justice? Which Rationality?* (Notre Dame: Univer-
    sity of Notre Dame Press, 1988).

26 Carol McMillan, *Women, Reason, and Nature* (Princeton , NJ: Princeton Uni-
    versity Press, 1982) 34ff.

27 Bernard Lonergan, *Method in Theology* (New York: Herder and Herder,
    1972) 34.

28 Ibid. 34, n. 5.

29 Sartre's dismantling of the Freudian notions of the unconscious and the
    censor in *Being and Nothingness* (1943: trans. Hazel E. Barnes [New York:
    Washington Square Press, 1966] 90–96 is based on a similar notion of unob-
    jectified consciousness. Sartre refers to this consciousness as pre-reflective or
    non-positional consciousness. He first provided a phenomenological des-
    cription of non-positional consciousness in his early work *The Transcendence
    of the Ego* (1936: trans. Forrest Williams and Robert Kirkpatrick [New York:
    Farrar, Straus and Giroux, 1957]).

    How Lonergan's acknowledgment of what is conscious but not objectified
    in 1972 is to be reconciled with his adoption of the Freudian notions of the
    unconscious and the censor in chapter 6 of *Insight* (1957) is a further ques-
    tion. See Bernard Lonergan, *Insight: A Study of Human Understanding*, vol. 3
    of *Collected Works of Bernard Lonergan*, ed. Frederick E. Crowe and Robert M.
    Doran (Toronto: University of Toronto Press, 1992) 212–31.

30 *Method in Theology* 6–13.

31 *Insight* 30–33.

32 Ibid. 237–38.

33 Morelli, *Anxiety* 96–100.

34 Common sense is not the exclusive domain of women; see Lonergan's chap-
    ters on common sense in *Insight*, chaps 6 and 7, esp. p. 196. Similarly,
    Lonergan does not differentiate patterns of experience on the basis of gen-
    der; see *Insight* 204–12.

35 In *Insight*, Lonergan distinguishes between the common sense of women
    and men, and it should be recalled that common sense is a specialization of
    intelligence: pp. 203, 444, 587. He also refers to the alertness of mind that
    enables young women (and men) to attend university, p. 311; and he states

that the goal of method is the emergence of explicit metaphysics in the minds of women (and men), p. 426.

Women and the Social Construction of Self-Appropriation

ABSTRACT *The purpose of this essay is to examine Lonergan's notion of self-appropriation in light of women's social and historical location. Lorraine Code's analysis of the traditional designation of women as non-knowers or, at best, receivers rather than discoverers of knowledge reveals the historical limitations set on the possibility of women engaging in self-appropriation. The empirical work of Belenky, Clinchy, Goldberger, and Tarule in* Women's Ways of Knowing *provides a descriptive analysis of the ways in which women understand themselves as knowers and the social structures that serve as obstacles to women's existential grasp of how they know. A close examination of Lonergan's understanding of community, belief, and the existential nature of self-appropriation shows that his heuristic position does account for the social location of knowers. At the same time, this empirical research provides powerful evidence of the social conditions of possibility for women's (self) knowledge. Further, Lonergan's explicit cognitional theory, grounded empirically in the knowing subject, can provide a normative framework for an explanatory interpretation of historical and empirical research on women's conceptions of themselves as knowers.*

One of the central components of Bernard's Lonergan's philosophy and theology is the notion of self-appropriation. In fact, he insists that cognitive and moral self-appropriation constitute the foundation, the starting-point, of any philosophy and, therefore, of any theological enterprise. Since confusions over how we know and whether we can know anything are at the root of many philosophical and theological debates, sorting out epistemological positions and counterpositions is a necessary beginning. And this sorting out is the fruit of attending to the operations that one engages in when one inquires, seeks to understand, has insights, weighs evidence and makes judgments, deliberates on courses of action, and makes decisions. Cognitive self-appropriation is a matter of applying the operations of inquiry to the subject of inquiry. Moral self-appropriation involves applying the same critical set of questions to oneself as a moral judge and actor.[1] Indeed, the central theme of both of Lonergan's major works, *Insight* and *Method in Theology*, consists of an invitation to the reader to engage in an experiment that only the reader herself can perform.[2]

In other words, Lonergan is concerned with *how* we know. He puts forward his analysis of the structure of knowing and then invites his readers to verify his theory. But the trick is that one does this, not by observing others, nor by purely logical deduction, but by attending to oneself as one operates.[3] Thus, self-appropriation becomes the means of verifying how we know: it results in a judgment: I am a knower and I know reality through a pattern of experiencing, understanding, judging facts, and judging values. It consists in heightening one's consciousness, not 'looking at' oneself as an object but becoming aware of oneself as one acts; increasing one's self-presence.[4] Lonergan insists that this verification of the process of knowing through self-appropriation will provide a powerful tool for all further tasks in philosophy, theology, indeed for grasping the world itself: 'Thoroughly understand what it is to understand, and not only will you understand the broad lines of all there is to be understood but you will possess a fixed base, an invariant pattern, opening upon all further developments of understanding.'[5]

In a similar attempt to re-orient philosophy and theology, feminist scholars in recent years have begun to attend to the ways in which knowing has been defined. In this case the task has been, not only to critique epistemologies within the domain of philosophy per se, but to show how various epistemological positions embody, wittingly or unwittingly, a patriarchal power structure. That is to say, processes of knowing have been defined by men, and these men have relegated women to a lower position in the epistemological domain. Feminists are discovering how philosophers in particular and socialization in general have defined women as non-knowers or as having inferior cognitive abilities.

The constructive side of this feminist critique involves women discovering for themselves how they know. Since knowing, the processes involved and the capabilities required, has for so long been delineated by men, women scholars are attempting to re-analyse knowing in light of women's experience.[6] While this scholarship covers a wide range of disciplines and approaches, much of this work shares Lonergan's attention to the concrete subject as the locus of epistemological verification. The feminist task has a more overt sociopolitical agenda and the technical 'self-appropriation' of

Lonergan is never adverted to. However, it is worth our while to attend to the work of feminists who are trying to 'appropriate' women's experience, and/or women's own understanding of their understanding.

The purpose of this paper is to examine the findings of feminist scholars with regard to women as knowers: how women have been treated, traditionally, as knowers, and how contemporary women understand themselves as knowers. By this review we will illumine the situation in which many women find themselves, the conditions that inhibit or contribute to the self-appropriation advocated by Lonergan. At the same time, we will raise questions with regard to Lonergan, pressing to expand his notion of self-appropriation in light of the empirical reality of contemporary women's experience.

1   Women's Ways of Knowing: Historical Analysis

The literature reviewing the history of philosophy and its legacy regarding women as [non] knowers is burgeoning. We will rely on an article by Lorraine Code to highlight some of the themes of this literature.[7] The first of these themes is that cognitive activity is communal and that 'the epistemic "location" of knowers and would-be knowers, in a time, a place, a culture, and a language, imposes constraints upon both the form and the content of knowledge.'[8] Different cognitive capacities, material resources, and cultural values affect and inform one's knowing, such that the world is known differently, and persons understand themselves as knowers differently, from one cognitive agent to the next. We are all cognitively 'located' within epistemic communities, and these epistemic communities in part define what and how we are able to know.

This emphasis on epistemic community is related to the critique of modern philosophy, which has generally assumed the isolation and autonomy of the cognitive agent. Whereas moral theory must acknowledge the social interaction of moral agents, epistemology has traditionally denied the interdependence of cognitive agents. 'The knowledge-seeker is conceived as solitary, on the assumption that people *are* and *should be* independent in cognitive activity.'[9] The 'solipsistic bias of traditional epistemology'[10] has resulted in the tendency to overlook the shared basis of knowledge. In fact, much of what we know we know because we have learned it from others. A key factor, then, in coming to know anything is to learn who is to be trusted as a source of knowledge.[11]

A central theme of Code's article is that the activity of knowing is closely tied to that of moral action. Thus, she speaks of 'epistemic responsibility' and of 'intellectual virtue.' However, the key to her article, and the argument of many feminists in reviewing the history of philosophy, is that women have been denied the opportunity to be epistemically responsible. '[T]he kind of moral responsibility women have been able to exercise has been *perceived to be* of a sort inferior to that possible for men.'[12] Code traces this difference back to Aristotle's discussion of virtue as something accruing to a citizen of the *polis*. Since women, by definition, were not citizens of the polis, virtue, including and especially intellectual virtue, was not something women could or should attain.'[13]

Thus emerges an argument central to much feminist literature. Women have been relegated to the private domain of the household and denied access to 'citizenship' in the public domain. Whether this stems remotely from Aristotle's emphasis on the *polis* or more proximately from post-indus-trialization economic structures, the division between public and private as male and female domains of activity and responsibility remains.'[14] The important point here is that this division has epistemic implications: 'For the fact that woman is restricted to dealing with things individual and private restricts those things she is in a position to *know* to things discoverable within the confines of this realm. Hence there is a constant, enclosed circle in female life where her morality, traditionally, is based in an excessively nar-row cognitive sphere: where the boundaries of her world are close about her, constraining both knowledge and action.'[15]

The restriction of women's cognitive capacities to the private realm has further implications for how women traditionally have gained their knowl-edge. Rather than being given opportunities to discover knowledge for themselves, women have traditionally been *taught*, been expected to receive knowledge from others. This restriction to learning by way of receiving knowledge from others leads over the course of time to inherited assump-tions that one cannot learn in any other way. Persistent socialization that sees women as incapable of making their own discoveries leads to women having diminished concepts of their cognitive abilities. Thus, for many women, exercising epistemic responsibility, developing intellectual virtue, involves a heroic courage that not only pursues the knowledge sought but affirms the capabilities of the knower as well. This is 'a form of courage that is difficult to sustain in the face of pervasive and *infectious* feeling on every side that one is bound not to succeed in one's enterprise, be it intellectual, moral, or other.'[16]

2   Women's Ways of Knowing: Empirical Research

These latter contentions, that women often are relegated to learning from others and that they distrust their own cognitive abilities, are borne out in the study conducted by Belenky, Clinchy, Goldberger, and Tarule.'[17] These researchers set out to gather empirical evidence on how women themselves understand their understanding. In effect, they have traced empirically the

self-appropriation of women in different social locations. The study took
place in the late 1970s and was modelled after the work of William Perry.[18]
Belenky et al. sought to replicate his work with the express purpose of
examining *women's* conceptions of themselves as knowers, and the attendant
but often implicit epistemologies involved.

Their study consisted of in-depth interviews of 135 women from a variety
of socio-economic situations. The interviews incorporated questions from
Perry, meant to establish epistemological positions. However, the questioning went far beyond this, on the assumption that the entire life situation
must be taken into account to understand women as knowers. The 135
subjects were drawn from academic institutions and social-agency training
programs. Ninety of the 135 were enrolled in educational institutions ranging from a prestigious 'ivy league' college to an urban community college
with a mixed ethnic and less advantaged clientele. In addition, forty-five
women interviewed were from family agencies dealing with clients seeking
help with parenting. Having gathered interview data, these researchers
coded the interview material into five classifications representing the distinct epistemological categories that they discerned.[19] We will briefly review
each of these perspectives.[20]

2.1 Silence

Though the researchers found only two or three subjects whom they could
designate as 'silent,' other women describe a period of silence in retrospect.
What stands out about these women is not their perspective on knowing
but the fact that they have none. The silent women live in a world cut off
from others, with little or no real communication. Words are not seen as
tools for dialogue but as weapons of might, used to diminish rather than
connect people. These women describe the barest experience of dialogue
with others and indicate no experience of dialogue with 'the self.'[21] Though
language is available to these women, the lack of representational thought
stands out (25–26). A lack of play in childhood seems tied to this absence
of symbolic images, as well as the belief that women are expected to be seen
but not heard (32).

What is most salient in these women's stories is their social location, the
role of authorities, the sex stereotypes involved, and the presence of violence. The silent women came from the youngest and the most socially,
economically, and educationally deprived segment of the research sample.
They were found in the social agencies, not the ivy-league colleges, and came
from families who themselves were isolated from community. The women
see themselves as passive, while others, the 'authorities,' are all-powerful.
The power accrued to authorities comes as a result of might not expertise.

Authorities are loud but never explain anything (27–29). Males are active, while women are passive and powerless: 'I didn't think I had the right to think. That probably goes back to my folks. When my father yelled, everybody automatically jumped. Every woman I ever saw, then, the man barked and the woman jumped. I just thought that women were no good and had to be told everything to do' (30). The presence of violence is tied to this notion of authority and lack of voice. In the families of silent women 'at least one parent routinely used violence rather than words for influencing others' behaviour' (32). While violence was apparent in the lives of women of other perspectives, these women seemed particularly impotent: they had no sense of themselves as intelligent initiators of change (29).

2.2 Received Knowledge

Unlike the silent women, women of this perspective see words as central tools in the knowing process (36). Listening becomes all important and is the vehicle of learning. Listening is a very active and demanding process and receiving knowledge from others can be quite liberating.[22] At the same time, received knowers have little confidence in their own ability to think or speak. Truth is 'out there' and comes from knowledgeable others; it cannot be discerned by any processes from within. Authorities are sources of truth, never to be questioned. And even these authorities do not generate their own answers; they too receive knowledge from others. Status is equated with truth, and a conflict in authorities leaves these women baffled.[23] Furthermore, there are no gray areas: things are either right or wrong, true or false. These women are intolerant of ambiguity and, in receiving knowledge, just simply accept it; there is no attempt to try to *understand* the idea (42).

Because women of this perspective rely so heavily on others for knowledge, their conceptions of themselves are largely tied to what others think. Just as knowledge about the world comes from others, so self-reflection is rare in these women. 'Who I am' is merely a reflection of 'what others think of me.' Self-appropriation, as Lonergan would have it, is practically impossible, since distance from others' expectations is rare.[24] Thus, these women typically conceive of themselves as caretakers, accepting the world as hierarchically arranged and dualistic (45–48). Add to this the expectation that women are not meant to be intellectually independent, and the 'fear of [intellectual] success' emerges: 'Women worry that if they were to develop their own powers it would be at the expense of others. Not only are they concerned to live up to the cultural standards that hold that women should be the listeners, subordinate, and unassertive; but they also worry that if they excel, those they love will automatically be penalized' (46).[25]

Exposure to diverse intellectual or cultural milieux can challenge received knowers to shift their perspective. Alternately, being thrust into roles of responsibility (parenthood, earning one's own living) can erode a simple trust in the 'truth' of 'them.' This shift often comes at a great cost, however. It is because their social worlds break down, and authorities are seen to be unreliable, that women are forced to look to themselves as generators of their own truths. Thus emerges 'subjective knowledge.'[26]

2.3 Subjective Knowledge

Belenky and her colleagues classify as 'subjective knowers' those who insist that there is an inner resource that contributes to their knowing. In most cases this involves a rejection of a simple dualism of right and wrong, as well as a nuanced assessment of authority as a locus of truth. In contrast to received knowers, who see truth as external to themselves, subjectivists conceive of truth as 'personal, private, and subjectively known or intuited' (54). One women refers to a portion of herself that 'I didn't even know I had – intuition, instinct, what I call my gut' (57).[27]

What is most striking is that this shift in epistemological perspective seems inevitably tied to a revolutionary change in personal life situation. It involves a shift to greater personal autonomy, yet it is not tied to any age, class, or ethnic group. What seems to link these women is that they identify this discovery of 'subjective' truth as a recent and profoundly liberating event in their lives (54, 56).[28] Indeed, what seems to come through most clearly in these stories is not only the current reliance on self for knowledge, but the past failure of male authority (57). Many of these women had had husbands or fathers who belittled them. Others angrily gave accounts of how their men had been disenfranchised through economic injustice or racism. Middle-class women recounted the emotional defections of fathers and husbands who were preoccupied with their own destinies. Most pervasive among these women was the loss of trust in male authority owing to sexual abuse or harassment. The discovery that male resources are not to be trusted was accompanied by a discovery of maternal authority, women mentors who could be trusted and who encouraged these women to trust their own abilities to know (60–62).[29]

For these women, affirming themselves as experts, relying on their own inner voice, is crucial. They lean towards an anti-rationalism that is suspicious of scientific expertise and they trust instead their feelings, intuitions, their 'gut' (71–75). Subjectivists rely on 'cafeteria style' means of determining truth, articulating no clear-cut procedures of verification. There is no absolute truth that is true for everyone; truth is absolute only for the person herself (69–70). Women of this epistemological stance are the ultimate relativists. However, while their position initially gives them courage and autonomy, it at times results in stubborn isolation. As women begin to discover that the inner voice can lie, and is not as reliable as first indicated, their subjectivist position breaks down. Some of them move on to procedural knowing.[30]

2.4 Procedural Knowledge

A much smaller group of women than those exhibiting 'subjectivism' fall into the category of procedural knowers. Most of these women are privileged, bright, white, and young, and all were involved in some formal educational institution (87, 93). The shift that occurred in their thinking came about as a result of further encounters with authorities, in this case benign authorities who challenged them to substantiate their opinions (88). Professors insisted on papers that *argued* a position rather than just *asserting* an opinion. Many of these women succumb initially to the demands of teachers out of practicality, the need for a college degree. But most come eventually to recognize the value of 'playing the game,' of learning how to think in rational, procedural terms.[31]

Procedural knowers engage in conscious, deliberate, and systematic analysis. They recognize that one's 'gut' is not infallible, that some 'truths' are truer than others, that they can know things that have never been seen or touched, and that expertise is to be trusted (93). The criteria for justifying an argument are 'objective' in that they relate to the object rather than simply reflecting the subject's point of view (89, 98–99). Attending to and understanding an object, be it a parent, a text, or a painting, are central (91). Learning is not a matter of memorizing right answers; in fact, teachers rarely provide the answers. Rather, access to knowledge involves learning a method, grasping the procedures that lie behind an assertion of truth.[32]

This shift is accompanied by a diminishment of 'voice.' Lacking both the derived authority of received knowers and the inner assurance of subjectivists, these women speak softly. 'The inner voice turns critical; ... because their ideas must measure up to certain objective standards, they speak in measured tones' (94). In a few cases, this emphasis on objectivity and the demands of procedure lead to personal alienation. In these cases some reclamation of the self is required and 'constructed knowledge' emerges.[33]

2.5 Constructed Knowledge

A handful of women in this study moved beyond procedural knowledge. These women seem caught between their own creative forces and the 'objective' procedures they have learned. They are seeking to reclaim the self as part of the process of knowing. Through periods of intensive self-reflection they try to grasp just 'how I want to think' (136). They discover a need to sort out what they have learned via others from what they themselves know to be true (137). There is a need to weave together reason and emotion, and objective and subjective knowing (134). But most central to this position is the discovery that '*All knowledge is constructed,* and *the knower is an intimate part of the known*' (137). Knowing is not a matter of merely attending to the object, it also involves constructing meaningful explanations.

Several corollaries are attached to this basic perspective. For one thing, for these women passion and intellect are not opposed, and the move into constructed knowing is accompanied by the unleashing of a passion for learning: knowing is no longer a cold, distant journey but a lively exciting quest (140–44). Within this quest there is a tolerance for ambiguity; the rigid dualisms are long gone (137). Further, 'real talk' is possible, in which people use words in a collaborative search for truth rather than as weapons or tools to impress others (144–46). In addition, the knowledge of experts is not ruled out of court, but taken with careful qualifications (139–41). Nevertheless, conflicts over 'voice' and silence remain, as constructivist women experience resistance to their abilities to think and articulate truth (146–48). Thus, though these women have moved to a very sophisticated and nuanced acceptance of themselves as knowers, they often find few who are interested in listening.

3   Lonergan's Self-Appropriation and Women's Ways of Knowing

Having reviewed the stories of women and how they think about their thinking, we now ask: What does this have to do with Lonergan's notion of self-appropriation? Lonergan speaks in the technical language of philosophy, addressing at a theoretical and explanatory level complex questions of epistemology. And his position on knowing does not rely on empirical verification through studies such as those of Belenky and her colleagues, but on each person attending to her own operating. Nevertheless, if his theory is correct, it should provide a framework in which to interpret these researchers' results, what Lonergan would call the 'upper blade' of any scientific or scholarly endeavour.[34] And the 'data' of this empirical study may be able to raise questions towards refining this theoretical framework as Lonergan outlines it.

Let us first deal with the questions that these findings might raise regarding Lonergan's notion of self-appropriation. The overriding message of feminist epistemology and *Women's Ways of Knowing* is that the social milieu in which women find themselves dictates how they conceive of themselves as knowers, and that a large part of their cognitive 'self-appropriation' depends on refuting false restrictions of their cognitive self-concepts. Does

Lonergan recognize the power of socialization and history in conditioning the possibilities of self-appropriation? Though a thorough defence of Lonergan's thought as *not* solipsistic is impossible here, a few indications from Lonergan can be drawn out.

As a first indication, it is clear that Lonergan recognizes that his own theory and its reliance on self-appropriation are only possible because of previous thinkers and owing to the current climate, which demands attention to interiority.[35] And though he does not explicitly outline his *own* narrative history and/or social location, it is clear that he recognizes the role of these in constituting the meaning of human acts:

> Human acts occur in sociocultural contexts: there is not only the action but also the human setup, the family and mores, the state and religion, the economy and technology, the law and education. None of these are mere products of nature: they have a determination from meaning; to change the meaning is to change the concrete setup.[36]

On community Lonergan says:

> The common meanings constitutive of communities are not the work of isolated individuals nor even of single generations. Common meanings have histories: they originate in single minds; they become common only through successful and widespread communication; they are transmitted to successive generations only through training and education. Slowly and gradually they are clarified, expressed, formulated, defined, only to be enriched and deepened and transformed, and no less often to be impoverished, emptied out, and deformed.[37]

While this illustrates Lonergan's general recognition of the role of community in meaning and self-definition, in his 1957 lectures on *Insight*, published as *Understanding and Being*, Lonergan explicitly relates communities of meaning to self-appropriation. Let us review at length several passages from a section in which he discusses the existential commitment involved in self-appropriation:

> Now there is a joker in this business of self-appropriation. We do not start out with a clean slate as we move towards self-appropriation. We already have our ideals of what knowledge is, and we want to do self-appropriation according to the ideal that is already operative in

us – not merely in terms of the spontaneous, natural ideal, but in terms of some explicit ideal ...

In other words, this business of self-appropriation is not a simple matter of moving in and finding the functionally operative tendencies that ground ideals. It is also a matter of pulling out the inadequate ideals that may be already existent and operative in us. There is a conflict, there is an existential element, there is a question of the subject, and it is a personal question that will not be the same for everyone.[38] ...

The kind of ideal you have at the present time is a function of your past experience, your past study, your past teachers, your past courses in philosophy.[39]

Thus, Lonergan recognizes that there may be a fundamental conflict between our spontaneous orientation to know and the messages/ideals we have received regarding our knowing. Lonergan in the above passage is referring to old philosophical ideals, of those trained in the thought of Descartes, Kant, Hegel, or whomever. But his point is no less true as applied to women's experience. In the case of women, historical analysis and empirical study reveal that the overriding ideal has been that of women as non-knowers or, at best, receivers of others' knowledge.

A further aspect of Lonergan's thought, often not discussed in relation to self-appropriation, adds refinement to this thesis. What the above passages allude to Lonergan speaks about elsewhere as 'belief.' Initially in *Insight*, and more extensively in his later works such as *Method in Theology*, Lonergan gives explicit emphasis to the fact that much of what we know we know by believing others.[40] Lonergan points out that there are two ways of gaining knowledge: (1) through discovering something for yourself or (2) through coming to believe the report of someone else's discovery. He points this out in contradiction to the modern assumption that reason is opposed to belief, the positivistic view that the discoveries of hard science are 'real facts,' whereas everything else is mere opinion.[41] Rather, Lonergan claims, even (and especially) science relies on the past discoveries of others. Thus, he illustrates the social and historical character of knowledge, the fact that human knowledge 'is not some individual possession but rather a common fund, from which each may draw by believing, to which each may contribute in the measure that he performs his cognitional operations properly and reports their results accurately.'[42]

This last phrase, the assumption that each may contribute to the common fund of human knowledge, reveals an assumption of a 'level playing field' as regards contributions to the public fund of knowledge. What studies reveal, however, is that there is much less than an equal opportunity when it comes to women, especially those disadvantaged by class and race barriers, in contributing to the public fund of knowledge. To the degree that women have been denied opportunities to legitimately and publicly discover things for themselves, they have not discovered that they themselves are discoverers. To the degree that society has set up expectations and stereotypes that denigrate women's capacities to know, women have not, except in rare and courageous exceptions, been free to discover facts for themselves.

Thus, in addition to the fact that knowledge flows in a dialectic between belief and immanent discovery, in addition to the ideal in which discovery and belief are mutually nourishing, there is the reality in which beliefs are distorted and inquiry becomes self-serving. While Lonergan does not use the particular example of women and knowing, he is surely aware of progress and decline in history, operative through bias, which skews belief and, in turn, distorts knowledge.[43]

Now, what becomes evident in examining the trends in 'women's ways of knowing' is that the distorted beliefs that have and still do oppress women are precisely beliefs about believing and discovery themselves. Historically, to the degree that women were considered cognitive agents at all, they were relegated to believing what others told them.[44] Many contemporary women, if they are not totally 'silent,' can only conceive of themselves as receivers of knowledge. Even those who move beyond this to some confidence in their own 'inner voice' find assertion of their role as 'discoverers' of knowledge to be radical, revolutionary, and requiring courageous changes in their communities of meaning. Thus, self-appropriation for women, even in its descriptive, untechnical form, seems to engage them in powerful existential struggles, not only with the operations they use in knowing, but with their roles as agents of their own discoveries rather than as mere receivers of others' knowledge.[45]

The implications of this discovery of agency are manifold. With regard to Lonergan's foundational position regarding self-appropriation, it means that what is implicit in Lonergan's thought needs to be made explicit. And it is precisely this: that self-appropriation involves not only verifying a particular set of operations as basic to what is involved in the knowledge of discovery, but also distinguishing clearly between the knowledge of discovery and the knowledge born of belief and, regarding the latter, heightening one's awareness of assumptions about knowing itself. This is not to deny but enhance the power of Lonergan's critical realism. Surely to attend to and affirm the fact that one knows not by 'looking' or by imagining but by experiencing, understanding, and judging is most basic. But just as basic is the affirmation that, in addition to the myth that 'knowing is like looking,' there is the myth that 'knowing is merely hearing,' that is, that merely believing others is the only route open to knowledge.

With regard to women's lives it becomes apparent that 'self-appropriation' can be a powerful tool for liberation. At the same time this analysis reveals clearly the 'conditions of possibility' for such a self-appropriation to take place. Basic material resources and structural opportunities are necessary before women can even begin to conceive of themselves as cognitive agents.[46] A community of dialogue in which language is seen as a tool for communication seens fundamental. Related to this is the absence of violence and/or the threat of violence.[47] While many women need to move beyond the myth of 'mere believing' it seems clear that the experience of benign authorities is necessary before any appropriation of reasoned discovery can take place. Most obviously, the full flowering of 'reason' (over against subjectivism) seems only to occur when opportunities of higher education are available: the inequality of 'life chances' promoted by classism and racism cannot be overlooked. Yet even the experience of the 'benign' authorities of higher education seems to be tainted with either the reality or fear of sexual harassment. The overwhelming presence of experienced sexual abuse or harassment among women of all epistemological perspectives is surely a central factor. To the degree that self-appropriation of oneself as a knower is dialectically related to appropriation of oneself as a believer, and to the degree that authentic believing rests on trustworthy authorities, the absence of 'safe' environments for women is a key obstacle to their self-appropriation. The presence of trustworthy female mentors, in a variety of contexts, seems directly tied to women's discovery of discovery.

We have been drawing out the implications of empirical/historical study in relation to Lonergan's advocacy of self-appropriation. Let me, now, point out how self-appropriation as an 'upper blade' of research might orient and aid that research. First, while we have been easily equating the stories of *Women's Ways of Knowing* with Lonergan's self-appropriation, there is a basic difference. Whereas Lonergan's invitation to self-appropriation aims at an *explanatory* account of knowing, the women interviewed by Belenky and her colleagues are giving *descriptive* accounts of knowing. They speak in a common-sense medium without any attempt at systematic definition of their terms or of the relations among those terms. While such a descriptive account, of how my knowing appears to me, is a necessary aspect of self-appropriation, Lonergan's notion involves verifying an explanatory account of knowing in which terms, in this case the concrete operations of knowing, are related systematically to one another in the recurrent and normative pattern outlined by Lonergan. This type of self-appropriation, while descriptive in its appeal to the concrete knower herself, has the added advantages of an explanatory account of knowing in that the elements are intelligibly related to one another and not just to the subject.[48]

More important, perhaps, is the role of the researchers themselves. Not only are they recounting women's descriptions of their knowing, they themselves are merely describing the results of their investigation. That is, the researchers make no attempt to *explain* explicitly the perspectives they discern and/or the relations among them. The study does not establish as correct one epistemological perspective over against others. The researchers disavow any attempt to explain these perspectives as developmentally related, insisting that these are not 'stages' but 'perspectives.'[49] Yet it is clear that there is a chronological sequence involved and that lower stages are related to the emergence of higher stages. More important, it is clear that the researchers have implicit assumptions about which perspectives are 'better' in both the sense of being 'more correct' and in the moral sense of promoting the well-being of women. The emergence of increasing autonomy and 'voice' seem to be the operative values here, while an epistemology that gives women both without isolating them from others stands as the highest ideal.[50] Yet the researchers never establish just where these norms come from or why they are foundational to their research. They appeal to others who have done similar work, merely asserting some assumptions and allowing others to remain tacit.

An explicit epistemology, grounded in the self-appropriation of the researchers themselves, could provide a better framework for such research. The power of Lonergan's position is that it is verifiable, not merely asserted. It is verifiable in the operating of the knower herself. Lonergan's position on knowing thus can provide an *empirically grounded* yet *normative* account of what knowing is and, therefore, what it ought to be. His explanatory account of knowing can provide a theoretical framework for an explicitly developmental theory.

To illustrate this point, let me suggest some ways in which Lonergan's account of knowing might clarify the descriptive categories that Belenky and her colleagues use. First, there is Lonergan's distinction between the world of immediacy of the infant and the world mediated by meaning and created by value, a world that we all enter around the age of two when we develop symbol systems, such as language. The emergence of mediated meaning relies heavily on role-playing and interaction with a community of meaning-makers and language-users. The women who describe 'silence' seem to be describing an abortive attempt to move into such a world mediated by meaning. A lack of contact with others, a lack of exposure to language as constructive, and/or participation in a community that prefers to hold them at a level of infantile immediacy, works against the growth of these women into a world where 'knowledge' is even possible. Since human consciousness is inherently oriented towards symbolic meaning-making and value-creating, it is no wonder that even the discovery of 'received knowledge' is experienced as liberative for some of the women that Belenky and her colleagues interviewed.

Second, Lonergan makes the distinction between the knowledge born of belief and the knowledge that we discover for ourselves, and points out that, developmentally, we live in a horizon of received truths before we hone our own skills for discovery. So the women categorized under 'Received Knowledge' describe the process of learning through belief.[51] For these women, the criterion of truth lies in others, in the knowledge that others have and can impart. This is indeed true of all knowledge that we receive through belief; others have made discoveries and it is their cognitive operations, their adherence to transcendental norms, that determines the truth or falsity of their claims. What is missing for women who conceive knowing as merely receiving knowledge is that (1) they overlook their own processes of discovery and (2) the extrinsicism of their 'realism' does not distinguish valid from invalid authorities as sources of knowledge. Truth is true, values are authentic, *because* they come from some 'other,' and others are reliable to the degree that they hold socially sanctioned roles of power.

Third, the women of 'Subjective Knowledge' have made the powerful discovery that there is another way to knowledge: that of discovery. This is a first move towards the recognition of what Lonergan would call 'authentic subjectivity.' It is the realization that the criterion of truth lies, not in some external voice or authority, but in the very constitution of human consciousness itself. Not all received truth is true, not all received values are authentic and, furthermore, the means for discerning between true and false beliefs lies within the subject herself. Cognitive skills are applied not only towards grasping the intelligibility of what is learned but also towards explicitly making judgments; judgments as to the correctness of various concrete truth claims and judgments as to the validity of various sources of received knowledge.[52]

What remains unclear at this stage is just exactly what the internal process of discovery entails. The women described by Belenky and her collegues, despite their brave move into the affirmation of themselves as knowers, still function with a sort of empiricism.[53] Knowing is more than believing, but it is simplistically described as mere sensation. The metaphor of knowing as mere looking is not as prevalant as the description of mere feeling: something is true because 'I know in my gut that it is right.' A critical-realist position would affirm the recognition by these women of the role of the subject, but would insist that knowing involves operations distinct from (yet reliant on) mere perception.[54]

The 'procedural knowers' begin to add some refinement to the subjectivist claim. Without denying the role of the subject in knowing, these women begin to recognize bias in themselves, and the way that this bias can misconstrue reality. The corrective to this bias involves recognizing, once again, the role of the object in knowing. Just as not all received knowledge is to be affirmed as true, neither is all subjective perception to be trusted. Instead, one must appeal to the evidence at hand, the data that the object provides in order to make a true judgment. Though these women do not give full-blown accounts of judgment as the fulfilling of certain conditions by sufficient evidence, objectivity as a possibility and as requiring an appeal to independent data figures prominently in their accounts of knowing. They are beginning to distinguish the *criterion* of truth, which lies within their own consciousness (their orientation towards intelligibility, truth, and value) from the *evidence* for affirming any truth claim, which exists independently of subjective processes.[55]

The final perspective, called 'Constructed Knowledge,' has few adherents, and functions – as all final stages do in developmental theory – as a kind of speculative ideal for the researchers. The few threads that the researchers pick up as increments beyond procedural knowing involve a discovery of the passion of knowing and a more accepting recognition of others as the source of knowledge, a nuanced view of epistemic authorities combined with a collaborative vision of the generation of truth. This I would affirm as another move towards the recognition of both (1) the valid dialectic between the roles of belief and discovery and (2) authentic subjectivity as the root of objectivity. This is the point at which an explicit self-appropriation on the part of the researchers, and/or the use of Lonergan's explanatory account of critical realism, can orient the theory of the emergence of women's conception of themselves as knowers towards a 'highest' stage constituted by a correct and verified critical realism.

Finally, let me appeal to the transcendental precepts: Be attentive, Be intelligent, Be reasonable, and Be responsible.[56] These norms, these imperatives, operate as inherent criteria for determining when our relevant questions have been answered, for defining the authentic subjectivity that constitutes the attainment of epistemic objectivity. Since human consciousness *is* ordered towards attentiveness, intelligence, truth, and value, the human subject *ought* to use her cognitive operations towards these ends. To the degree that any set of cultural meanings, any designated gender roles, any social structures, civil laws, political systems, or economic configurations prohibit the free unfolding of a woman's exercise of her capacities for intellectual or moral self-transcendence, those systems and meanings need to be changed.

4   Conclusion

The purpose of this paper has been to examine Lonergan's advocacy of self-appropriation in light of women's social and historical location. Several conclusions emerge. On the one hand, the fact that gender, race, and class set clear conditions on the possibility of women's cognitive and moral self-appropriation comes to the fore. This in turn implies the need to understand Lonergan's notion of self-appropriation in light of his notions of community, belief, and existential commitment. Though Lonergan never specifically treats the question of women and knowing, his framework certainly allows for recognition of bias regarding knowing, a bias that may be the result of socio-economic, gendered conditions as much as it is a result of philosophical ideas. Concretely, it seems that women have inherited a bias in favour of either silence or a conception of knowing as believing. Yet more concretely, breaking out beyond these limits to a discovery of themselves as discoverers requires fulfilment of concrete conditions of material resources, educational opportunities, 'safe' environments, and trustworthy mentors. On the other hand, it is possible that Lonergan's meticulous explanation of the processes of knowing, and his advertance to verification in the knower herself, could move both historical and empirical studies of women's ways of knowing forward to a more explicit delineation of the criteria of valid knowing and the ideal of human flourishing operative in feminist theory.[57]

Notes

1 See Bernard Lonergan, *Method in Theology* (New York: Seabury Press, 1972) 14–15; and *Collection*, vol. 4 of *Collected Works of Bernard Lonergan*, ed. F.E. Crowe and R.M. Doran (Toronto: University of Toronto Press, 1988) 208.

2 See the Introduction to *Insight: A Study of Human Understanding*, vol. 3 of *Collected Works of Bernard Lonergan*, ed. F.E. Crowe and R.M. Doran (Toronto: University of Toronto Press, 1992), where Lonergan refers to this experiment, saying: 'It will consist in one's own rational self-consciousness clearly and distinctly taking possession of itself as rational self-consciousness' (13). In *Insight* Lonergan uses phrases such as 'appropriation of rational self-consciousness' rather than 'self-appropriation' as such. The one exception to this usage is when he describes *Insight* as an 'essay in aid of self-appropriation' (16). In *Understanding and Being*, vol. 5 of *Collected Works of Bernard Lonergan*, ed. E.A. Morelli and M.D. Morelli (Toronto: University of Toronto Press, 1990), which is a published set of lectures given in the summer of 1957 on *Insight*, 'self-appropriation' becomes the dominant theme. See also Lonergan's appeal to the reader's self-involvement in *Method*, 7, 14.

3 On self-appropriation as verification, see *Understanding and Being* 263, 272–73. See also the key chapter (11) in *Insight*, 'Self-Affirmation of the Knower.'

4 See *Method* 14–15, 262. Cf. *Collection* 210.

5 *Insight* 22. See also *Method*, where Lonergan claims that the primary function of philosophy is 'to promote the self-appropriation that cuts to the root of philosophic differences and incomprehensions' (95).

6 See, for example: Alison M. Jagger and Susan R. Bordo, eds, *Gender/Body/ Knowledge: Feminist Reconstructions of Being and Knowing* (New Brunswick, NJ: Rutgers University Press, 1989); Sandra Harding, *Whose Science? Which Rationality? Thinking from Women's Lives* (Ithaca, NY: Cornell University Press, 1991); Lorraine Code, *What Can She Know? Feminist Theory and the Construction of Knowledge* (Ithaca, NY: Cornell University Press, 1991); and Evelyn Fox Keller, *Reflections on Gender and Science* (New Haven, CT: Yale University Press, 1985). See also discussions of these works in articles by M. Vertin and P. Kidder in this volume.

7 Lorraine Code, 'Responsibility and the Epistemic Community: Woman's Place,' *Social Research* 50 (1983) 537–55.

8 Ibid. 537.

9 Ibid. 540. Though Code insists that moral theory necessarily takes stock of social interaction, much of modern moral theory is based on the independence and autonomy of moral agents, an assumption criticized regularly by feminists. Just as Code criticizes epistemological assumptions that the cognitive agent is independent of others, so the whole question of the role of autonomy in moral deliberation has generated great debate in feminist circles. See, for example, Thomas E. Hill, 'The Importance of Autonomy ,' and Diane T. Meyers, 'The Socialized Individual and Individual Autonomy,' in E.F. Kittay and D.T. Meyers, eds, *Women and Moral Theory* (New York: Rowman and Littlefield, 1987).

10 Code, 'Responsibility' 541.

11 Ibid. 542. In Code's discussion of epistemic community here she is emphasizing exactly what Lonergan insists upon in his discussion of 'belief' as a source of knowledge. See Lonergan, *Method* 41–47 and 'Method: Trend and Variations,' in F.E. Crowe, ed., *A Third Collection* (New York: Paulist Press, 1985) 13–22, esp. 17–19.

12 'Responsibility' 543.

13 Code relates assumptions about male/female differences in cognitive and moral abilities to Aristotle's emphasis on the *polis*. Others have traced the assumptions of women's inferiority in moral and cognitive domains through other thinkers. Genevieve Lloyd, for example, treats Philo, Augustine, and Aquinas before engaging in a longer analysis of the fruits of Cartesian thought for a 'complementarity' that masks an assumption of female inferiority. See G. Lloyd, 'Reason, Gender, and Morality in the History of Philosophy,' *Social Research* 50 (1983) 490–513. For a review of the same sort of analysis regarding social-contract theory, see S. Benhabib, 'The Generalized and the Concrete Other: The Kohlberg-Gilligan Controversy and Moral Theory,' in Kittay and Meyers, eds, *Women and Moral Theory*, 154–77.

14 See Jean Bethke Elshtain, *Public and Private: Women in Western Political Thought* (Princeton: Princeton University Press, 1981), and Mary O'Brien,

The Politics of Reproduction (London: Routledge and Kegan Paul, 1981).

15 'Responsibility' 545. Code makes a note at this point that Jane Austen's women are clear illustrations of this constraint. She also goes on to note the attendant fear that it would be dangerous to allow women into the public intellectual domain because of their seductive nature. Thus, Elshstain cites Rousseau's insistence that women wield their power privately (*Public and Private* 159). The image of woman as temptress and the association between women and (unwieldy, dangerous) sexual powers, in contrast to self-controlled rationality, is evident throughout history. Though this is another strong current in feminist analysis of the history of ideas, we cannot develop it at any great length here.

16 'Responsibility' 550.

17 M.F. Belenky, B.M. Clinchy, N.R. Goldberger, and J.M. Tarule, *Women's Ways of Knowing: The Development of Self, Voice, and Mind* (New York: Basic Books, 1986).

18 Perry traced the way in which students' conceptions of knowing evolved, but his work focussed mainly on privileged white males. See William Perry, *Forms of Intellectual and Ethical Development in College Years* (New York: Holt and Rinehart, 1970). See also idem, 'Cognitive and Ethical Growth: The Making of Meaning,' in A. Chickering, ed., *The Modern American College* (San Francisco: Jossey-Boss, 1981) 76–116.

19 For a further discussion of the sample used and the coding system devised, see Belenky et al., *Women's Ways of Knowing* 11–16. While they present these perspectives in order, and record how some subjects seemed to develop from one perspective to another, the researchers disavow any claims that these are stages in a developmental sequence.

20 To facilitate this review I have inserted relevant page references in parentheses in the text. All these citations refer to Belenky et al. and their study. These notes contain further examples or other references.

21 For example, Belenky et al. cite the following: 'When asked to finish the sentence, "My conscience bothers me if ...," Cindy, a pregnant fifteen-year-old, wrote, "someone picks on me" ' (25).

22 An example is the story of Ann, whose experience of childbirth catapulted her into a need to learn. Her discovery of the workers at the social agency who seemed to know everything she needed to know regarding babies was a very profound experience. Note that their provision of knowledge was combined with a confidence in Ann's own intellectual abilities, a combination that served to change Ann's life. See ibid. 35–36.

23 When asked why professors are always more or less right, Angela replies: 'They have books to look at. Things you look up in a book, you normally get the right answer' (ibid. 39). When asked what they would do if two advisers

at the children's centre gave them opposite advice, both Ann and Rachel were confused. Ann denies that this could ever happen and Rachel finally says she would gather the facts from the 'right studies.' But if the studies conflict? Rachel finds this incomprehensible, but ultimately says she would opt for the one that 'most people believe in.' See ibid. 41.

24 A college freshmen reports: 'Everything I say about myself is what other people tell me I am. You get a pretty good idea of yourself from the comments that other people are saying about you' (ibid. 48). Thus, the power of social definitions of 'knowers' is revealed. As Belenky et al. point out, since women of this perspective are so vulnerable to others' opinions, if authorities define women as 'stupid' or of inferior intellectual abilities, women internalize this as a cognitive self-definition. If, however, authorities encourage women to use their intellects, and treat them as equal and capable cognitive agents, women will begin to believe in themselves and discover their own processes of knowing. See ibid. 49 and chap. 9.

25 On fear of success in women, see M.S. Horner, 'Towards an Understanding of Achievement-Related Conflicts in Women,' *Journal of Social Issues* 28 (1972) 157–76. See also G. Sassen, 'Success Anxiety in Women: A Constructivist Interpretation of Its Source and Its Significance,' *Harvard Educational Review* 50 (1980) 13–24.

26 Belenky et al. have a further section in the chapter on received knowing, comparing their findings about [female] 'received knowers' with Perry's élite [male] sample of what he calls 'dualists.' The most interesting comparison lies in the conception of authorities. While for both groups authorities are the source of truth, Perry's male subjects tend to identify with these authorities and dichotomize 'the familiar world of Authority-right-we as against the alien world of illegitimate-wrong-others' (Perry, *Forms of Development* 59, as quoted in Belenky et al. 43). The women studied by Belenky et al. tend to describe these authorities *as* 'other.' They are awed by authority but do not identify with it; they, rather, see it as 'authority-right-they.' For example, women spoke of science professors who communicated their conviction that women couldn't do science, or indicated experiences in which authorities wielded power to extract sexual favours. The lack of female mentors to communicate a positive sense of intellectual authority is thus problematic. See Belenky et al. 43–45.

27 Belenky et al. note that there remains an implicit dualism in many of these subjectivists: 'In fact, subjectivism is dualistic in the sense that there is still the conviction that there are right answers; the fountain of truth simply has shifted locale. Truth now resides within the person and can negate answers that the outside world supplies' (54). That the 'subjectivism' labelled by Belenky et al. is a single, discrete, epistemological position seems doubtful.

Rather, as they themselves admit (55), it is a loosely defined term, a kind of 'catch-all' label that links a group of women together. Likewise, just what these women mean, and what these researchers mean, by 'intuition' remains vague. A footnote on page 55 refers to the philosophical tradition of intuitivism, but just how the common-sense usage of it here relates to this tradition is not made clear. Cf. Elizabeth Morelli's article on women's intuition in this volume.

28 The example given by Belenky et al. is that of a Columbian-American woman named Inez, who had been subject to incest as a child and to an abusive marriage as an adult. She did not believe that a woman could 'think and be smart.' The turning-point came when she returned home to California to discover that her father was known and accepted by the entire local community as a child molester. Her anger propelled her to leave her past behind entirely, and she now claims, 'I can only know with my gut. I've got it tuned to a point where I think and feel all at the same time and I know what is right' (53). See ibid. 52–53, 56–57.

29 Though these researchers did not initially set out to chart experiences of sexual harassment, they found it to be such a pervasive theme that they began to survey women on this issue. Based on a sample of seventy-five subjects, 38 per cent of women in schools and colleges and 65 per cent of women contacted through social agencies said that they had been subject to either incest, rape, or sexual seduction by males in authority over them. Among the college women, one in five had a history of childhood incest. Among women from the social agencies, which draw on a population in which drug and alcohol abuse is prevalent, one out of every two women had been subject to incest. Incidence of sexual abuse was not limited to any one epistemological group. However, among subjectivists the sense of outrage was most prominent, accompanied by a recognition of previous naïvete and docile submission. See ibid. 58–60. Note especially the footnote on page 59 indicating the many other studies that confirm the findings here.

30 Again, the authors compare their female 'subjectivists' with Perry's male subjects at the stage that he calls 'multiplists.' These male college students exhibited the traditional relativistic and rebellious stance of many young adults leaving a homogenous home environment. Belenky et al. found that their middle-class and upper-class women in college fit neatly into Perry's category. The *difference* they found between Perry's men and their women lay in the confidence with which their subjects asserted their new-found perspective. Whereas the male subjects would brazenly insist on their views over against parents, teachers, and administrators, the women 'hidden multiplists' were often lonely and reticent to express their quiet but passionate differences with authority. This difference is best summarized in the oft-repeated phrase of the men, 'I have a *right* to my own opinion,' in contrast

with the more common female version, 'It's *just* my opinion.' See ibid.
62–68.

31 One of the clearest examples given is that of Naomi, who struggled with the
demands of an art-history course. Initially she objected to required work on
the basis that art history was a merely subjective topic in which there is no
right or wrong. Though she could have a profound response to a Van Gogh
painting, 'Wow!' did not constitute a paper that could be graded. The professor eventually provided a five-page guide and Naomi came to see the usefulness of a guided set of criteria: 'They give us a way to analyse paintings.
Then we analyze the painting and come to a conclusion. There are certain
criteria that you judge your evaluation on – the composition, texture, color,
lighting, how the artist expresses his feelings, what the medium is' (ibid. 89).
No matter what Naomi's personal reaction to a painting, she had to justify
her response in relation to the *object*, the painting itself.

32 Belenky et al. point out that there is a negative side to the emphasis on
procedure. The form of an argument ends up taking precedence over the
content, such that one student insists: 'It does not matter ... whether you
decide to have your baby or abort it. It matters only that you think the decision through thoroughly' (95). This emphasis on method can verge on what
Mary Daly labels 'methodolatry.' Acceptable procedures within a certain
institution can limit women's access to the knowledge they need. An ideology of methodology can assert that only certain types of arguments are
acceptable, and when women or other minorities do not easily adopt these
methods, they are left out of the sphere of acceptable knowledge. See ibid.
95–96. See also M. Daly, *Beyond God the Father* (Boston: Beacon Press,
1973).

33 Belenky and her colleagues devote an entire chapter (6) to a distinction
within procedural knowledge, between 'separate' and 'connected' knowing.
Separate knowing seems to fulfil the modern philosophic images of objectivity as distance from the object, a kind of 'empty head' assumption about
objectivity. Connected knowers can be equally attuned to the need for
'objective' criteria of truth, but grasp the truth by connecting with the object
they are seeking to understand. The former group seem to be those most
immersed in the demands of an alienating academia; it is these who find a
need to reconcile their 'selves' with their academic pursuits, and who often
become constructivists. While this chapter is fascinating, and reflects current
feminist discussions of connection versus autonomy, it is not clear just why
these two are discrete categories and, if they are, why they do not form two
discrete epistemological positions. That is, why are these two styles *within* an
epistemological perspective rather than distinct perspectives themselves?
The authors simply assert these themes as descriptive and give no account as
to the basis of their categories here.

34 See Lonergan's discussion of heuristic method in *Insight* 337–38, 546, 554, and 600–601.

35 See, for example, Lonergan's article 'Dimensions of Meaning,' *Collection* 232–45.

36 Lonergan, *Collection* 225. I believe that this recognition of the social location of the knower/actor is precisely what Lonergan is asserting when he later discusses, in *Method in Theology*, the 'constitutive function of meaning' (see *Method* 76–91).

37 Lonergan, *Collection* 227.

38 Lonergan goes on here to point out why having a seminar on the subject is so important. There is a need for interaction such that false ideals of knowing can be highlighted and eradicated. It is interesting to note that the study of Belenky et al. bears out the fact that isolation, rather than leading to any sort of self-appropriation, only hinders it. The 'silent' women suffered mostly from isolation from communities of dialogue and collaborative knowledge. For those such as Ann, who moved out of silence, a key catalyst was entrance into a community of learning and dialogue, such that she gained the ability to speak about herself as a learner, even if in an unsophisticated or unnuanced way. See Belenky et al., *Women's Ways of Knowing* 35–36.

39 Lonergan, *Understanding and Being* 17–18.

40 Lonergan, *Method* 41–47. Interestingly, Lonergan attaches a note to his subtitle for this section. He alludes to his earlier discussion of belief in *Insight* 703–18, and then comments: 'The same facts are treated by sociologists under the heading of the sociology of knowledge' (41, n. 15).

41 Lonergan, *Method* 42–43.

42 Ibid. 43. See also 'Method: Trend and Variations,' in *A Third Collection*.

43 On progress and decline in relation to belief, see Lonergan, *Method* 44, 52–55. See also the sections on bias and the dialetic of community, *Insight* 242–60.

44 Note Code's emphasis: 'Excluded from public intellectual debate, woman is more restricted than "real" members of the epistemic community to reliance upon testimony *chosen for her*: to the tutelage of her patrons, friends, and lovers. Her possibilities for circumspection are fewer than those available to men. Hence the distance she can acquire from her own cognitive endeavors to cast a critical eye upon them ... and the scope of her possible epistemic responsibility is, accordingly, narrowed. She is *more than* naturally reliant upon acquiring knowledge from others, ... more at the mercy of those she is *permitted* to trust, than is man, who at least is *in a position* to choose more widely, however well or badly he may do this' 'Responsibility' (547).

45 Note that though my emphasis here is on the move beyond received knowing, Belenky et al. indicate that there is a sort of 'self-appropriation,' which is

very liberating, when women move from silence to the rudimentary discovery that they can *receive* knowledge. Clearly, one must be able to conceive of oneself as a receiver of knowledge (the knowledge born of belief) before one can move beyond that to a critical self-appropriation of oneself as a discoverer of knowledge. And, equally clearly, this initial discovery has life-changing implications. See the story of Ann (Belenky et al., *Women's Ways of Knowing* 35–36), as discussed in n. 22 above.

46 See Alison Moore's study of the relation between basic social and material resources and women's conception of themselves as moral agents: 'Moral Agency of Women in a Battered Women's Shelter,' *Annual of the Society of Christian Ethics*, 1990, 131–47. See also Belenky and her colleagues' discussion of Liz and Mimi, and how their opportunities to move beyond 'silence' were entirely different owing to their differing socio-economic class. Though both suffered from the sexual abuse of a tyrannical father, Liz managed to transcend her circumstances thanks to financial resources that gave her opportunities to find other sources of strength and growth. Mimi, lacking such resources, reacted by running away from home, an action that ultimately landed her in a detention centre (*Women's Ways of Knowing* 160–62).

47 The presence of domestic violence within the lives of the 'silent' women, and even amongst the 'received knowers,' is overwhelming. Comparing Moore's study of battered women and their sense of agency with portions of Belenky et al. (cf. 27–28, 32) makes it clear that there is a profound connection between the socialization of women as *receivers* of knowledge and the social acceptance of *violence* against women. While teaching women to be receivers of knowledge has value in itself, restricting them to this role, while appearing benign, may in fact have tragic social implications. The flip side of this connection is that asserting one's ability to discover one's own truth presents a direct challenge to the (sometimes violent) power that men wield in women's lives. Thus, Code's allusion to the courage required to assert oneself as a knower is no mere conjecture but has its concrete reality: the existential commitment of self-appropriation, alluded to by Lonergan, can put some women at the risk of losing their lives.

48 For a discussion of explanation and description, see Lonergan, *Insight* 316–24, 357–59. On common sense, see *Understanding and Being* 85–88. On the role of description and explanation in self-appropriation, see ibid. 141–42.

49 *Women's Ways of Knowing* 15.

50 It is quite obvious that they disapprove of the circumstances that promote 'silence' and that the emergence of voice and autonomy is positive as the various perspectives unfold. See, for example, comments on page 55 that indicate that subjective knowing is 'another step toward the kind of maturity that we call connected knowing.' See also their comment on page 87 about

the voice of reason (procedural knowing) as a 'humbler, yet ultimately more powerful' voice than those previously heard. The researchers clearly welcome the emergence of the voice of reason over against subjectivists, expressing concern over the stubborn isolation of some subjectivists and welcoming the reorientation towards the object. At the same time they express concern over the alienation that can occur when women are, through higher education, socialized into a separate kind of knowing. The reintegration of self and other, object and subject, reason and emotion, that takes place in constructed knowledge serves as a final ideal towards which they, clearly, would advocate the movement of other women.

51 Note that all persons, once they move out of the immediate world of the infant into the world mediated by meaning, use the cognitive operations Lonergan designates as experiencing, understanding, judging, and deliberating. The fact that 'receiving knowers' do not describe themselves as discoverers does not mean that they do not operate with these cognitive processes. They simply do not objectify (or 'appropriate') these processes in any way. The point is that the development recorded in this study is not from an absence of cognitive operations towards acquiring cognitive operations. The operations are given. What develops is skill in using these operations habitually and the ability to articulate just what these operations are.

52 There seems to be little refinement at this point as to various authorities and their relative authenticity. All 'others' seem to be rejected as sources of knowledge; only the self can be a valid generator of truth. External authorities are accepted only to the degree that they agree with internal, subjectively discerned truth. Alternately, because of past negative experience with male authority, gender becomes the sole criterion for authentic authority: only women can be trusted. It is interesting to note that as women move into other, more nuanced perspectives on their own cognitive processes, their perspectives on authorities and external sources of knowledge also becomes more refined. On the fact that believing another person is itself a value judgment and a choice, and on the process by which one revises one's mistaken beliefs, see Lonergan, *Method* 44–47. See also Lonergan's article, 'Dialectic of Authority' in *Third Collection*.

53 This group of women is large in number and, I suspect, diverse in the ways they would delineate their cognitive processes. It is possible, upon further analysis, to find within this group those who would fit the category 'idealist' as well as 'empiricist.' Perhaps some of these women would affirm, descriptively, the incidence of insights beyond mere perception. What they clearly don't seem to have recognized is the role of judgment, and the part that appealing to objective evidence plays in their cognition.

54 See the discussion of women's intuition in the article by Elizabeth Morelli in this volume.

55 The difference that the researchers note between 'separate' and 'connected' procedural knowing would relate, I contend, to different notions of objectivity operative in our culture and educational institutions today. To the degree that objectivity is conceived of as a kind of value-neutrality or 'empty-headedness,' objective knowing will be considered impossible unless one separates one's head from one's heart, one's passionate questioning from the objects of one's questions. To the degree that objectivity is a fruit of authentic subjectivity, I would argue (following Lonergan), objective knowing will involve connecting one's desire to one's questions, engaging in creative exploration of the intended objects of one's questions until the internal exigence for truth or value is satisfied. This latter, dynamic, view of objectivity as the fruit of authentic subjectivity yields a very different notion of method than the former notion of objectivity. It therefore avoids or answers some of the concerns of Belenky et al., reflecting Mary Daly, about 'methodolatry.' See n. 33 above and Lonergan's first chapter of *Method*.

56 On the transcendental notions as operative inherently in human consciousness, see Lonergan, *Method* 23–25, 34–35, 282. On these notions operative as transcendental precepts, see ibid. 53, 55, 231–32.

57 I would like to thank the faculty of the Department of Religion and Religious Education at the Catholic University of America for their discussion of an earlier draft of this paper. I would especially like to thank Sr Margaret Mary Kelleher for her insightful comments and Patricia DeFerrari for her careful proofreading.

Authentic Feminist Doctrine

ABSTRACT   *There are many conflicting 'feminist' doctrines. If women's interests are to be truly served, then the task is not simply to reduce disagreement but to collaborate on determining which feminist doctrines are 'authentic.' Bernard Lonergan provides an analysis of authenticity and its relation to power, authority, conversion, and historical change that gives concrete guidelines for that collaboration.*

In particular, Lonergan promotes a triple consciousness-raising that authenticity normally produces – becoming aware of the mystery of life, recognizing the injustice that shapes the routines of one's life, and waking up to the philosophic issues involved in recognizing that not all authorities who point the way to justice are authentic.

Feminists today face many challenges. There are male-dominated institutions to undo. There are millions of men to convert. There are millions of women to convert as well. That conversion means taking a new stand on a variety of feminist doctrines ranging from politics, parenthood, and pornography to self-image and religious affiliation. For example:

- Forbidding a person to hold any office because of gender is wrong.
- That women and men often complement each other does not mean that women and men *must* complement each other.
- An authentic liberation of women will be simultaneously a liberation of men.
- Pornography demeans men as well as women.
- Every woman has an inviolable right over her own body.

- Nothing will be more effective for women's liberation than the unity of women.
- A lesbian has as much right to raise a child as a heterosexual woman.
- Women have a right to an abortion on demand.
- Hierarchical authority structures are intrinsically anti-women.
- A person bears God's image no less by being female.

It is not just the variety of these doctrines, however, that makes women's liberation difficult. It is also the disagreements among feminists about doctrines like those listed above and about various approaches to doctrines: reformist, revolutionary, anarchist, and various kinds of hermeneutics, each with its own rules for reading history and probing the female and male psyches. Such disagreement can occur even within feminists when the doctrine one espouses belies the behaviour one exhibits. We all know women who champion women's rights but in reality are just trying to get a higher seat in an unchanged patriarchal structure. They will elbow out any other women to get there first, all in the name of feminism.

Frustration over lack of consensus drives some women to gather a social force based on mere numbers. They can forget how typical it is for partisan groups to divert their original charisms away from the social objectives that initially attracted generous recruits, to pour their energies instead into activities designed to eliminate competition, and to squander their intellectual capital on identity-maintenance. When feminists conceive the task of women's liberation as chiefly a matter of power blocs rather than respectable doctrine, newcomers to the movement lose touch with the question that energized its founders: Which of our doctrines can change the course of history for the true betterment of women?

So it will not be enough to eliminate internal contradictions; fascists dream as much. The liberal agenda of recognizing women's rights to self-determination is necessary, but it is not sufficient to spell out how to exercise those rights for women's true well-being. There are likely some feminist doctrines that ultimately degrade women and some 'non-feminist' doctrines that are actually in women's best interests. The problem is that feminists disagree on what 'degrades' a woman and what 'best interests' means. So, beyond the variety and even the contradictions among doctrines, there is the ultimate question of which doctrines are objectively the best.

Like other authors, I will use the word 'authentic' to refer to those doctrines, as yet unspecified, that will most closely approximate what is objectively best for women. But although I will begin by using the term in its general, heuristic sense, readers will find that Lonergan gives the term a very concrete and strategically useful meaning.

Bernard Lonergan has much to offer to feminism. Whether anyone accepts his entire philosophy of critical realism, he at least provides an insightful analysis of how both authentic and unauthentic doctrines play a critical role in effecting the historical changes that feminists hope to bring about. Also, he roots that analysis in a verifiable model of the wholesome person – which promises to give common ground for sorting out differences by identifying what 'best interests' and 'degrade' mean concretely.

Still, it is important to understand what Lonergan aimed to accomplish by his philosophy of critical realism. He recognized that the categories commonly used in theology were based on a classical, static view of the person and the world. The empirical and developmental categories used by the natural sciences enabled scientists to make fantastic improvements in material standards of living. But the human sciences (such as anthropology, psychology, sociology, political science, philosophy, and theology) still lacked empirically grounded categories that might bring about equally effective psychological, social, and spiritual improvements in standards of living. Lonergan's critical realism aims to generate and critique the models of person and community underlying all efforts to improve global common life.

Like many feminist thinkers, Lonergan also recognized that the categories we use to talk about social problems ought to be free of hidden value judgments. He saw that these categories should have the power to explain the causes of problems, not merely to describe them. His method of assuring such value-free and explanatory categories is to define them by referring to verifiable, conscious human acts. In other words, his approach to setting the human sciences on solid footing is to define and verify the dynamic process by which humans ask questions, and then to define scientific categories in terms that are related to this dynamic process. No doubt, the reader unfamiliar with Lonergan would like a few good examples here of how he grounds key terms by reference to the questioning person. So, by way of giving these examples, and to lay out the parts of Lonergan's work that support authentic feminist doctrines, I will discuss how he defines and interrelates seven key categories: doctrines, belief, power, authority, authenticity, conversion, and historical change.

1   Doctrines, Beliefs, Power, and Authority

Normally *doctrines* are used to create a community, to direct and limit the community's activities, and to serve as a test for belonging. They may be taken as absolute by a community's members, but if we hope to test doctrines for authenticity, it is better to regard them as neither right nor wrong but just as taught opinions. In his *Method in Theology*, Lonergan listed many types of doctrines (original sources, interpretations of original sources, official church doctrines, non-official teachings of theologians, and doctrines on methodology). But he proposed a further type of doctrine, namely, one that relies on the personal conversion of the theologian to select doctrines from among the choices presented by a critical analysis of current and traditional doctrines.[1]

It will help here if I clear up two common misunderstandings about what Lonergan meant by doctrines. The first regards *belief*. The cognitional theory he presented in *Insight*[2] focused chiefly on how new knowledge enters the world rather than on the ordinary way we know, namely, through believing someone else. So one could get the impression that what he meant by doctrines are strictly those new opinions that someone has worked out to meet present needs. Feminism itself faces a Sophie's Choice about how to deal with male-privileging beliefs. One can reject all beliefs that concern women (along with the language and institutions that bear them) and start all over with new doctrines to meet present needs – a task so big it may never come to completion. Or else one can prefer to accept all beliefs that concern women (along with the supporting language and institutions) except those that clearly damage women's rights and roles in society – a task that risks naïve accommodation to hidden oppressive structures. Lonergan chose this second option.

Lonergan's analysis of how we learn concluded that 'starting over' to learn about reality is impossible. The mind does not begin from a clean slate and gradually add pieces of knowledge. We are born in a flowing river of questions and answers. The mind raises questions that follow upon answers reached upstream by our forebears. Trying to get back to the beginning of everything we know, in an effort to avoid all bias, would certainly mean ignoring all the worthwhile answers built up over the ages. The problem, he insisted, is not the mistaken belief anyway; it is the mistaken believer. The penchant for bias in us all dooms any approach that would begin by discounting belief in general. This is because bias is an intellectual blind spot, and no one has a guarantee that fresh looks will not overlook the same covert injustices as old beliefs.[3]

If Lonergan preferred accepting inherited beliefs, how does he avoid a naïve accommodation to hidden oppressive structures? One starts by identifying a single mistaken belief in one's personal set of beliefs, analysing how it got there, and uprooting related beliefs. Writers experience this when a sharp-eyed editor points out a sentence that contains one error and they end up deleting kilobytes of text. But this is only the personal side of the task.

Lonergan's strategy, of which I will give a fuller account only after clarifying the above seven categories, involves a collaborative discipline that clarifies the nature of authenticity and uses that clarification to spot biases and devise remedies. Rather than start over recreating civilization, Lonergan recommended a method for starting where we find ourselves, namely, having grown up believing a million opinions, some of which will probably carry an anti-woman bias but which are also vulnerable in the long run to the scrutiny of the questioning mind.

A second common misunderstanding of Lonergan regards *power*. Newcomers to his work often think of his brand of doctrines as dry principles or truths to which one makes an assent. After all, he repeatedly pointed out that this assent to truths occurs on the level of consciousness where one says Yes or No, True or False. This can sound individualistic and without any incitement of human passion or achievement of social change.

A closer look, however, will show that for Lonergan doctrines are about exercising power in history. Those who frame doctrines ask questions very similar to those asked by a historian. His functional speciality 'History' aims at settling what social movements have been developing; the speciality 'Doctrines' settles what social changes ought to develop, and on what principles. Both specialize on the same level of consciousness, the level at which we aim to settle the truth.[4] Where historians ask, 'What historical trends have merged here?' the framers of doctrine ask, 'What historical trends *ought* to be emerging here?' Where historians ask, 'What propositions about society and the person underlay this historical development?' the framers of doctrine ask, 'What propositions about society and the person should underlie authentic future historical development?' In other words, Lonergan takes doctrines to mean those value judgments and propositions aimed at shaping history: 'Doctrines are not just doctrines. They are constitutive both of the individual Christian and of the Christian community. They can strengthen or burden the individual's allegiance. They can unite or disrupt. They can confer authority and power. They can be associated with what is congenial or what is alien to a given polity or culture.'[5] Because he was writing on method in theology, Lonergan usually used the theological term 'doctrines' to refer to a community's operative values and principles. But where he extended his analysis to methods in other branches of human studies, he used the term 'policy.' Corresponding to his doctrines in theology, he identified a specific kind of policy-maker in human studies. The policy-maker's task is to 'devise procedures both for the liquidation of the evil effects [of ideology] and for remedying the alienation that is their source.' The policy-maker will also 'apply the best available knowledge and the most efficient techniques to coordinate group action.'[6] So, by 'doctrine' Lonergan included what social and political disciplines call 'policy,' but he also aimed to identify those doctrines or policies that rely on a policy-maker's personal conversion in choosing from among existing or proposed policies that have the power to change history for the better.

Philosophers have batted the idea of power around for thousands of years, but in widely different contexts. It was in a letter to a friend that Lord Acton wrote his famous line, 'Power tends to corrupt; absolute power corrupts absolutely.' Bernard Loomer, then Professor of Philosophical Theology at the University of Chicago Divinity School, was exercising a phenomenological method when he distinguished two models of power: relational power and unilateral power, tagging them respectively as female and male styles of authority.[7] Lonergan has indicated that neither common-sense wisdom (of the type found in Lord Acton's letter) nor phenomenological models (of the type found in Loomer) give a sufficiently normative procedure for resolving differences in doctrine. What is needed is an understanding of authenticity and how it is the presence or absence of authenticity that accounts for the misuse of power. His approach is neither to discredit power nor to describe it in phenomenological models. Rather, he begins empirically by taking power to be simply the ability to get things done, analysing why accomplishments so often fall short of hopes, and locating the root cause of the misuse of power in a lack of authenticity.[8]

To the extent that one imagines the source of power as brute force and violence, then the muscular brute and the terrorist with the Uzi become the chief carriers of power. But if one takes power as the ability to get things done, then the chief source of power in any civilization is human cooperation. Cooperation, for Lonergan, extends both vertically down the ages and horizontally at any given place and time. So the essential carrier of power becomes the community, both as it carries on a tradition and as it interlocks millions of present functions, each contributing to the standard of living.

The idea that the community is the essential carrier of power has a direct impact on the meaning of *authority*. Normally, we look for sound doctrine by relying on some kind of authority, and we frustrate that pursuit by relying on the wrong kind of authority. But there is a danger here of picturing authority essentially as some person. Lonergan was careful to distinguish between authorities and authority. 'The authorities are the officials to whom certain offices have been entrusted and certain powers delegated. But authority belongs to the community.'[9] If power is the ability to get things done, and power relies on cooperation, then the word of authority resides in 'all ways of cooperating that at any time are commonly understood and commonly accepted.' In a world of cooperating communities, authority is the invisible but very real set of agreements and values that underpin the concrete way society functions. The women and men we call authorities are the persons to whom the essential authority – the community's functioning agreements and values – have been entrusted. 'Authorized' by the community, they are also the persons who are accountable to the community for how they carry out this trust.

The feminist today hears voices from many kinds of authorities, each authorized by certain communities and each subject to its own kinds of limits. For example, some feminists regard the *Diary of Anne Frank* as an authoritative feminist source. But it is one thing to be moved by her reflections and quite another to translate them into authentic doctrine for today. For another example, because certain people hold high offices, or have earned respect by their personal charism, their teachings command attention. Margaret Thatcher and Susan Sontag command respect because of their positions as politician and philosopher, respectively. But the respect they command should not automatically extend to everything they think, say, or do. Or think of those feminists who promote only those people who happen to be women, as if being a victim of sexism automatically makes one a trustworthy authority. Or, finally, take the argument that women have authority simply because they experience life in a way different than men do. While many would accept this as true, few can say with precision what those ways of experiencing are, and feminists need that precision in order to scrutinize doctrines for gender-related bias.[10]

In all these different kinds of authoritative voices, in the traditions represented by these authorities, and in each woman and man who listens to them, the essential question is not correct doctrine anyway. Lonergan sides with the philosopher Eric Voegelin in pointing out that 'nothing can be achieved by pitting right doctrine against wrong doctrine.'[11] What is needed is an analysis of authenticity and its absence. What is needed is a restoration of what Voegelin calls 'the classical experience of reason,' the experience of questions about meaning in the face of life and death.[12] A restoration of this classical experience of reason would mean educating the young to ask about the engendering experiences that lay behind historical developments and political positions.

Let me sum up some of Lonergan's contribution to the questions of doctrines, beliefs, power, and authority. A doctrine that bears the power to affect history may or may not be authentic. But the authenticity of a doctrine stems from authenticity in the tradition, in the authorities, and in those who believe the officials. If some believe that history will be affected adversely by this or that doctrine, Lonergan would not recommend louder counter-preaching or vote-gathering or enemy-bashing. He would recommend a critical return to the experiences that engendered the doctrines and a commitment to cooperation as the best base of power. We can see both approaches today in the unresolved questions on abortion. While many people on each side seem to prefer the strategy of 'pitting right doctrine against wrong doctrine,' there are some who recognize the presence of life's mystery and death's meaning here and who are determined to remain close to women's experience in the matter and to search cooperatively for wise solutions.

2   Authenticity and Historical Process

If the root of unauthentic doctrines is the unauthentic person, then we ask, What makes a person authentic? Lonergan defined *authenticity* as obedience to one's inner norms for raising questions. He identified these norms as five 'transcendental precepts': Be attentive, Be intelligent, Be reasonable, Be responsible, and Be in love.[13] By 'precepts' Lonergan does not mean external directives; he means the spontaneous urges in us to pay attention, to understand, to settle true from false, to settle right from wrong, and to love. 'Transcendental' refers to how these precepts keep transcending the individual realities around us in an openness to any experience, to complete understanding, to all truth, to the best there may be, and to the fullness of love. Authenticity, then, is an internal obedience to five distinguishable voices that put us in touch with reality. Unauthenticity is its opposite at each level: being obtuse or oblivious, being stupid or short-sighted, being silly or unrealistic, being irresponsible or merely fun-loving, and being hateful or hard-hearted.

This authenticity and its absence are the ultimate drivers behind historical process, according to Lonergan. First, authenticity drives historical progress. The transcendental precepts flood people's consciousness with questions about potentialities, about meaning, about truth, about values, and about persons. When they act authentically, obeying these inner urges, they avoid twisting these questions by bias, they more frequently experience good ideas, they express these good ideas as doctrines, which, in turn drive good action, and history enjoys a progressive turn. At the same time, unfortunately, unauthenticity is driving historical decline. Fear, egotism, the need to belong to a group, or intellectual laziness can hinder the working of the transcendental precepts in people. That is, they can divert their attention, restrict their intelligence, narrow their reason, frustrate their responsibility, and lace their love with bitterness. Good ideas are suppressed, biased doctrines are preached, and history suffers from ill-conceived action.[14]

By this analysis, Lonergan combined two familiar but distinct explanations of why personal and social problems persist, citing Sir Karl Popper and Bertrand Russell as typical representatives. On the side of Sir Karl Popper, some hold that people are basically good, but simply not intelligent enough. On the side of Bertrand Russell, others hold that people are intelligent enough, but basically bad.[15] By his focus on five inner drives towards authenticity, Lonergan would say that people are potentially attentive, intelligent, reasonable, responsible and loving, but frequently obtuse, stupid, silly, irresponsible, and hateful. In other words, capable of intelligence and goodness but often unintelligent and wicked.

This analysis also runs contrary to the popular opinion that what is needed to meet social problems is more creativity. Lonergan located the cause of social decline not in any lack of creativity in shaping doctrines; unauthentic people are always creative in rationalizing their behaviour. The problem is that their creativity has been only partially guided by authenticity; it has been guided also by the urge to dominate, to be secure, comfortable, or honoured, and so on. In short, human creativity is constantly in need of healing.[16]

Note that inner obedience to the transcendental precepts does not guarantee unbiased doctrines. There is no sure-fire formula that will declare one doctrine authentic and another unauthentic. What Lonergan offers here is an invitation to his readers to analyse how they form judgments (either about their own opinions or someone else's) and to discover personally how they rely on these inner voices of authenticity to test for bias. He expects that by understanding the role of authenticity in their own opinion-filtering process, they will possess a language for talking about authenticity to others and, what is most essential, they will have understood from personal experience how all doctrines begin, are refined, are passed on, are accepted or rejected, and are replaced.

In 'Theology and Praxis,' Lonergan described his approach 'as basically a praxis.'[17] But he was careful to point out that by praxis he meant 'attention to the responsible freedom of human conduct,' not simply 'practicality.' That is, he takes praxis to mean precisely the regular scrutiny of one's consciousness for signs of unauthenticity. In a rare reference to the liberation of women, he voiced the opinion that the theology of liberation on which some feminists rely uses 'praxis' to mean mere practicality. His remark reads as a thinly veiled critique of feminist theologies insofar as they try to convert theology into a tool for some distinct, already accepted end.[18] He was afraid, I believe, that too many feminists accept their inherited agendas without question. The foundation for social improvements, in his view, is the authentic subject, not some canonized doctrine, policy, authority, or agenda.[19]

3   Conversion: The Root of Authenticity

Normally, authenticity leads a person to three fundamental choices about reality. Lonergan referred to these choices as 'conversions,' although they do not necessarily occur at a known point in time, nor does the converted person always call them conversions. People usually experience these conversions and put them into effect without ever describing them to anyone.

There are many works describing and praising conversion, but Lonergan is among the few who attempt an explanation of what constitutes a conversion. For him, the conversion experience is essentially an experience of a liberation from certain limits to the kinds of questions a person can ask. Under (1) an affective conversion, a woman does not restrict her love to the things and people around her. She experiences and relies on a love for transcendent mystery in everyday life. Under (2) a moral conversion, a man does not restrict action to what benefits himself. He focuses on objective worth. Under (3) an intellectual conversion, a woman does not restrict reality ahead of time by any a priori certitudes about what can possibly be real. She investigates reality with a readiness for anything.

Each conversion sets that person in a larger world of quite different questions, difficult though they be to answer. While she or he easily understands the more restricted world defined by the old presuppositions, someone living in that restricted world seldom grasps the meaning of the new questions. Living in different worlds, people are unable to make fundamental contact with each other, and this, Lonergan holds, accounts for the most intractable differences between people. More to our topic, the presence or absence of conversion defines the most radical differences found among people who frame, transpose, or accept doctrines. So a clear account of the workings of conversion should also account for any essential differences between authentic and unauthentic feminist doctrines.

3.1 Affective Conversion

Originally, Lonergan referred to affective conversion as 'religious conversion.'[20] The change makes sense: the names for the other two conversions refer to realms of consciousness – intellectual and moral – and the realm of consciousness where a religion normally finds its home is in human affectivity. Besides, the expression 'religious conversion' can imply that such a conversion necessitates belonging to a religion. It seems more clear to refer to this conversion sheerly in terms of consciousness rather than sociocultural institutions. By keeping our focus on the interior events that constitute such a conversion rather than on any institutionalization and symbolization of it, we stay in touch with the engendering experiences of any religion. We also may stand at a clear vantage from which to keep our own religion honest.

Still, the expression 'affective conversion' runs the danger of connoting strictly the emotions, and Lonergan meant something larger than that. He wanted to refer to that part of love that is concerned about ultimate meanings and what is ultimately worthwhile.

As I see it, the pilot light for affective conversion is human wonder, particularly as it illuminates the mystery of life. Falling in love then fuels this flame of wonder. As our affectivity is ignited, other mysteries of life beckon us to walk forward. Teenagers gaze up at the stars and wonder why the universe is structured the way it is. They contemplate how every single thing might have been different. They feel a conviction that the universe is sending a message to them, a message of reassurance about life. Young adults face the terror of possibilities – the plasticity of their present potential and the choices that will set them on one-way streets into the future. They marvel at the miracle of birth and the mystery of death. Older adults realize that they will never fully unleash the energies of their love or fully harness the powers of their hate. Their hearts carry hurts side-by-side with a genuine wish that they could find forgiveness to give. Seniors reflect on lost opportunities and reluctantly endure the slow losses to their metabolisms just when they begin to enjoy slow gains in true wisdom. They quietly acknowledge the eternal quality of each moment, whether remembered or forgotten. They await death not with fear and trepidation but with a deep hope that all manner of thing shall be well.

Driven by wonder about this 'fated call to a dreaded holiness,'[21] some people pursue religion. Not all feminists pursue religion, of course, but an authentic feminist, Lonergan might say, would at least allow questions about the mystery of life into consciousness and would consciously act in ways that honour life's mystery. Authenticity should lead even those who pursue religion to criticize any religious doctrines that are biased. Only if we remain conscious of these engendering experiences of wonder and mystery can we appropriately criticize any doctrines – religious or otherwise – that profess to say what is worth doing and what is really true. The messages of the Bible or Koran mean nothing significant unless we welcome them as divine words about the mysteries of life that ignite our wonder.

For Lonergan, love for life's ultimates is the peak of other human loves – love of self, friends, family, and country. Like an engine, it drives and energizes these more tangible loves. It facilitates a more faithful obedience to the precept 'Be in love.' The eye of love sees goodness and possibilities where the eye of ethics sees only rights and duties. It is because love reveals values overlooked by logic and reason that affective conversion is an essential element in discriminating between authentic and unauthentic doctrines, feminist or otherwise.

Concretely, this means that a person in love is statistically more likely to resolve problems than a person who is bitter about life and blind to its mystery. Most of us, of course, have a partially converted affectivity. We all know people (including ourselves) whose high-minded ethics constipates their passionate love. We know (and belong to) groups whose very camaraderie squelches questions about integrity, goals, and group style. Worse, we know people who limit their affectivity to love of comfort, money, a big name, and a boast that 'I did it my way.' All these forms of imprisoned hearts imprison minds as well, and when the imprisoned mind goes around solving problems no one is surprised to see the problems multiply.

3.2 Moral Conversion

Moral conversion means looking to true value rather than mere subjective satisfaction when deciding what is good. The very possibility of two opposing criteria for deciding what is good indicates that there is a radical ambiguity in the word 'good.' The ambiguity cannot be resolved by logic or persuasion. If we take good to mean whatever satisfies and comforts us, and nothing else, then we also consider this very criterion to be good. If, however, we think of the good as whatever is objectively worthwhile, disregarding subjective comforts, we also consider this criterion good. This is why it takes a conversion, not a definition or a logical deduction to move from the criterion of satisfaction to the criterion of true value.

Consider a woman reading a doctrine with which we began: 'Forbidding a person to hold any office because of gender is wrong.' This is a value judgment. She may be inclined to agree because she wants a job in pastoral ministry ordinarily held by a man. But, thus far, her reason for agreeing lacks authenticity. She has yet to face the question whether the value judgment is true in itself, prescinding from any personal payoff. Is it truly wrong to forbid a woman to hold any office just because of her gender?

The question leads to a shock if she opens her eyes and sees that this practice is objectively wrong. She may have been hesitant about supporting, say, women's ordination because of the great difficulty in educating a congregation to accept such a change. But her focus can suddenly rest on the simple wrongness of the prohibition, leaving all the difficulties on the fuzzy periphery. Now she will be ready to fight for women's ordination even if she is convinced that, given the present administration and all likely successors, she will never hold the office for which she is qualified.

3.3 Intellectual Conversion

To understand Lonergan's intellectual conversion, it is necessary to understand his distinction between the world of immediacy and the world that is mediated by meaning and motivated by values. The world of immediacy is the world we experience through the five senses; it seems real because you can see it, pound on it, sometimes hear and smell it. The world mediated by meaning and motivated by values is the larger world of friendships, agreements, enmities, laws, language, customs, and the history of everything we think we understand. You cannot see or touch them. These entities are constituted not by paper or sounds but by acts of meaning, particularly by imagination, insights, and verifications. They are driven by acts of evaluation, particularly by feelings, appreciation, and promises.

In this larger world, a living memory of those meanings is essential. Think of what would happen if everyone were suddenly struck with amnesia.[22] No one could read or write. No one would even understand what reading is. No one could remember the laws and customs that govern everyday life. No one would know who their parents, children, or friends were. No one would understand that he or she was expected to hold down a job, let alone how that job contributed to the commonweal. This is the world mediated by acts of meaning and value. We discussed this world earlier when we pointed out two realms of power. In the world of immediacy, power is just physical force. In the world mediated by acts of meaning and value, power is the ability to get things done, and its source is human cooperation.

What is more, we engage this invisible but very real world by our own acts of meaning and value. And while these acts depend materially on the five senses, they depend formally on our own acts of insight, judgment, and evaluation. These, in turn, depend on the questions that happen to occur to us. The essence of an intellectual conversion is the realization that the final criterion by which we grasp meaning and appreciate values is not some sort of observation, but the absence of relevant questions occurring to us. To realize that everything we take to be real or good depends on the drying up of one's questions about the matter at hand, rather than on some kind of look at what is 'out there' with one's eyes, 'is a matter of personal philosophic experience, of moving out of a world of sense and arriving, dazed and disoriented for a while, into a universe of being.'[23] The shock reverberates more deeply when one realizes that everything in this larger world is subject to interpretation, and that the same friendships, laws, words, and customs can and will be interpreted differently by the very people they affect most deeply.

Interpretations can differ for a variety of reasons, and Lonergan addressed these differences through distinctions made among the conscious acts of persons, not through classifications of the results of those interpretations. That is, a major reason why people think different thoughts is that they think in different manners. Common sense is not art. Science is not scholarship. Mysticism is not philosophy. These different realms of meaning subdivide the world of meanings and values, so that common-sense people with no differentiation of consciousness may talk about art, science, scholarship, mysticism, and philosophy, but they quite literally do not know what they are talking about.

Still, the most radical differences between people will pivot on the presence or absence of Lonergan's threefold conversion. The differences are radical because, as we indicated, mere logic cannot bridge the gap between the converted and the unconverted viewpoints. These two viewpoints attach radically different meanings to love, to what is worthwhile, and to what can be real. Common parlance often describes disagreements as 'we're talking different languages about the same realities.' The more radical problem here is precisely that we may be talking the same language, but about different realities.

By recognizing the horizons of these different worlds, the intellectually converted person already possesses the means for ascertaining whether two apparently opposed doctrines stem merely from different realms of meaning or are radically opposed owing to the absence of conversion on one side. More than that, only when the intellectually converted person grasps the various manners in which meaning is mediated in the realms of science, scholarship, and philosophy, will she or he be sufficiently enabled to criticize the categories on which people rely for their analyses of social problems.

The discovery that the words we use to talk about issues carry unwanted baggage marks a crucial development in one's intellectual conversion.[24] Typically, the more descriptive the word, the more the baggage; the more explanatory the word, the more useful it is for an in-depth understanding of the problem. Take, for example, the descriptive rhetoric used by many feminists that divides the world between oppressors and oppressed. Several twentieth-century developments of mind should take them beyond such an adversarial view. In the human sciences, psychology and sociology have identified a cycle of abuse by which victims become victimizers, the oppressed become oppressors. In politics, Mahatma Gandhi saw that the oppressor/oppressed dichotomy was a dangerous misconception of the problem of enslavements. The real driver of historical events here is a cycle of abuse, not an oppressor. Granted, no one can see a cycle; it lacks the vividness of a wicked Simon Legree twisting his moustache and cracking his whip. But while anyone with imagination can picture someone to blame, it takes an intellectual conversion to identify an invisible yet very real process for which many parties share responsibility. We often see this difference when we compare those people who are ready to analyse a problem from a systemic perspective to those who are incapable of anything but pointing the finger of blame.

4   Authentic Strategies

What strategy might Lonergan have proposed to move from that triple conversion to shaping history? One might think the answer is obvious; namely, review policies and doctrines that regard women with a view to reducing surface differences to fundamental differences. Then identify and promote those policies and doctrines that are legitimate, namely, those rooted in affective, moral, and intellectual conversion.

But Lonergan was aware that things are not that simple. He often pointed out, for example, that authenticity is usually a matter of withdrawing from unauthenticity, correcting errors, abolishing silliness, and repenting of one's sins. What he means is that we do not identify authenticity as if it were anyone's permanent possession. 'Authenticity is reached only by long and sustained fidelity to the transcendental precepts. It exists only as a cumulative product.'[25] So we should not canonize persons or doctrines. We should take a critical rather than a promotional approach to all authorities. What counts is uprooting unauthenticity; the authenticity of doctrines will cumulatively increase as a result.

Yet uprooting unauthenticity is not simple either. A person can be authentic within an undifferentiated or partially differentiated consciousness, but unauthentic outside of familiar realms of meaning. This is the sin of backwardness, of not being familiar enough with, say, realms of scholarship or art or philosophy to contribute intelligently to the commonweal. Or a person may be authentically faithful to an unauthentic tradition, which Lonergan names 'minor authenticity.'[26] Or a person may fall short of Lonergan's three-dimensional conversion. Add that to the phenomenon that these varieties of unauthenticity can be carried by the tradition, by those officials currently in power, or by anyone who accepts their doctrines, and one may well conclude with Lonergan, 'Inquiry into the legitimacy of authority or authorities is complex, lengthy, tedious, and often inconclusive.'[27]

'A more effective approach is to adopt a more synthetic viewpoint,' he continues. This viewpoint results from a three-step analysis of the workings of history that Lonergan had worked out in 1938.[28] Recall the first two steps I discussed in the section on authenticity and historical process: One, there is progress in history when people obey the transcendental precepts. Two, there is also decline in history when people disobey the transcendental precepts. Step three adds self-sacrificing love as a further element, a yet closer approximation to concrete reality. This kind of love has the power to heal the damage done by disobedience to the transcendental precepts.

Relying on his own analysis of the psyche, he points out that a person in love is statistically more likely to forgive and forget, to take responsibility even at high personal cost, to face reality rather than nurse a myth, to be functionally more insightful than the egotist, and to notice the elements in experience that beg attention. Furthermore, being in love tends to promote affective conversion, which in turn promotes moral conversion, which promotes intellectual conversion.[29]

Complementing the infrastructure of being in love, Lonergan identified religion as a necessary superstructure for making that self-sacrificing love an effective force in history. Lonergan credited Toynbee for evidence that religions have very often provided civilizations with the doctrine of self-sacrificing love that has helped them transcend mutual animosities. 'To my mind,' Lonergan stated, 'the only solution is religious.' But here he meant religion not as any existing institution, but only insofar as religion provides a faith that sees beyond rationalizations, a message of hope that a liberation from history's shackles is possible, and the command of neighbourly love that alone can break the vicious circle of mutual retributions.[30]

In the meantime, while Lonergan would not discourage going for the philosophic jugular where differences stem from lack of conversion (as he himself did with regard to doctrines on Christology), where the nature of the differences is unclear or less fundamental, he preferred a dialogical approach: 'it can be more helpful, especially when oppositions are less radical, for the investigators to move beyond dialectic to dialogue, to transpose issues from a conflict of statements to an encounter of persons. For every person is an embodiment of natural right. Every person can reveal to any other his or her natural propensity to seek understanding, to judge reasonably, to evaluate fairly, to be open to friendship. While the dialectic of history coldly relates our conflicts, dialogue adds the principle that prompts us to cure them, the natural right that is the inmost core of our being.'[31] In other words, he is betting. Lonergan gambles that a person who roots his/her opinions in the 'natural propensity' to authenticity will listen carefully to the other person, despite some fundamental-looking disagreements. He hopes that as individuals and as groups we would cross sociocultural boundaries and enter the world of others. And not the narrow world of doctrine, but the larger world of everyday experience, practical concern, and concrete loves. To connect at the level of person is not a strange, élitist experience. It is the kind of meeting with which everyone is familiar – the experience of raising common questions about common concerns and letting go of questions that silently measure the other's worth.

It would not have surprised me if Lonergan had related the current feminist concern for consciousness-raising to his own concern for conversion and promoted a triple consciousness-raising. In the first kind of consciousness-raising, one wakes up to the mystery of life and usually seeks out some religious framework within which to grow in faith, in hope, and in genuine charity. The second kind makes women wake up and see the injustice that shapes the routines of their lives (and men to see their role in this injustice). This is the conversion most feminists speak about, a type of moral conversion. The third kind makes both women and men wake up to the problem that not all authorities who point the way to justice are authentic.

It makes them explore, as we have done above, the underlying philosophic issues surrounding doctrines, belief, power, authority, authenticity, historical process, conversion, and religion.

Taken together, these conversions provide a person with an internal standard of authenticity with which to size up authorities. Gloria Steinem, in her *Revolution from Within*,[32] calls women to a deeper sense of self-esteem. I think Lonergan would have agreed with her general approach, but would have gone further by pointing out the process by which self-esteem is actually reached: obedience to the transcendental precepts.

Finally, Lonergan also might have given a new definition to women's liberation. If affective, moral, and intellectual conversions liberate a person to ask fundamental questions about mystery, values, and reality, then the radical liberation of women should be identified not with a social structure but with a personal process of conversion. Woman's liberation would have the following features:

- It will be a liberation from bias, not 'oppression.' It is a liberation from limits on the questions one is able to pose.
- It should be taught as a praxis by which one tests the quality of inspirations, not merely their doctrinal content. It should be taught to women and men.
- It should result more often in the critique of authorities than their promotion. That critique focuses less on blame and more on understanding.
- It should also critique the categories used by the human sciences to analyse history and promote current policy, especially those categories stemming from mere proverbial wisdom or from purely descriptive phenomenological models.
- It should find the origin and testing ground of doctrines in concrete experience. It should downplay feminist doctrines in favour of feminist questions.
- It should avoid pitting doctrines against doctrines and focus instead on mutual encounter and dialogue.
- It should support education that teaches the rules that govern the realms of art, scholarship, science, philosophy, and spirituality, and how each realm affects the commonweal.
- It should find an ally in religion without exempting that religion from scrutiny for bias.
- Finally, it should result in doctrines or policies aimed not at triumphing over enemies but in the kind of cooperation that alone exercises lasting power in history.

Notes

1 *Method in Theology* (New York: Herder and Herder, 1972) 295–98.
2 *Insight: A Study of Human Understanding* (London: Longmans, Green, and Co., 1957).
3 See 'Belief: Today's Issue,' in W.F.J. Ryan and B.J. Tyrrell, eds, *A Second Collection* (London: Darton, Longman and Todd, 1974) 87–99.
4 See *Method in Theology* chap. 5 (pp. 125–57) for how Lonergan relates these two functional specialities.
5 Ibid. 319.
6 Ibid. 365, 367.
7 See 'Two Kinds of Power,' in *Criterion* 15:1 (University of Chicago Divinity School: Winter, 1976) 12–24.
8 His most concentrated analysis of power can be found in his 'Dialectic of Authority,' in F.E. Crowe, ed., *A Third Collection* (New York: Paulist Press, 1985).
9 See ibid., 7, for this and other citations in this paragraph.
10 We have all heard the argument that only a woman can have a woman's experience. This datum begs expansion. Experience needs insight to become understanding. Understanding needs judgment to become verified. Responsibility alone draws one out of the cognitive world and brings about real change. If women also understand, judge, and decide differently than men do, these differences also have to be considered. In *Women's Ways of Knowing* (New York: Harper Collins/Basic Books, 1986), M.F. Belenky et al. struggle with how to classify different modes of knowing; they settle on phenomenological models.
11 See 'Theology and Praxis,' in *A Third Collection* 188.
12 'Reason: The Classical Experience,' *Southern Review*, 1974, 237–64.
13 *Method in Theology* 20, 53, 55 and passim.
14 See 'Mission and the Spirit,' in *A Third Collection* 31–32, and its footnote. For a fuller view, see his 'Healing and Creating in History,' 100–109 in the same volume.
15 'Healing and Creating in History,' esp. 100–101.
16 Ibid. 100–109.
17 'Theology and Praxis,' in *A Third Collection* 196. See also, in ibid., 159–61, 163 (from 'The Ongoing Genesis of Methods'), and 246 (from 'Unity and Plurality').
18 *A Third Collection* 184–201.
19 We could also describe Lonergan's theology as a 'theology of discernment,' where discernment focuses on how a person deals with his or her questions and not strictly on the content of doctrines. As a Jesuit, Lonergan was

trained in a medieval spirituality rooted in discernment of personal inspirations ('spirits'). One tested the authenticity of an inspiration not so much by its content as by the quality of the experience. So, for example, a monk might feel inspired to pray an extra hour on his knees. But if the inspiration struck him with some agitation (the metaphor proposed was how falling water spatters on stone), the monk should ignore the inspiration because its source was probably an evil spirit. Notice here that the content of the inspiration was quite good; it was the quality of consciousness that indicated some lack of authenticity. See, among many translations, L. Puhl, trans., *The Spiritual Exercises of St. Ignatius* (Westminster, MD: Newman Press, 1951) para. 335. This Jesuit tradition of attending to the quality of the experience more than the content of an inspiration may have influenced Lonergan's insistence that the problem with biased doctrine lies not in what it says but in unauthenticity in those espousing it.

20 The change is evident in a 1977 address to the American Catholic Philosophic Association, published as 'Natural Right and Historical Mindedness.' Still, he reverts to 'religious conversion' in his address published as 'Unity and Plurality.' He does so, I believe, because here he is addressing his audience on a specifically religious topic – the 'wide divergence of doctrines ... being expressed by Catholic theologians,' while in 1977 he was addressing a more philosophic question and audience. See *A Third Collection* 176, 179, 180; cf. 247.

21 *Method in Theology* 113; see also 240.

22 Lonergan proposes this experiment to convey what it means to say that we are historical beings. Ibid. 181.

23 'The Subject,' in *A Second Collection* 79.

24 Prior even to this critique of categories, an intellectual conversion carries the ability to recognize the difference between an insight and a concept, between a real assent and a notional assent, between a value judgment and a feeling, between desire and love. This requires what Lonergan calls an 'interiority analysis' that results not merely in understanding these concepts but in understanding these events as they occur in one's psyche.

25 'Dialectic of Authority' 8.

26 *Method in Theology* 80.

27 'Dialectic of Authority' 9.

28 '*Insight* Revisited,' in *A Second Collection* 271–72.

29 See *Method in Theology* 243 for how the conversions are related to each other.

30 'The Ongoing Genesis of Method,' in *A Third Collection* 158. On religion as suprastructure, see 'Prolegomena to the Study of the Emerging Religious Consciousness of our Time,' in ibid. 71.

31 The 'natural right' he is talking about is precisely the propensity to seek

understanding, judge reasonably, evaluate fairly, and be open to friendship. See 'Natural Right and Historical Mindedness' 182. See also his brief references to dialogue on pp. 159, 162. I have translated this passage slightly to maintain consistent spelling and non-exclusive pronouns.

32 Boston: Little, Brown, 1992.

Lonergan's Transcendental Precepts and the Foundations of Christian Feminist Ethics

ABSTRACT *This study explicates Lonergan's 'transcendental precepts' in light of the current search of feminist theoreticians for surer foundations. Lonergan's transcendental precepts, which I take to summarize the implications of his view of human consciousness for the task of becoming authentic, are Be attentive, Be intelligent, Be reasonable, Be responsible, and Be loving. Each epitomizes the work of a given level or depth of consciousness. Each may be considered a further call of God upon our consciences, which makes the precepts as a bloc especially relevant to feminist ethics. In explicating the precepts, I stress the transcendental nature of human consciousness itself – how we are always being called beyond present attainments to face further questions, to grow to a further level of maturity. I conclude that the precepts sketch a radical program that undercuts the privileges and challenges the biases of any group, male-chauvinist or feminist, and that, by bringing their own hard-won convictions to bear on Lonergan's theories, challenging him on such matters as historicity, the social construction of reality, and the omni-relevance of feelings, feminists can provoke a good dialogue, fraught with implications for the reform or further progress of 'Lonerganism,' that might make the two camps ongoing partners.*

Since 1966, when I began Ph.D. studies at Boston College, Bernard Lonergan has been a deep source of orientation for all my work. My Ph.D. dissertation (1970) dealt with his analysis of the human person, and his views of human consciousness determined that my basic cognitional theory has become transcendental and intellectualist: that is, we are oriented to God by the very build of our spirits; we best appropriate what human beings can of the structures the transcendent deity has built into creation by striving for a critical realism. As well, critical realism best squares with the Roman Catholic faith that Lonergan and I share, making central provision for the analogy of being, definition of theology as faith seeking understanding, sense that faith is the knowledge born of religious love, and love of the cardinal Christian mysteries – the Trinity, the Incarnation, and Grace – on which Lonergan expended most of his labour as a dogmatic and systematic Catholic theologian. Thus, I come to a topic like the one announced in my title as a committed Lonerganian. I do not haunt the (very useful) circles that discuss and publish first-order Lonerganiana (works by the master himself or by others directly focused on his projects), but I have taken to mind, heart, and soul his basic view of reality.

In a recent book I took up the challenge of responding theologically to the current state of the art of Christian feminist ethics.[1] While I found much to praise in the significant quantity of literature that Christian feminists have generated in the last decade or so, I also found much to lament. Principally, I lamented an ignorance or repudiation of traditional Christology, which seemed to me to render many authors either lightweight or unbalanced. Not accepting the full divinity and humanity of Christ as the key hermeneutic for human studies, they produced works I found embarrassingly superficial or truculently heretical. Now, I would not be misunderstood. My book is not an act of war. I did find much to praise in the recent work of Christian feminist ethicists. But, contrasting my dissatisfactions with their work with my admiration for the teachings and example of Bernard Lonergan, as the present occasion invites me to do, I want to suggest how Lonergan's cogency and depth, as represented by his 'transcendental precepts,' might aid feminist scholars trying to secure the foundations of a moral inquiry faithful to both their demand that women receive a justice equal to that accorded men and to the promise of Christian faith that no purely human justice approaches the fulfilment that God holds out to us (which eye has not seen, ear has not heard, and so on).

At the outset, I should indicate my agreement with feminist analysts who claim that Lonergan is bound to present feminists with significant obstacles, especially on first acquaintance.[2] While deeper acquaintance tends to lessen many of these obstacles, or to make one realize that one's feminist objections have to be expressed with greater nuance, Lonergan remains a man of his time and clerical culture. None the less, he elaborated a developmental, open-ended view of knowledge, rooted in the dynamics of both external history and personal consciousness. So, he should be among the first to admit that feminists have a solid right to challenge traditional Christian ethical positions, including his own, and that women's different historical experience, sociological positioning, psychological formation, and the rest bear directly on what a fully adequate contemporary Christian ethics requires.

Moreover, some feminist thinkers themselves have lamented the lack of foundational clarity, the nearly promiscuous taking up and laying down of theoretical positions, that now characterizes many works labelled feminist.[3] While we can point to feminist studies that are meticulously scholarly,[4] they tend to employ traditional historical methodologies, where rigour is fairly clearly defined. My impression is that, on the whole, efforts to delineate specifically feminist theory and methodology tend to be less impressive, in large part because of their failure to handle well the critical (epistemological) demands bound to arise. But, delineating such demands and showing how to meet them has been one of Lonergan's greatest strengths. Thus, serious study of Lonergan's claims about how all human beings think ought to be very stimulating for feminist theoreticians. For the rest of this article, let me explicate positively one small portion of the domain that such claims cover, Lonergan's transcendental precepts. I shall avoid invidious comparisons to what I consider less mature feminist foundational efforts, try to ease problems that feminists are likely to suspect simply from hearing the precepts articulated, and indicate the liberation I think Lonergan's great depth might bring to many ethical inquiries.

1   The First Three Precepts

As I lay them out here,[5] Lonergan offers us five transcendental precepts. The first three deal with knowing. The last two deal with deciding and embracing. A 'transcendental precept' is a rule, a bit of advice, an admonition, a directive that a wise person follows because it applies always and everywhere. The 'transcendental' aspect of the precept is this constant applicability, its status as a simple expression of what we simply are as human beings, how we simply are constituted to perform. The force of the precept depends on its perspicuity, its credibility. In the spiritual life we cannot honestly accept or employ rules, directives, that we do not agree with wholeheartedly, either because we agree with the observation and logic they manifest, or because we revere the authority offering them to us. We are dealing, then, with five imperatives whose force readers will have to judge for themselves. I shall do the best I can, in the limited space available, to suggest whence Lonergan derives these imperatives. The full argument behind them, though, builds through the many hundreds of pages in which Lonergan exposed his views of both human consciousness and the divine mysteries. *Insight* and *Method in Theology* are the writings most directly relevant, but to catch the full theological resonance these precepts carry one would also have to consult Lonergan's texts on the Trinity and Christology.[6]

The first three transcendental precepts are: Be attentive. Be intelligent. Be reasonable. Though they appear to be simplicity itself, a little background may be helpful. In Lonergan's analysis of human consciousness, it has several levels. First comes experience. Second comes understanding. Third comes judgment. The second level develops on the basis of the first and engages more of our humanity, more of the spirituality (capacity for knowing and loving) enfleshed in our bodies. The third level develops on the basis of the first two and is a still further engagment, a still richer advance into our human potential. The precepts summarize what is required of us to prosecute successfully the work of each level of consciousness.

Experience is awareness. It need not be direct, in the sense that we are focusing only or fully clearly on a particular matter. It can be oblique, in the sense that we have a peripheral awareness. It can be reflex, because we are examining critically something that has come to our attention. For an example of Lonergan's approach to experience, awareness, and so the need to be attentive, let us go to the biblical beginnings. Eve is in the garden, and though her thoughts are on marketing the zucchini, which even in Paradise proliferate excessively, she is peripherally aware of the apples growing redly and greenly all around her. Along comes a sidewinding conversationalist, quite intriguing, and she focuses on one of the apple trees directly, giving it all her attention. Indeed, she thinks about the low fellow's proposal, running through some of the permutations its suggested use of the singular apple tree might generate.

The point is that we can attend in several different modes. In the measure that we want to understand a given problem or situation, we will attend fully, with no distractions. We will make all of our self present and let no detail of the matter at hand escape us. Relatedly, in the measure that we want to understand life, ourselves, the human condition, the apparent will of God for us, we will assume a habitual posture of full attention. We will discipline ourselves to give every matter at hand as much of our awareness, our sensible perception, our intuition, as we can. The more fully attentive we manage to make ourselves, the less life and God's designs will pass us by, the more we are likely to grasp reality as it actually is and make judgments that enable us to negotiate it well. Thus, Zen masters have always stressed attention. The beginning of wisdom, East and West, has been not only fear of the Lord but also getting one's consciousness together, becoming 'one-pointed,' learning how to be fully present to any important matter at hand.

Be intelligent. Think hard about the yield of your attention, the data your experience is generating. Discipline your brain, stir your imagination, push the data this way, pull them that way. Rearrange the images you have been using to configure the data. Make lists, diagrams, cross-checks, arguments pro and con. Remember that Aristotle said that insight is a grasp of form in imagination. We understand when a pattern leaps forth from the data, giving them a plausible coherence. Set in this pattern, they seem to make sense, hand over meaning. The harder we have been pursuing this meaning, the more desperately we have wanted it, the more exhilarating our insight will be. Thus, Archimedes never stopped for his towel when he raced from the bath. He had to test his hypothesis straightaway. It seemed to make sense. The doors apparently had swung open, solving his problem. And he could not help loving the light that had flashed in the insight. He could not help blessing the bath water that had not only relaxed him into having that insight but been a major clue, a key new image for how to determine the gold content of the crown.

Archimedes was intelligent, not just in the sense that God had given him a high IQ. He was intelligent because he worked at his problem, bestirred his good mind, pushed himself hard (the strong will of his sovereign was a great prod, but ultimately scientists, indeed all genuine intellectuals, are moved most by what Lonergan called 'the pure desire to know'). Lonergan says to any person wanting to become authentic, mature, fully 'realized': throw aside your old, lazy, unexamined images, ideas, assumptions. Deal with your problem afresh. Get into it, live with it, let it eat at your innards, start to haunt your dreams. Bend all your wit towards cracking it. That's the way to advance. Even if you never solve a given problem, you will be developing habits, stretching capacities, that will serve you splendidly in the future. (College teachers will recognize here the only valid response to students' whining about having to grapple with materials initially above them. It is a tough response to sell, but the simple fact is that we only become intelligent, learn to think quickly, accurately, well, by working very hard at it, constantly being drawn on. Knowledge maketh a bloody entrance – not only because we have to learn many unpleasant things about ourselves, but also because we remain dull as long as we are not working hard to be intelligent.)

However, being intelligent is less than half the full ideal. In Lonergan's view, insights are a dime a dozen. A great many more patterns, possible solutions, spring to mind than actually fit the case. The gap between a fresh hypothesis and whatever we should call one that has been verified (a theory, a law, a proven solution) is enormously significant. It is the distance from 'might be' to 'is.' In some cases it is Kant's famous difference between 10,000 thalers in his mind and 10,000 in his pocket. So it is imperative that we be reasonable – critical, inclined to review data, reasoning, assumptions; suspicious of our initial burst of light; in a word; judicious. For Lonergan 'reasonable' is not the genteel middle-mindedness of tried, and so somewhat cynical, diplomats. It is not the lowest common denominator for which negotiators often settle. It is the expression of our human spirit's insistence on adequate grounds. If we are serious about determing the truth of a given proposition, the verification of a given hypothesis, we will not rest until we reach a 'virtually unconditioned.' This is a cause and state of affairs that depends on nothing outside itself except God. (Only God is absolutely unconditioned.) This is the end of the chain of research, the smoking gun, the exact information or indisputable argument that clinches the matter and tells us what we must judge: yes, the hypothesis stands verified, the bright idea is sound; or no, it is clear beyond doubt that the hypothesis has been falsified, the argument has a fatal flaw.

Judgment is a reflective process whose ultimate ground is God's creation of us as incarnate spirits and so trustworthy knowers. For critical realists, in the judgmental process the human spirit shows its limited but real, dependable capacity for knowing how some things really do stand, what in some cases actually is true or false beyond reasonable doubt. This is not a popular epistemological position in a post-Kantian, relativistic age. Still, anyone willing to take up Lonergan's challenge to self-appropriation[7] is bound to come away with an enriched appreciation of how being reasonable, insisting that we meet our inmost demands for sufficient grounds, adequate explanation, is a primary expression of our status as images of the divine.

2   The Last Two Precepts

Precepts four and five in Lonergan's list of transcendental imperatives for the journey to human authenticity are: Be responsible. Be loving. We are responsible when we act in accord with what we judge to be so or not so. Authenticity, being moral or ethical, entails doing what we know we should, agreeing to no gap between preaching and practice. Any time we reach a virtually unconditioned, and so pass a judgment on which we know we can rely, we raise a further question, 'What are we going to do about this?' In speculative matters, the existential, personally engaging implications may not be dramatic. Shifting from a Ptolemaic to a Copernican view of the universe need not have changed what scientists ate for lunch or where they banked their money. Shifting from a classical to a modern view of human nature could bring more thunder and lightning. If in consequence of this shift one no longer thinks that natural law validly determines that 'artificial' contraception is always immoral, one's sexual morality can change, probably has to change, significantly.

The liberation theologians have been the major proponents for the primacy of praxis in theology. Lonergan would want considerable nuance placed on their thesis, but on his own grounds he would have to agree that decision, engagement, doing, making commitments, and following through on them is the next, inalienable step that judgments often reveal. We have to embrace the truth, or we remain divided, people who think one thing and do another. Human consciousness itself is 'transcendental' in the sense that it is always going beyond previous positions, is always feeling a call to appropriate what it has experienced, understood, and judged more deeply, accepting fuller responsibility for consequences, entailments, implications. If a feminist can show that many traditional nexuses of experience, understanding, and judgment were imbalanced because of a neglect of data coming from or bearing on women, half the human race, then the responsible Lonerganian has to review such nexuses and, if the feminist's argument is found to hold up, revise them thoroughly. Equally, if the old judgments led to political or ecclesiastical positions concerning women's roles in social or religious life (for instance, concerning suffrage or eligibility for orders), and the old judgments now stand exposed as inadequate, then the political and ecclesiastical positions they grounded have to come up for review.

The only responsible activity is to put into practice positions compatible with an adequate nexus of relevant experience, understanding, and judgment. For example, not to rethink practical positions when one has become persuaded that traditional ones rested on a classical view of consciousness, human nature, history, doctrine, and the like, and one is convinced that that classical view is no longer defensible, is to show oneself inauthentic – moved by considerations other than the truth, what is so, what one's best judgments have revealed to be the structure of God's reality.

Obviously, the way I am pitching my explication of the transcendental precept to be responsible amounts to a challenge to conservatives of various stripes to examine their consciousnesses regarding their policies towards women. However, the precepts are remorseless, cutting across all ideological lines. If a feminist should find that her nexus of experience, understanding, and judgment has been bent by bias or oversight, she or he has a grave responsibility to review the cognitional past and reset the practical future in light of what removing such a bias or oversight requires. We cannot knowingly tolerate a dichotomy between what we say to ourselves is so and what we try to put into practice. We have constantly to try to act as we are intellectually, incarnate what we judge, tolerate less and less difference between self and persona. God requires this of us. God wants justice – doing the truth, rendering all creatures their due. Such justice may include a new due that religious conversion may reveal. If we become convinced that the goods of the earth come from God as intended for all the earth's people, in such wise that no particular group has the right to superfluities while others lack necessities, then our social agenda has to clarify. We have to become people who work for a redistribution of the goods of the earth, so that the equity the Creator intended will come closer to realization. It is another question, dispensible on the present occasion, how the sinfulness of human beings ought to enter into our calculations of what is possible, realistically expectable, in matters of economic justice. Sufficient for the present occasion is making very clear the Lonerganian position that we will not be ethical until we have harmonized what we do with what we judge, know, and experience.

The fifth transcendental precept, Be loving, takes us to the core of the human person, where the vocation that a Christian theologian such as Lonergan espies becomes the well-spring of a deep *metanoia*. If one can say that embracing Lonergan's critical realism usually entails a conversion from relativistic cognitional theories (occasionally from idealistic ones), and that embracing Lonergan's view of responsibility can entail a conversion from irrational, usually self-centred ethical foundations, one has to say in boldface that embracing Lonergan's view that the transcendental outreach of human consciousness results in a call to love unconditionally, without restraint, every good that comes across one's horizon entails the most profound of conversions, that to religion (which Lonergan understands as opening oneself to a transcendent divinity, a Truth and Goodness without limit and so not restricted in the hold it has on our allegiance, because it is precisely what we have been made to find for our fulfilment).

The true is also the good. Truth and goodness are convertible. For an intellectualist anthropology, we are made to embrace the truth as a good ordered to our human nature. We cannot call the truth false or evil without denaturing ourselves. The absurd tangles into which Marxist regimes have often gotten themselves by trying to make the truth political (by insisting that truth is not what is so but what the ruling powers consider expedient) is probably the best and most chilling example of what is at stake here. Similar, unfortunately, is some of the thought, argumentation, and rhetoric one comes across in defence of unabridged rights to abortion. The double-speak that George Orwell satirized more than a half-century ago has continued to develop in post-Orwellian, contemporary politics. Language is a good index of our will to abide by the truth, to love what is actually so, not what we find convenient or demanded by dogma.

Religious groups get no exemption on this point, as they get no exemption on any other generated by Lonergan's transcendental precepts. If a church makes decisions and indicates what goods its followers ought to love on the basis of dogma in a pejorative sense – positions more imposed by authority than justified by reason and good practical effects – it is neither responsible nor religious. Violating both the fourth and fifth transcendental precepts, it is inauthentic, and those followers who discover its inauthenticity have an obligation to reject whatever in its dogmatic positions they cannot square with the truth and goodness their consciences feel bound to honour. This is radical religion – more radical than many churchpeople find comfortable.

Once again, the same rigorous standard would apply to a feminist group, whether an informal political coalition or a spiritual coven, that showed itself unwilling to stretch and love goodness wherever found, unwilling to love the unlimited goodness and truth as which 'God' appears in most secular consciousnesses. That feminist group would be inauthentic, unethical, on such points, and any honest member would have to demur. The further question (virtually always, Lonergan would note wryly, there is a further question) is whether one should stay in the group and try to reform it or should shake the dust from one's feet and take a hike. In many cases, this is a tough question, very hard to answer. Therefore, it is legitimate to keep chewing it over until one gets sufficient clarity to answer it boldly and take decisive action. It is not legitimate to pass it by, or bury the group's inauthenticity under the rug as a peccadillo. That is the way to bend one's own conscience towards inauthenticity and spiritual pain, and to make oneself partially responsible for the evils that result from the group's biases, inauthenticities, hatreds of the truth, and will to power even at the cost of the truth.

In summary, then, the fourth and fifth transcendental precepts take us to the hard-core, truly foundational ethical issues. As well, they open the door to the Christian proposition that God is light in whom there is no darkness at all, that God is love, and that our best indication of what these propositions mean is the life (work, personality, teaching), death, and resurrection of Jesus the Christ. They lay down a level surface, on which all people can play, regardless of sex, age, race, religion, economic or social status, even previous ethical history. They remind us that the only truly significant game in town, our response to God's call to authenticity, must be played on this surface. So doing, they also remind us that the enormous reality that we hardly ever find this level surface is precisely what Christian theologians ought to be spotlighting when they speak of 'original sin': the tilt, the warp, the imbalance, the pre-present injustice that taints all the situations into which we move, into which we are born. That is truly a sobering consideration, the neglect of which renders many secular ethicists, feminists often included, embarrassingly superficial.

3   Further Reflections for Feminists

I have indicated how Lonergan's transcendental precepts illumine the foundations of the entire authentic life that human beings of good will strive to develop, from learning to be attentive to learning to love without prejudice whatever good comes into their awareness. While all the precepts are provocative, in my opinion feminists will profit most from attending to precepts three and four. For foundational work in any area, but perhaps especially the area of ethics with which I have been most concerned, realizing the depth and detachment to which we are called if we wish to make authentic judgments, and realizing further the self-denial entailed in acting upon such judgments, sets the feminist project of self-realization in a much more demanding, ascetical, and admirable light than what I usually see proposed under the banner 'I am woman.' The imperative to love is a huge further step, fraught with religious, indeed specifically Christian obligations, but two considerations keep me from pressing it upon feminists with full ardour. One is that most women, and many feminist men, realize that love is the crux of human authenticity and fulfilment. With or without stereotype, this is not a hard point to sell. The other consideration is that so many feminists are allergic to religion, for good autobiographic or historical reasons, that going lightly with the implications of the fifth precept allows one to postpone for a later day full discussion of where authentic judgments and decisions lead. That later day has to come, or spiritual development remains retarded, but I believe it should be possible to begin a fruitful dialogue with secular feminist ethicists simply by spotlighting precepts three and four.

In such a dialogue, I would urge feminists to challenge Lonerganians and the structures implied by the transcendental precepts on such matters as historicity, the sociology of knowledge, and the place of emotions.

First, I believe that Lonergan's work provides very well for historicity, and so relativity, and so for the need to revise biases and oversights regnant, even canonized, in the past – for example, express or tacit convictions that women are inferior to men.

Second, I believe that Lonergan could accept half of what feminists urge when they ask for the priority of a sociological reading of knowledge over an individualistic one, distinguishing between a sensitivity to the *Weltgeist* pressing on any of our views and the (unacceptable) position that the social is the concrete locus of consciousness and conscience, not the individual person. We greatly need the sensitivity to the social construction of reality. The majority of people take their sense of reality from the buzz going round the block. However, until we accomplish a further evolutionary leap, perhaps the one that Teilhard de Chardin foresaw when he spoke of the 'hyperpersonal' or some mystics intuit is latent in the Christian understanding of the 'Mystical Body' of Christ, individual human beings will remain the concrete sensoria for the voice of God. This is a simple fact: there is no party, organization, or group possessing a directive awareness, intelligence, judgment, faculty of decision, or loving heart that composes a unified consciousness and can be held responsible *en bloc* (not simply as a legal fiction, rather as a natural whole with a single responsible centre) for what it thinks and does. It is not true that because the fathers have eaten sour grapes the children's teeth have to stay on edge. We can stand up to the group-think of our time, the Nazi propaganda of our era of German history, even the

Maoist cant of our Khmer Rouge cadre. It is difficult to do this, but we are human beings, not ants or termites. God holds each of us individually responsible for our lives, however much the divine wisdom and mercy mitigate individual responsibility because of powerful social forces.[8]

Third, Lonergan provides an important place for feelings in the discernment of values, but feminists would be wise to push Lonerganians so that feelings would colour the entire rise of consciousness from awareness to unrestricted loving, the whole existential call to transcend current limitations, face further questions and decisions, and so respond well to God's call to authenticity (which finally can require faith: a knowledge born of religious love, by submitting oneself to the divine mystery that the processes of consciousness reveal and/or the beauty of an individual icon of the divine such as Jesus or the Buddha). Lonergan too easily appears to be a rationalist, and even after one has defended him well against this charge, on the basis of his own writings, feminists are right to applaud those Lonerganian disciples who have delved into such matters as 'psychological conversion': the shifts in feelings, the reconceptions of emotional maturity, that following the drive to authenticity can require.[9]

It is more than twenty-five years since I first found myself exhilarated by the work of Bernard Lonergan, nearly twenty years since I taught my first course on 'Women and Religion,' at Penn State, more than fifteen years since I published my first article drawing on both Lonergan and feminist sources, more than ten years since I first published a book in which Lonerganian convictions worked below the surface of a study of women and religion.[10] Thus, for a large portion of my professional career I have been interested in a substantive dialogue between the two poles of thought being examined in this volume. It is curious that it has taken so long for this dialogue to become explicit – an indication, perhaps, of the powerful resistances that have existed in both camps, and of the courage that Cynthia Crysdale has shown in challenging us to overcome them. I am sure I join many others in thanking her for both this courage and the labour involved in producing this volume. My own contribution has been a labour of love – a grateful obeisance to a master and mistress I have long found delightful to serve.

Notes

1 Denise Lardner Carmody, *Virtuous Woman: Theological Reflections on Christian Feminist Ethics* (Maryknoll, NY: Oribs Books, 1992).
2 See Cynthia S.W. Crysdale, 'Lonergan and Feminism,' *Theological Studies* 53:2 (June 1992) 234–56.
3 For example, see Sheila Greeve Davaney, 'Problems with Feminist Theory:

Historicity and the Search for Sure Foundations,' in Paula M. Cooey, Sharon A. Farmer, and Mary Ellen Ross, eds, *Embodied Love: Sexuality and Relationship as Feminist Values* (San Francisco: Harper and Row, 1987) 79–95, and Lisa Sowle Cahill, 'Feminist Ethics,' *Theological Studies* 51: 1 (March 1990) 63–64.

4 I have in mind the recent works of Gerda Lerner.

5 See *Method in Theology* (New York: Herder and Herder, 1972) 53 and passim. I have added the precept, Be loving, in view of Lonergan's treatment of religion in chapter 4 (see ibid. 101–24, esp. 105–12).

6 See *Divinarum Personarum: Conceptio Analogica*, 2 vols (Rome: Gregorian University Press, 1964), *De Verbo Incarnato* (Rome: Gregorian University Press, 1964), and *De Constitutione Christi Ontologica et Psychologica* (Rome: Gregorian University Press, 1964).

7 See *Insight* (New York: Philosophical Library, 1958) chaps 9–11 (esp. 11, pp. 319–47).

8 See Eric Voegelin, 'Reason: The Classic Experience,' in his *Anamnesis* (Notre Dame, IN: University of Notre Dame Press, 1978).

9 I have in mind especially the work of Robert Doran, S.J.

10 See Denise Lardner Carmody, 'Feminist Redemption: Doris Lessing and Bernard Lonergan,' *Andover Newton Quarterly* 16 (1975) 119–30, and *Women and World Religions* (Nashville: Abingdon Press, 1979).

Emergent Probability and the Ecofeminist Critique of Hierarchy

ABSTRACT *The ecofeminist critique of patriarchal hierarchies has challenged classical notions of world order and raised questions about the kind of relationship human communities should have to nature. In* Insight *Bernard Lonergan develops a viewpoint in which the normative core of the classical notion of nature is retrieved without a surrender to the distortions of patriarchal hierarchy. Yet Lonergan's notion of world process remains hierarchical. The notion of emergent probability provides an explanatory key for establishing an undistorted yet hierarchical notion of world order that pertains to both the processes of nature and the dynamics of human history. The viewpoint that emerges provides a context for the proper understanding of the relationship between human history and nature and provides clues for understanding how human communities can authentically appropriate natural processes.*

At the heart of the feminist project has been the task of exposing to the culture at large the concrete and systematic subordination of women. Feminist analysis suggests that this situation is the consequence of a patriarchal hierarchy that is deeply embedded in the contemporary cultural matrix. In Letha Dawson Scanzoni's view, the justification of this hierarchy, at least in the Western world, rests on the classicist notion of world order that Arthur Lovejoy aptly named 'the great chain of being.'[1] This notion of the 'great chain of being' had its origins in ancient Greek philosophy, its expansion in the neo-Platonist atmosphere of late antiquity, and its flowering in medieval Christendom.[2] Scanzoni argues that this hierarchy was conceived as static, permanent, and divinely ordained. The 'chain' is constituted by a vast number of beings, graded on a scale of increasing approximation to divine perfection. On this scale, living matter is higher than non-living matter, animals are higher than plants, and human beings are higher than animals yet lower than the angels. According to this scheme, the relationship between the human race and nature was one in which 'man' was master and nature subservient.[3] In the prevailing theology this mastery over nature was justified because God made 'man' in his image and granted 'him' dominance over the natural world.[4] This pattern of mastery extends to the entire cultural matrix. Consequently, there perdured a complex chain of unequal relationships of the master/servant type.[5]

In Rosemary Ruether's view, concomitant with this hierarchical viewpoint is a dualistic conception of the relationship of mind and body rooted in gender bias. In this dualism mind is identified with a superior spiritual order, while the body is identified with an inferior natural world. Spiritual or intellectual progress occurs through the mastery of the morally inferior bodily nature. The consequence of this conception is an unhealthy splitting apart of mind and body. This fissure breaks along gender lines so that male-female dualism combines with body-spirit dualism. Thus, in the patriarchal hierarchy, men's activity is identified with the higher calling of mind, women's activity is identified with their bodies and hence with nature. Ruether writes: 'The psychic traits of intellectuality, transcendent spirit, and autonomous will that were identified with the male left the woman with the contrary traits of bodiliness, sensuality, and subjugation.'[6] This skewering of gender relationships links men's mastery over nature with a presumed right to rule over women. These assumptions infected the social matrix and the ideologies that justified its structure. Elisabeth Schüssler Fiorenza writes: 'This attempt to see human nature and Christian Discipleship expressed in two essentially different modes of being human led in tradition and theology to the denigration of women and to the glorification and mythologization of the feminine.'[7] Women are fit to nurture men to adulthood, but unfit for the higher tasks of making history. Men, by contrast, whose 'nature' it is to be rational, transcendent, and free, are suited for the higher intellectual and spiritual vocations, which include those public functions concerned with economic and political power. Even in the domestic sphere this relation of dominance perdured, as man is considered head of the household and woman subject to his rule.

As an alternative to the prescribed order of the master/servant hierarchy, Scanzoni, like Ruether, proposes a *negotiated* order in which females and males mutually respect and appreciate one another and care about each individual's preferences, needs, concerns, dreams, fears, pains, interests, talents, and aspirations.'[8] Yet, while the classical culture in which the hierarchical world-view flowered is largely a thing of the past, the personal and social consequences of its distortions have reverberated into this century, and the negotiated order of mutual respect between men and women, grounded in a healthy integration of mind and body, still does not prevail. Ruether writes: 'The subjugation of the female by the male is the primary psychic model for this chauvinism and its parellel expressions in oppressor-oppressed relationships between social classes, races, and nations. It is this most basic symbolism of power that has misdirected men's psychic energy into the building of the Pentagon of Power, from the pyramids of ancient Egypt to the North American puzzle-palace on the Potomac.'[9] Women's sphere of activity is still restricted, their power minimized, and their intellectual development frustrated. Underpinning this state of affairs is the implicit repression of women's power that can and does erupt in violence. Moreover, this violence against women can be linked to the violence against nature that degrades our ecosystem.[10] The split between mind and body becomes the rationale of prevailing ideologies for the neglect or exploitation of nature.[11]

There is widespread agreement about the destructive aspects of patriarchal hierarchies. Feminist responses have, however, been complex and varied. Simone de Beauvoir expresses the view of many when she rejects as sexist the view that women are closer to nature than men.[12] For liberal feminists this stand fits in well with the political goal of securing equal rights with men and fair access to economic resources.[13] In order to create a place in the corridors of power, women must assert their right to be identified with the higher nature of intellect and freedom, and overcome, or at least minimize, the traditional identification of women with biological functions and domestic roles. Despite ideological differences with liberals, socialist feminists too have generally rejected the identification of women with nature as a distorted product of the ideology of capitalist domination.[14] For cultural feminists, however, whose project it is to create and celebrate a distinctly feminist culture, the identification of women with nature has been a central, if controversial, issue.[15] Many cultural feminists emphasize women's special connection with nature.[16] Cora Twohig-Moengangongo, for instance, writes: 'A feminist insight, shared with indigenous people, calls us back to our senses. Here, in our bodies, in our earth, we welcome the symbols and feelings, given to and re-membered in psychic consciousness from within the pulsing flow of life.'[17] This connection has borne fruit in the special role cultural feminists have had in the ecological movement. The ecofeminism movement, which emerged out of this linkage, is an effort to restore our integral connection with nature.[18] It challenges the feminist movement as a whole to reconsider the significance of the relationship of humanity in general and women in particular to nature. Ecofeminists seek an alternative feminist vision of world order that would overcome the false dualisms of body/mind and nature/history inherent to patriarchal hierarchies. Ynestra King writes: '[T]he problem of connecting humanity to nature will still have to be acknowledged and solved. In our mythology of complementarity, men and women have led vicarious lives, where women had feelings and led instinctual lives and men engaged in the projects illuminated by reason. Feminism has exposed the extent to which it was all a lie.'[19] The question arises: 'How do we change the self-concept of a society from the drives toward possession, conquest, and accumulation to the values of reciprocity and acceptance of mutual limitation?'[20]

To expose a lie or to right a distorted relationship assumes that we have some notion of what the relationship ought to be. In this respect Bernard Lonergan's thought invites us to a comprehensive viewpoint that anticipates the features of an undistorted relationship between mind and body. This viewpoint would acknowledge the need to reverse distorted dualisms and to create a cultural matrix oriented by reciprocity and negotiated mutuality.[21] In this context, Patrick Byrne has argued that Lonergan's *Insight* constitutes an authentic retrieval of a normative core of the notion of nature – a retrieval accomplished without surrendering to the ideological distortions of patriarchical hierarchy.[22] Lonergan's retrieval depends upon an integration of classical notions of normativity with the advances of the natural sciences. In this new context, the normative operation of the mind in history does not result in the domination of nature. This new synthesis opens up ways to restore the relationship of mind to body, men to women, and nature to history, ways that honour these connections and overcome the destructive dualisms that have prevailed to date. If Byrne is correct, then Lonergan's understanding of the relationship between nature and history could prove fruitful for exploring the questions that have been brought to the fore by ecofeminists.

There is, however, the question of whether or not Lonergan's notion of world process is truly amenable to the values of reciprocity and mutuality championed by ecofeminists writers. Crucial to his efforts is the notion of emergent probability. On Lonergan's account, emergent probability is the immanent intelligibility of world process. What follows from his explanation of emergent probability is the notion of world process as constituted by a succession of 'higher forms.'[23] This suggests that Lonergan's retrieval of the normative core of the notion of nature includes a hierarchical explanation of world process.[24] This in turn raises the concern that Lonergan's retrieval reaffirms the distortions of the classical 'great chain of being.' Is Lonergan's understanding of world process, then, a reaffirmation of the false norms of patriarchical hierarchy in modern dress, or does it signal a significant advance? Are hierarchical notions always inimical to the values of negotiated mutuality? Because the analysis of hierarchies has tremendous importance in the feminist hermeneutic of suspicion, the central task of this paper will be to address this question. In the process I hope to offer an illustration of the constructive role that the notion of emergent probability might play in the task of appropriating genuine connections between mind and body, nature and history.

1   Emergent Probability and the Intelligibility of Nature

If human beings are a concrete unity of mind and body, then it is by virtue of the mind that there is history, while it is through the body that we maintain our connection to nature. The notion of emergent probability provides an intelligible connection between the two. We begin our analysis of the connection by considering emergent probability as it pertains to natural process.

The notion of emergent probability is the novel product of Lonergan's attempt to understand world order as a dynamic and evolutionary process.[25] We can locate his efforts generally in the broad sweep of his project to bring traditional theology up 'to the level of the times.' Of relevance are his reckoning with developments in the physical and chemical sciences, Darwin's theory of evolution, and secular philosophies of history. The germ of the idea is already present in Lonergan's efforts to forge a theory of history in the 1930s.[26] Essential elements of the notion inform his seminal article 'Finality, Love, Marriage,' published in 1942, in which Lonergan applies his understanding of world process to human sexuality and marriage.[27] In *Insight* Lonergan offers his most extensive treatment of the notion of world process.[28] He returns to the problem as late as 1976 in the article 'Mission and the Spirit.'[29]

In *Insight* Lonergan arrives at the notion of emergent probability in the wake of his investigation of the complementarity of classical and statistical methods of inquiry in the sciences.[30] While classical methods anticipate a constant system to be discovered, statistical methods anticipate that there will be data that will not conform to system. Laws of the classical type abstract from specific circumstances to arrive at abstract and general laws that state, through some correlation or function, the relationship of things to one another. To take an elementary example, Boyle's Law states that the pressure and volume of a gas are inversely proportional to one another or $PV = k$, where P is pressure, V is volume, and k is a constant of proportionality. This law states precisely the correlation between the pressure and volume of gases.[31] However, the actual results obtaining from particular investigations may deviate from the ideal on account of factors, such as temperature, that pertain to a particular situation. Statistical laws, thus, consider these very concrete situations from which classical laws abstract. They establish the ideal frequencies for the occurrences of events of a particular kind. While such frequencies can anticipate ideal norms, any particular event can deviate from the norm. Thus, in a coin toss we can expect that 50 per cent of the time heads will turn up but we cannot with certainty determine whether any particular toss will be heads or tails. We expect the results to be random. If we were to toss the coin and always get heads, we would suspect someone had tampered with the coin. Consequently, statistical laws take randomness as a given, the very something from which classical laws abstract.[32]

For Lonergan, classical and statistical laws are complementary. On the one hand, while classical laws abstract from events, still those laws are verified in events. On the other hand, statistical laws regard events that are specified by the correlations and functions generated by classical methods. Moreover, when classical and statistical laws are applied to dynamic processes in which we can anticipate the emergence of novel events and species, chance and randomness are found to be compatible with the notion that events have determinate causes. It is by virtue of unsystematic or random elements that new species and schemes of events occur.[33] For example, if factors in the environment are appropriate, chance variations produce adaptive features in a species. Over time successful adaption produces identifiable species variations, subspecies, and eventually the emergence of entirely new species.[34] With Darwin, then, Lonergan acknowledges probability as explanatory in evolutionary theory. He understands Darwin's notion of chance variation to be an instance of the probability of emergence, and natural selection as an instance of the probability of survival.[35]

The general notion of emergent probability '[r]esults from the combination of the conditioned series of schemes with their respective probabilities of emergence and survival.'[36] Schemes of recurrence are a series of related and recurrent events of a particular kind. Such schemes are possible because the 'divergent series of positive conditions for an event might coil around in a circle.'[37] The series of events would be so related such that the 'fulfilment of the conditions for each would be the occurrence of the others.'[38] Examples of such recurrent schemes would include the solar system, the nitrogen cycle, and the digestive system. Such schemes come into existence, survive over time, and break down in accordance with a certain schedule of probabilities. Thus, there was a time when our solar system was not and its continued existence is a matter not of certainty but of probability. Moreover, prior schemes condition the emergence and survival of later schemes. Thus, emergent probability is not about single schemes but a conditioning series of schemes. The solar system is one of the prior series of schemes that conditions the emergence of the earth's weather systems. Weather systems condition the emergence and survival of life on earth. Living species exist in specific environments and are connected to each other in various ecologies. Plant life is a condition in the environment for the emergence and survival of animal life. Conditioned schemes also admit of breakdown and therefore schemes and species may cease to exist. There occur as well blind alleys in world process.[39] Through statistical methods we can work out, given sufficient data, the probability schedules for the emergence, length of survival, and breakdown of conditioned schemes.

The world order that emerges from an understanding of the dynamics of emergent probability is a '[l]ong series of discontinuities reaching from subatomic particles to mankind.'[40] It is an open-ended, flexible, yet indeterminately directed process in which there is the emergence, survival, and breakdown of a conditioned series of schemes of recurrence and things, operating according to certain schedules of probability.[41] Lonergan distinguishes four successive levels of schemes and things in the non-human environment. These four levels are the physical, the chemical, the biological, and the psychic.[42] Each level has its own laws that we cannot simply deduce from the laws of other levels. Schemes at each level have a horizontal finality proportional to that level and a vertical finality orientated to a higher end.[43] Thus, the adequate explanation of any particular series of events in the environment may involve a number of sciences. For instance, the evaporation of H_2O is integral to weather schemes; however, by virtue of its role as a conditioning scheme in the survival of biological species, the water cycle contributes to the higher ends of life. Changes in the frequency of waterfall produce changes in those higher schemes. A significant drop in waterfall over time will produce changes in the water table. Such changes can alter the reproductive rates of some plant species of a marshland. Many animal species that are well adapted to the schemes of a marshland environment will not survive if a drop in the amount of rainfall leads to significant changes in the distribution of plant species in the marshland ecology. Different species will come to inhabit the new and drier habitat. Where red-winged blackbirds once sang, starlings now shriek. Thus, the explanation of changes in the population of certain bird species in a marshland undergoing transformation to a field ecology will involve forays into meteorology, earth sciences, chemistry, plant ecology, ornithology, and so forth. Thus, in continuity with the traditional classical hierarchy, Lonergan acknowledges that lower levels can be instruments of higher levels, but he adds the evolutionary notion that lower levels somehow participate in higher-level organization. He writes: 'Subatomic particles somehow enter into the elements of the periodic table; chemical elements enter into chemical compounds, compounds into cells, cells in myriad combinations and configurations into the constitution of plant and animal life.'[44] A red-winged blackbird is a functioning aggregation of aggregates of aggregates of aggregates. The lower aggregates are physical, chemical, biological, and the controlling aggregation is zoological.[45]

In order to survive, what emerges must integrate the coincidental manifolds of the prior conditioning schemes; they cannot violate the integrity of the schemes by which they are conditioned.[46] The open-ended finality of world process therefore tends to both greater differentiation and increased systematization. Greater differentiation occurs with the actual emergence of conditioned schemes and things. Increased systematization occurs because the emergence of higher-level schemes and things integrates coincidental events on the lower levels. On Lonergan's account, we cannot explain this complex of distinct levels of organization in terms of the laws of one level. Each level is truly distinct: the laws of physics and chemistry cannot adequately explain cellular division in plants; and the laws of physics, chemistry, and genetics cannot adequately explain animal flight behaviour. At the same time, however, Lonergan acknowledges a relationship among distinct levels. Thus, genetics is a factor in a complete explanation of animal flight behaviour, and such behaviour depends upon the maintenance of the lower schemes of chemistry and physics.

Lonergan affirms a hierarchical organization to world process: there emerges an ongoing succession of higher genera and species. It is, however, important to note two things that are relevant to our discussion. First, the hierarchy that follows from the notion of emergent probability is not static, as in the notion of 'the great chain of being.' The science that underlies this latter conception is Aristotelian, but Lonergan's account rests on the methods of modern empirical science. In contrasting his own view with that of Aristotle's, Lonergan notes: 'Not only did Aristotle fail to grasp the abstract laws of the classical type, but explicitly he repudiated the possibility of a theory of probability.'[47] Aristotle's basic distinction was between the necessary and the contingent. For him the laws of the heavens were necessary, while all earthly activity was contingent. But, from the viewpoint of emergent probability, Lonergan writes: 'The alleged necessary movements of the heavens are merely schemes of recurrence that arose through the unfolding of probabilities and will survive in accord with probabilities.'[48] Likewise, terrestrial activities can be explained in terms of the unfolding of a similar, if more complex, set of probabilities. In this way, the notion of emergent probability opens up the possibility of an explanatory account of world process as dynamic, an account that includes disproportionate levels of being, and that avoids the static conclusions of 'the great chain of being.' Still, while Lonergan's account of world process is dynamic, he regards the design of emergent probability as relatively invariant. By this he means that, although the actual explanatory account may be refined or vary in presentation, there is excluded a radical revision that would shift the fundamental terms and relations of the explanatory account. Lonergan bases his claim on the invariant features of cognitional process that are relevant to all knowing and therefore relevant to scientific method and its heuristic anticipations. Therefore, he writes: 'They [the fundamental terms and relations of the explanatory account] rest on the scientist's necessary presupposition that there are classical and statistical laws to be determined.'[49]

Second, the world-view that recognizes emergent probability is an alternative to various reductionist views of nature. This point must be emphasized in light of the criticism of mechanistic science voiced by feminists regarding prevailing practice in the sciences. Such criticism notes the part played by the natural sciences in perpetuating the domination of nature and connects such domination with the gender bias of patriarchy. Lonergan, for his part, contrasts his view with both mechanistic determinism and indeterminism. Mechanistic determinism allows that there are laws of the classical kind that would determine events.[50] In doing so it disallows the role of the non-systematic in relationships among things and events.[51] Indeterminism, on the other hand, points to the laws of Quantum Mechanics to disavow mechanistic determinism.[52] Lonergan's account, by contrast, accepts the duality of two distinct modes of empirical investigation, the classical and the statistical, and relates them to a single world-view. If Lonergan's view is to be rejected, then, either we are left with some form of reductionist science, or we must discover some other way of differentiating the complexities that exist in scientific methods and in natural processes themselves.

2   Emergent Probability and Human Living

Not only does emergent probability apply to natural processes, it is also applicable to human living.[53] Human beings are made up of a controlled aggregation of aggregates of physical, chemical, biological, and psychic schemes, where the controlling aggregation is a set of higher-order schemes that are not only intelligible but intelligent. In other words, we have molecules, chemical processes, cells, a sensitive psyche, and intelligence. Thus, the sounds produced by the manipulation of breath through the larynx can be more than expression of biological exigencies; they can be the intelligent communication of words. From the zoologist's perspective, there are coincidental features of sound production, such as variation in voice quality, pitch, and intensity, that, from the perspective of the human sciences, human beings exploit to communicate ideas, to dramatically express meaning in conversation, or to artistically shape a song. Lonergan writes: 'As in the animal, so also in man, there exist the exigencies of underlying materials, and the pattern of experience has to meet those exigencies by granting them psychic representation and conscious integration. The biological cannot be ignored and yet, in man, it can be transformed.'[54]

This transformation is possible because the capacity of human intelligence goes far beyond what is possible in other animals.[55] Dogs, for instance, are conscious, but only intermittently. Their 'knowing' is a kind of sensitive integration orientated primarily to the biological exigencies of survival and reproduction.[56] They can, for instance, tell harmful foods from useful ones.[57] They are capable of solving problems through a limited use of imagination.[58] Because human beings have bodies and live in environments, they also are subject to biological schemes of recurrence and respond to the exigencies of those processes. In human beings, however, there operates a further recurrent scheme of acts that constitutes human intelligence. Because of the capacity to ask intelligent questions, human beings are orientated to higher ends than the biological. For what is coincidental to acts of sense, demands intelligent organization from the standpoint of the questioner. Asking questions lifts human beings above sensitive patterns of experience into an intentional world orientated towards beauty, understanding, truth, and goodness which transforms sensitive spontaneities.

Consequently, human beings can exploit flexibility in the psyche for the purposes of constituting their world with meaning and can shape it according to chosen values.[59] While the dog's use of intelligence is restricted to making connections in the immediate environment, human intelligence employs the free images that emerge in the conscious flow to move beyond the 'already out there here now' world of immediate experience. Direct insights organize into a unity presentations that were merely coincidental aggregates at the empirical level. Direct insights can be expressed, in hunches, hypotheses, or concepts. Further truth questions arise and initial insights are sublated by a set of acts that lead to a judgment as to the correctness of hypotheses that emerge from these insights. Reflective insights thus function to compare the data with the various possible answers to the questions asked. Judgments of fact follow. These judgments, in turn, become part of the habitual texture of thought mediating perception of the conscious flow.[60] Moreover, the same basic process can be applied to transform situations according to the demands of responsible living, because the recurrent and cumulative process that reaches a judgment of fact can also reach a judgment of value. This capacity for intelligence, and its potential for liberating us from confinement to the immediate world of the senses, is universal in human beings regardless of culture or gender. Lonergan assigns no special privilege. Thus, while in the history of patriarchal culture the natural superiority of men for rational thought has been advocated, there is no evidence in Lonergan's account of the cognitional process to justify this position.

We note that emergent probability applies to the operation of intelligence. There is a recurrent pattern of acts; there is an element of randomness in the emergence of questions and the occurrence of insights, which can be accorded certain schedules of probability. Moreover, as the cognitional process unfolds, sense data will be integrated by higher levels and the laws operating on the lower empirical level will not be violated or dominated. Seeing still functions in ensuring survival, but it also serves higher ends.[61] However, the unfolding of cognitional process is not automatic. For human intelligence is linked to freedom of choice. Humans are the only creatures that choose. This makes human beings radically different from other animals because, not only are human beings subject to the lower conditioning manifolds, they can also create the conditions of their own existence. Our intelligence allows us to grasp ways of creatively transforming ourselves and our environment. Our capacity to judge means we can distinguish fact from fiction. These judgments in turn become the underlying manifold for our choices. But authentic choices do not follow automatically from the exercise of our intelligence and freedom. We can opt not to follow their demands. For this reason human beings do not always act authentically. Our thinking can be defective, our judgments biased, and our choices poor.

Lonergan argues that there is an authentic or normative functioning to the cognitional process. This conclusion is of crucial significance in figuring out how intelligence can have the capacity for transforming nature in a non-destructive way. The structure of the process itself provides the clue. Lonergan roots his basic position in the claim that cognitional process functions according to an invariant pattern with its own built-in norms that do not have to be invented.[62] While both experience and questions vary, the fundamental structure by which questions process the data to produce results does not vary. Human knowing is a recurrent sequence of acts occurring in the context of a four-levelled structure; experience, understanding, judgment, and decision. Questions precede answers, direct insights provide the required leaps that organize the data, the expression of insights are submitted to the scrutiny of reason, which verifies the products of understanding. Only when all the conditions of the question itself are met can we proceed to judgment of the facts. The products of the process are cumulative and progressive insofar as knowers act in accordance with the demands to be attentive, intelligent, reasonable, and responsible.

Moreover, just as the operation of emergent probability in nature generates an ordered series of discontinuities, its operation in human intelligence generates an analogous set of higher viewpoints. Insights coalesce into viewpoints that integrate conditioning schemes in such a way that functioning is normally spontaneous and habitual. Yet the basic drive of human questioning remains, and settled schemes can be submitted to questions so that further insights reveal the shortcomings of established patterns. Thus, a higher viewpoint that would integrate what is unintelligible in the context of the previous integration is sought.[63] Such a higher viewpoint is not a logical consequence of established schemes, but must be a 'leap' that changes the context of inquiry. Human development is therefore marked by stages. Examples of such a succession of higher viewpoints might be the stages of moral development put forward by Kohlberg or the stages of meaning proposed by Lonergan.[64] Thus, analogous to the hierarchies of nature that are studied by natural scientists are the stages of human meaning studied by human scientists.

It remains, however, that we experience a conscious tension between the operations of intelligence and the spontaneous and polymorphous desires of our sensitive living. For while our eyes delight in what we see, intelligence demands that we direct our attention to what is relevant to the question at hand. Moreover, the same basic tension would perdure between established routines and the exigencies of operators that would adapt to new situations. The benefit of habit is stability and its inertial tendency is to maintain the status quo. Questions, by contrast, intend the discovery of something new. This can disrupt established routines. There is, then, both a unity and a duality to be grasped in human beings; a unity expressed in the 'I' that survives various changes and developments in the person and a duality expressed in the tension between the operations of mind and body.[65] Human beings are both intelligent and sensitive and, whereas the finality of intellect is to intelligent order, no less are there other desires originating in biological processes and represented and integrated in psychic components of humankind. This is the reason there is a duality in human nature that is consciously experienced as a tension between the quite distinct demands of sensitive living and the desire to know. This duality is a permanent feature of human living; we cannot live (and therefore think) without a body but we cannot be human without a mind and will. In human beings nature and spirit meet. The proper negotiation of this fundamental tension is, I believe, of crucial importance for establishing an authentic relationship between mind and body that, when subsumed in the collaborative context of the species, would pertain as well to the relationship of nature and history.

3   Emergent Probability and History

To the larger arena of history we now must turn, for it is only through collaboration that the human species advances in any significant way. Because of the fact of human solidarity, the recurrent schemes of the subject are set in a communal context. Individuals are members of a community of meaning first; it is only over time that they develop as unique persons.[66]

Because human beings live in groups, common needs set common goals and the capacity for intelligent operation is turned to the task of ensuring that these needs are met. Therefore, the role of human beings in transforming natural schemes is accomplished cooperatively.

Humans beings spontaneously cooperate in procuring the particular goods that are desired. This cooperation is a function of human intersubjectivity and its product in intersubjective communities. Lonergan writes: 'As the members of the hive or herd belong together and function together, so too men are social animals and the primordial basis of their community is not the discovery of an idea but a spontaneous intersubjectivity.'[67] Practical intelligence has its origins in intersubjectivity, but it goes beyond it to create and maintain over time a good of order that ensures a regular supply of particular goods.[68] Its product is civil community. The recurrent intervention of intelligence creates the tools, the exchange patterns, and the institutions that constitute the good of order. The challenges of living in a particular environment provoke creative responses. Technologies advance that necessitate the development of new economic arrangements. New economies require the development of a polity that can order the developing differentiation of roles and social classes. The development of technologies and capital formation '[i]nterpose their schemes of recurrence between man and the rhythms of nature [and] economics and politics are vast structures of interdependence invented by practical intelligence for the mastery not of nature but of man.'[69] Thus, whereas intersubjective communities provide the material for civil community, the development of a civil community mediates over time the patters of the intersubjective communities it would integrate. In this way human communities transform both their natural environment and the conditioning biological schemes of their own interrelating.

Beyond the good of order that practical intelligence produces, culture expresses, reflects, and communicates the common meanings and values that orientate this order, and submits it to the scrutiny of a higher criticism. Culture stands beyond practicality, for we do not live by bread alone. 'Delight and suffering, laughter and tears, joy and sorrow, aspiration and frustration, achievement and failure, wit and humour, stand not within practicality but above it.'[70] Culture is that capacity to seek meaning and value that appeals to the exigencies of mind and the true desires of the heart. It expresses itself in painting, music, stories, dance, drama, sport, a philosophy, a literature, and a history. Lonergan further distinguishes a cultural infrastructure and a cultural superstructure.[71] The cultural infrastructure communicates meaning and value in the drama of everyday living. The cultural superstructure is a higher viewpoint that develops with the emergence of the reflexive procedures of theory.[72] It is the product of the reflection of human beings on the meaning of living. Both infrastructure and superstructure condition the development of persons, so that the values that orientate human cooperation are discovered, communicated, and fostered.[73]

As in his analysis of the human subject, Lonergan finds there is both a unity and a duality to be grasped in human community. Unity in community is a matter of solidarity. Human beings respond to spontaneous fears and desires. Though each has his or her own desires and fears, the bonds of intersubjectivity make the experience of each resonate with the experience of others. Furthermore, practical intelligence creates common sense. But intersubjectivity and practical intelligence possess different properties and different tendencies. Lonergan writes: 'Yet to both [intersubjectivity and practical intelligence] *by his very nature* man is committed. Intelligence cannot but devise general solutions and general rules. The individual is intelligent and so he cannot enjoy peace of mind unless he subsumes his own feelings and actions under the general rules that he regards as intelligent. Yet feelings and spontaneous action have their home in the intersubjective group *and it is only with an effort and then only in favoured times that the intersubjective groups fit harmoniously within the larger pattern of social order.*'[74] Thus, corresponding to the duality of sensitive psyche and the finality of intelligence in the subject there is the duality of intersubjectivity and practical intelligence in human community. As in the individual the poles of the duality act to condition and orientate communal schemes. Intersubjective groups provide the material to be ordered, while practical intelligence generates the ideas that mediate the demands of intersubjective groups. Human beings are, therefore, the originators and legislators of social systems in which the satisfactions of each group are to be measured as they contribute to the satisfactions of all.

Just as judgment in the knowing subject determines whether an idea is true or not, so the task of cultural community is to reflect upon and communicate the meanings of intersubjective community and the social order. Lonergan writes: '[M]an is a compound-in-tension of intelligence and intersubjectivity, and it is only through the parallel compound of a culture that his tendencies to aberration can be offset proximately and effectively.'[75] Ideally culture orientates the civil order to a higher calling than the practical. In human history, because cultural meaning is the outcome of creative responsibility, the authentic orientation of history is in the direction of greater personal liberty that will be concretely expressed in personal relationships of mutual respect and love.[76] But communities can be inauthentic as well as authentic and culture can become a slave to the practical expediency of civil community. When this happens the community loses its primary source of self-criticism and decline inevitably follows. Consequently, in our efforts to restore a proper relationship between human communities and nature we must pay close critical attention to the role a culture plays in shaping human community and therefore in transforming nature. For the roots of the distortions of patriarchy are pre-eminently cultural and therefore their reversal will be accomplished primarily through the aegis of culture.

4   The Authentic Transformation of Nature in History

To this point we have suggested that, starting with the notion of emergent probability as the immanent intelligibility of world process, we might envisage a dynamically formal structure in nature, the intellect, and history.[77] With respect to non-human nature, Lonergan differentiates four distinct genera: the physical, the chemical, the botanical, and the zoological. With human beings, Lonergan adds a fifth genus, intelligence, and recognizes the occurrence of a succession of higher viewpoints following upon its normal development. This succession of viewpoints pertains to both personal development and the communal progress of history. In this evolving process, emerging higher levels exploit the coincidental events of lower levels. Higher levels integrate lower-level schemes for higher ends, but in the process the schemes of lower levels must be respected. Thus, authentic control in the movement of history is intelligent control, and intelligent control demands that we pay attention to the schemes of nature and exercise responsibility towards them. We find the root of Lonergan's view in his account of human cognition, from which he derives the basic analogy for his position on world process. This account of human cognition is normative in conception, as is its expansion to the communal schemes of recurrence that constitute the human environment. When human beings follow inherent norms they will be attentive to experience, intelligent in questioning, rational in judgment, and responsible in their decisions. This being the case, there is then a finality that goes beyond the regularity of biological schemes.[78] The exigencies of the human person so conceived provide operative norms for the effective and positive transformation of our natural environment (including our bodily selves). The transformation would be effective in history as a consequence of the transposition of these basic operative norms to a cooperative context. Thus, Lonergan's basic positions expand to provide us with a heuristic structure for anticipating the responsible transformation of nature through the exercise of human intelligence.[79]

Does such transformation mean the domination of nature by humankind? This might be the case if we were utterly unable to grasp how lower-level schemes might be integrated by higher-level operations, or if we dogmatically asserted that there is not an intelligible connection between the schemes of nature and those of history. This is the case in world-views that assert an unbridgeable divide between mind and body, nature and history. Such claims mar the whole tradition from Descartes to Kant, which separates mind from body and nature from history. Such a position underlies any ideology that would justify the exploitation of natural resources without regard to the integrity of ecosystems. This, however, is not the import of Lonergan's position. For him, lower levels provide the materials to be integrated by higher levels; higher levels normatively transform the lower-level schemes. This relationship is to higher ends, but it is not a relationship of domination. It is a matter of the 'long, hard uphill climb, [which] is the creative process itself.'[80] The still remote fruit of this long climb would be a nuanced control of the material of nature within the larger context of the responsible implementation of human goals.[81] All persons have neural demands and psychic tendencies that operate in human development. It follows from this that the distinctive neural demands and psychic schemes of the two genders merit attention in any responsible and sufficiently nuanced control of history. To make this claim does not, however, restrict us to our biology or psychic make-up, because all persons also have the capacity to intelligently direct developments that originate in the underlying manifolds. These manifolds have been profoundly shaped or misshaped by the cultural meanings assigned to sexual differentiation. Therefore, although the reversal of patriarchal bias involves paying attention to underlying lower manifolds, this attention must be paid in a dialectical context that would consider how these neural demands and psychic tendencies have been shaped or misshaped in our cultural histories.

There is, however, a further issue relevant to understanding the connection of ongoing human development to the integrity of natural schemes, whether we are thinking of bodily functions or the environment. Indeed it is a crucial point. Because human beings have the capacity to choose whether or not to follow the exigencies inherent in the structure of human consciousness, development can be distorted. Thus, the finality of human intelligence and the demands of sensitive living do not always coexist in harmony. This lack of harmony can occur for fundamentally different reasons. A primary reason is the lag between sensitive integration and the demands of intellect.[82] Lonergan discusses three aspects of this lag in his treatment of human development. In the first place, because human beings are a unity, there is a law of integration relevant to human development.[83] While the initiative in human development may be organic, psychic, intellectual, or external, it remains fragmentary until there is a corresponding integration on other levels.[84] For this reason any psychic differences pertaining to women and men need to be taken into account. In the second place, there is a law of limitation and transcendence. This law follows from the inherent and permanent conscious tension in human beings between the subjects that we currently are, constituted by existing laws, habits, spontaneities, and schemes, and the demand for ongoing development of new laws, habits, spontaneities, and schemes. This tension is rooted in the contrary demands of intelligence, orientated in detachment to unrestricted inquiry, and the inertial tendencies of our sensitive psyche as self-interested animals in a habitat.[85] This tension, however, cannot be met by suppressing the exigencies of either. For while intelligence mediates the inertial tendencies of our spontaneities, still intelligence needs the cooperation of those selfsame inertial tendencies to sustain its quest. Third, to meet the heightened tension of the law of limitation and transcendence, Lonergan proposes the law of genuineness. Genuineness is fundamentally the admission into consciousness of the tension of limitation and transcendence, and is therefore the 'necessary condition of the harmonious co-operation of conscious and unconscious components of development.'[86] The admission is necessary to avoid a conflict between conscious and unconscious components of development. Such genuineness demands complete authenticity. While such a goal goes beyond what we might expect of human achievement, still it sets an ideal for negotiating the tension between the conscious and unconscious components of our development.

Another reason for discontinuity in human living is that while nature can be genuinely appropriated and integrated in human living, it can also be ignored and violated. Where harmonious relations might obtain between our bodily selves and our intellects, fragmentation commonly occurs. Lonergan refers to such distortion when he writes of dramatic, individual, group, and general bias that infect human living to produce the social surd.[87] There is the personal neurosis of dramatic bias that prevents needed insights. Preconscious dramatic bias results from a scotosis, or blind spot, in the individual psyche. The scotosis interferes with the conscious representation of neural demands and blocks the emergence of helpful insights. Undesired insights and repressed neural demands are re-routed in the psyche to emerge attached to incongruous objects. Because the repression is preconscious the person affected may be unaware of the source of the difficulty, even though its effects hinder personal development. The result can be a failure to intelligently assess problems that demand attention. Thus, dramatic bias affects the recognition and communication of particular needs as well as the performance of tasks. It produces a distortion in common sense and, accordingly, affects those schemes that promote the good of order. Moreover, there are egoists who ignore the question of how their actions will affect others and use their intelligence to further their own ends. Such egoists ought to ask how their actions affect the just order of the community, but they do not. But bias is not restricted to individuals. There are groups who defend their own interests at the expense of others. Class bias, racism, and sexism are instances of such group bias. Furthermore, all groups suffer from general bias, the tendency to disregard the long-term viewpoint in favour of immediate practical results. Our present environmental degradation is one consequence of such collective short-term thinking. Characteristic of all bias is the exclusion of needed insights that are required for real development of persons and communities. It is rooted in the failure of persons to be authentic, to consistently follow the inherent exigencies to be attentive, intelligent, reasonable, and responsible. Inauthenticity is, after all, rooted in the failure to follow these transcendental precepts. Such inauthenticity spreads to infect theories about the human condition and ultimately the entire social structure. When bias is a dominant factor in the situation, the result is inequality. If the situation remains uncorrected there is eventually the breakdown of social order, where hatred and fear become the rule rather than the exception. Fear leads to control by dominant minorities who offer stability at the cost of human liberty.

Our history is a product of both authenticity and inauthenticity. Where ideally (or normatively) an intelligent situation should prevail, there is the complex of the social surd. This fact must be taken into account in determining the value of Lonergan's hierarchical notion of world order. Are hierarchies inherently distorted? If we follow the analysis of prevailing gender-biased hierarchical social structures, we would conclude that hierarchies are always distorted. If we accepted a static notion of world order as normative, we would be correct to conclude that such a notion does not take into account the patent evidence that world process is dynamic. Again, we would be quite right in rejecting hierarchical notions. For bad theory applied to concrete living produces disastrous results in the longer term. However, arguing from existing practice does not lead us to a negative assessment of Lonergan's notion of world process. Lonergan does not start with existing social practice: he grounds his approach in the normative exigencies of human intelligence. These exigencies follow from the praxis of the human mind itself. Therefore, Lonergan's account is not a description of current cultural meanings or social practices; it is the basis for a criticism of them. Indeed, the most insidious bias of all is the general bias of common sense, which would make theory conform to current practice. Lonergan is unequivocal in this regard. He writes: 'A civilization in declines digs its own grave with a relentless consistency. It cannot be argued out of its self-destructive ways, for argument has a theoretical major premise, theoretical major premises are asked to conform to matters of fact, and the facts in the situation produced by decline more and more are the absurdities that proceed from inattention, oversight, unreasonableness, and irresponsibility.'[88] Progress is a matter of obeying the transcendental precepts: Be attentive, Be intelligent, Be reasonable, Be responsible. To obey these would be to reject what is wrong with current practice. Lonergan's effort is precisely to develop a formally dynamic account of world process that does justice to its complexity while avoiding reductionism. He writes: 'The challenge of history is for man progressively to restrict the realm of chance or fate or destiny and progressively to enlarge the realm of conscious grasp and deliberate choice.'[89]

We can now coil around to the question with which we began this paper. Lonergan's account of world process does reaffirm, in its admission of higher and lower aggregates, hierarchical aspects of the 'great chain of being.' Still, such an affirmation does not lead to the justification of distorted patriarchal structures. We need to distinguish between distorted, impoverished notions of hierarchy and an understanding of hierarchy that results from the adequate differentiation of the complexities of world process. Unless subatomic particles and human beings are to be regarded as of the same complexity, then to be adequate that account of world process must acknowledge higher and lower forms. Because Lonergan's account acknowledges the real disproportion between the various levels and between non-human nature and history, he can suggest how relations ought to obtain between these disproportions in human development. In this matter, he offers us the laws of integration, limitation and transcendence, and genuineness. I would argue that, far from denying the values of mutuality between the sexes and respect for natural processes, these three laws applied to our dealings with nature and our bodies offer a uniquely valuable heuristic tool for understanding how such values may be implemented. What the feminist critique rightfully condemns are notions of hierarchy, rooted in bias and wrong-headed theory, that impoverish human creativity, bias the social-cultural matrix, and block personal development. The key is to distinguish hierarchies that enrich from those that impoverish.

It remains that the reach of authentic human desire far outdistances human achievement. Consequently, human history with all its shortcomings is ultimately the material for divine artistry.[90] It is only though the supernatural mystery of divine healing, and the creative human cooperation with that mystery, that the problem of reversing the distorted structures of patriarchy will ultimately be met. This is not to underestimate the difficulty of that reversal. In this we can concur with Rosemary Ruether when she writes: 'The work of fostering religious consciousness which is explicitly incompatible with sexism will require an extraordinary degree of creative rage, love, and hope.'[91] This concurs with a sentence from the concluding chapter of *Insight*: 'The antecedent willingness of charity has to mount from an affective to an effective determination to discover and to implement in all things the intelligibility of universal order that is God's concept and choice.'[92] A significant component of an effective determination of charity in the present world is an understanding of the structure whereby human beings act to effectively transform and integrate nature through the responsible use of our intelligence.

Notes

1 See Letha Dawson Scanzoni, 'The Great Chain of Being and the Chain of Command,' in Mary I. Buckley and Janet Kalven, eds, *Women Spirit Bonding* (New York: Pilgrim Press, 1984) 41–55. Arthur J. Lovejoy's original (and more positive) account is in *The Great Chain of Being* (Cambridge, MA: Harvard University Press, 1936).

2 Scanzoni, 'The Great Chain of Being' 41, and Rosemary Radford Ruether, 'Motherearth and the Megamachine: A Theology of Liberation in a Feminine, Somatic and Ecological Perspective,' in Carol Christ and Judith Plaskow, eds, *Women Spirit Rising* (New York: Harper and Row, 1979) 43–52.

3 The term 'nature' can be problematic, especially as it comes to include the notion of human nature. I will use the term 'nature' in a restricted sense to refer to those physical, chemical, botanical, and zoological schemes and things studied by natural scientists. This would include what we refer to descriptively as 'the body' and 'the environment.' Lonergan makes a similar distinction in setting forth the differences between history and natural science in his discussion of history as a functional speciality. See *Method in Theology* (London: Darton, Longman, and Todd, 1972) 1975–80. See 'Finality, Love, Marriage,' in *Collected Works of Bernard Lonergan*, vol. 4, ed. Frederick E. Crowe and Robert M. Doran (Toronto: University of Toronto Press, 1988) 38. A fully explanatory context, in accord within the expectations of Lonergan's heuristic perspective, would sublate a descriptive use of the term 'nature' into the larger explanatory context suggested in Patrick H. Byrne, '*Insight* and the Retrieval of Nature,' in Fred Lawrence, ed., *Lonergan Workshop* 8 (Atlanta: Scholars Press, 1990) 1–59.

4 Both Carolyn Merchant, *The Death of Nature: Women, Ecology and the Scientific Revolution* (San Francisco: Harper and Row, 1989 [1980]), and Rosemary Radford Ruether, *New Women / New Earth: Sexist Ideologies and Human Liberation* (New York: Seabury, 1975), connect the domination of nature with the distortions of patriarchal culture. Before Darwin, mastery over nature in the Christian West was often justified by appeal to biblical texts, especially Genesis 1:28. Many authors claim that a Judaeo-Christian assumption about the relationships of human beings to nature is at the root of the ecological crisis. This is certainly the view found in Lynn White's influential article 'The Historical Roots of Our Ecological Crisis,' *Science* 155 (10 March 1967) 1203–1207. This interpretation of the role of the biblical tradition in the ecological crisis has recently been challenged by Cameron Wybrow, *The Bible,*

Baconism, and the Mastery of Nature: The Old Testament and its Modern Misreading (New York: Peter Lang, 1991). His careful exegesis of the biblical texts is a helpful preliminary for developing a theology of nature.

5 See Scanzoni, 'The Great Chain of Being' 41.

6 Ruether, 'Motherearth and the Megamachine' 44. See also Elisabeth Schüssler Fiorenza, 'Feminist Spirituality, Christian Identity and Catholic Vision,' in Christ and Plaskow, eds, *Women Spirit Rising*; and J.B. Miller, 'The Construction of Anger in Women and Men,' in *Work in Progress*, Stone Center for Developmental Services and Studies, Wellesley College, MA, no. 83–01 (1983).

7 Elisabeth Schüssler Fiorenza, 'Feminist Spirituality' 141.

8 Scanzoni, 'The Great Chain of Being' 53–54.

9 Ruether, 'Motherearth and the Megamachine' 46.

10 Scanzoni writes: ' "Chain ideology" leads to a climate that accepts, legitimatizes, and promotes control, coercion, domination, and even violence in human relationships. Such a climate characterizes militarism with its nuclear muscle-flexing. It is manifest in a irreverent disregard for the natural environment that ruthlessly depletes nature resources' ('The Great Chain of Being').

11 I understand an ideology to be a theoretical distortion rooted in a disregard of the transcendental precepts. Lonergan writes in *Method*: 'The term, alienation, is used in many different senses. But on the present analysis the basic form of alienation is man's disregard of the transcendental precepts, Be attentive, Be intelligent, Be reasonable, Be responsible. Again, the basic form of ideology is a doctrine that justifies such alienation. From these basic forms all others can be derived' (55).

12 Cited in Ynestra King, 'Making the World Live: Feminism and the Domination of Nature,' in Buckley and Kalven, eds, *Women Spirit Bonding* 55–57.

13 See Elizabeth Fox-Genovese, *Feminism Without Illusion* (Chapel Hill: University of North Carolina Press, 1991) for a discussion of these issues. There has been increasing attention paid to environmental issues by liberal feminists. See Carolyn Merchant, 'Ecofeminism and Feminist Theory,' in Irene Diamond and Gloria Feman Orenstein, eds, *Reweaving the World* (San Francisco: Sierra Club, 1990) 100–105. Merchant notes distinct liberal, Marxist, radical, and socialist feminist approaches to environmental issues.

14 See Joan Griscom, 'On Healing the Nature/History Split in Feminist Thought,' in Barbara Hilkert Andolsen, Christine E. Gudorf, and Mary Pellauer eds, *Women's Consciousness, Women's Conscience: A Reader in Feminist Ethics* (Minneapolis: Winston Press, 1985) 86–87.

15 See Ynestra King, 'Healing the Wounds: Feminism, Ecology, and the Nature/Culture Dualism,' in Diamond and Orenstein, eds, *Reweaving the World* 106–21.

16 See Ynestra King, 'Healing the Wounds' and 'Making the World Live: Feminism and the Domination of Nature,' in Buckley and Kalven, eds, *Women Spirit Bonding*, 56–64; Ruether, *New Women / New Earth*; Charlene Sprentnak, 'Ecofeminism: Our Roots and Flowering,' in Diamond and Orenstein, eds, *Reweaving the World* 3–14; Charlotte Bunch, 'Beyond Either/Or Feminist Options,' *Quest* 3 (1976) 2–17; Hallie Iglehart, 'Unnatural Divorce of Spirituality and Politics,' *Quest* 4 (1978) 12–24; Starhawk, 'Immanence: Uniting the Spiritual and the Political,' in *Women Spirit Bonding*; and Cara Twohig-Moengangongo, 'Bernard Lonergan and Feminism: A Conversation,' *Canadian Theological Society Newsletter* 10:2 (1991) 5–8. For an opposing view see Sherry B. Ortner, 'Is Female to Male as Nature to Culture?' in Michelle Zimbalist Rosaldo and Louise Lamphere, eds, *Women Culture and Society* (Stanford: Stanford University Press, 1974) 67–87.
17 'Bernard Lonergan and Feminism' 8.
18 For an introduction to the ecofeminism movement see Irene Diamond and Gloria Feman Orenstein, eds, *Reweaving the World* (San Francisco: Sierra Club, 1990).
19 'Healing the Wounds' 116.
20 Ruether, *New Women / New Earth* 204–205.
21 Lonergan invites us to the task of self-appropriating the conscious and intentional operations implicit in our knowing. This raising of consciousness is a capacity available to all human beings, irrespective of gender, and its results can be submitted to the exigencies of critical thought. The particular benefit of Lonergan's work for feminist thinkers is not in the pre-existing answers it would provide, but in the integral heuristic structure it offers for setting questions. In this fashion. Lonergan's work can be helpful, as have Marx's or Hegel's, as a structure of heuristic anticipations for feminist analysis.
22 '*Insight* and the Retrieval of Nature'
23 See *Insight: A Study of Human Understanding*, 2d ed. (New York: Philosophical Library, 1958) 209.
24 This is confirmed in Lonergan's work 'Finality, Love, Marriage,' published in 1942. He writes: 'The hierarchy of ends in marriage can be understood only in the context of the more general hierarchy in human process' (37). As late as 'Mission and the Spirit,' in Frederick E. Crowe, ed. *A Third Collection* (New York and Mahwah: Paulist Press, 1985) 23–34, Lonergan still uses explicitly hierarchical language. He writes: 'Vertical finality is to an end higher than the proportionate end. It supposes a hierarchy of entities and ends' (24).
25 Lonergan's account is in *Insight* 115–39. He contrasts the world-view of emergent probability with the Aristotelian, Galilean, Darwinian, and Indeterminist world-views. For an excellent account of Lonergan's notion of emergent probability see Philip McShane, *Randomness, Statistics and Emerg-*

ence (Dublin: Gill and Macmillan, 1970). Kenneth R. Melchin explores the relevance of emergent probability to human affairs in *History, Ethics and Emergent Probability: Ethics, Society and History in the Work of Bernard Lonergan* (Lanham, MD: University Press of America, 1987).

26 See, for instance, Bernard Lonergan, 'Panton Anakaphalaiôsis,' in *Method: Journal of Lonergan Studies* 9 (1991), 140–72. 'Panton Anakaphalaiôsis' was originally written in 1935. For an account of this and other relevant documents from this period see my *The Origins of Lonergan's Notion of the Dialectic of History* (Lanham, MD: University Press of America, 1993).

27 'Finality, Love, Marriage' 17–52. See also the article by M. Frohlich in this volume.

28 See n. 25 above.

29 *A Third Collection* 21–34. 'Mission and the Spirit' was originally published in Peter Huizing and William Bassett, eds, *Experience of the Spirit: To Edward Schillebeeckx on His Sixtieth Birthday (Concilium* 9:10, 1976) 69–78.

30 On classical and statistical heuristic structures see *Insight* 35–69.

31 Lonergan discusses in some detail the process of abstraction as it relates to the formation of classical laws in *Insight* 35–46. The important point to keep in mind is that the successful results of classical procedures aim not merely to describe but to explain. Consequently, procedures move beyond a description of the relation of things to the observer to state exactly the relationship of things to each other.

32 Confusion about the difference between these two kinds of method mire philosophical discussions concerning the natural sciences. For an extended reflection on the role of chance and randomness in evolutionary process see McShane, *Randomness, Statistics and Emergence* 100–247.

33 David Oyler writes in 'Emergence in Complex Systems,' *Method: Journal of Lonergan Studies* 2 (1983) 47–59: '[W]e should not confuse unsystematic with complete disorder. Though there may be no set of laws which fully explains the existence of a situation, there are laws operating in the situation. In short, unsystematic processes have positive results. The conditions are assembled for the next situation. Because the unsystematic process is not completely disordered, it can be a cause of future processes and situations' (51).

34 On the connection between natural selection and adaption see Ernest Mayr, *Toward a New Philosophy of Biology: Observation of an Evolutionist* (Cambridge, MA: Harvard University Press, 1988) 127–60.

35 Although Lonergan agrees with Darwin on the significance of probability for understanding evolution, Lonergan's notion of emergent probability is, I believe, a significant advance on Darwin's understanding of randomness in evolutionary process. For Lonergan's account of the differences between his theory of emergent probability and Darwin's account of evolution see *Insight*

132–34. For a sympathetic account of Lonergan's advances in evolutionary theory see McShane, *Randomness, Statistics and Emergence* 206–47. For a defence of Darwin's position see Stephen Jay Gould, *Ever Since Darwin* (New York: W.W. Norton, 1977). Gould is quite right when he argues that the major stumbling-block to the general acceptance of natural selection has not been the difficulty of the argument but the radically materialist philosophy that if affirms. As we might expect, Lonergan does not accept Darwin's materialism, which would reduce all diversity to a matter of material complexity. Instead, the view that would obtain from emergent probability would differentiate various disproportionate levels of complexity, including non-material levels resulting from the evolutionary process. In Lonergan's account psychic and intellectual levels emerge out of material complexity yet cannot be explained simply as instances of material complexity.

36 *Insight* 122.

37 Ibid. 118.

38 Ibid.

39 For Lonergan's discussion of breakdowns and blind alleys in world process see *Insight* 127.

40 'Mission and the Spirit' 23. Although this notion of hierarchical discontinuities has not received widespread acceptance in the sciences, some philosophers of science have begun to recognize that differences among the sciences cannot be assembled into a unified theory based on methods of one science and that, consequently, there is a hierarchical organization of the various sciences. See, for instance, Ernest Mayr, *Toward a New Philosophy of Biology* 8–36.

41 *Insight* 125–28.

42 It should be noted that, following Lonergan, the taxonomy of animal species is properly considered at the psychic level. The relevant differences are those of an animal's sensitive psychology or behaviour. A particular animal species is an aggregation of physical, chemical, biological, and psychic schemes in a unity which is that particular species; see *Insight* 262–67. On this and related issues see Philip McShane, 'Zoology and the Future of Philosophers,' in *The Shaping of Foundations: Being at Home in the Transcendental Method* (Lanham, MD: University Press of America, 1976), 79–95, and 'Insight and the Strategy of Biology,' in *Lonergan's Challenge to the University and the Economy* (Lanham, MD: University Press of America, 1980) 42–59.

43 On horizontal and vertical finality see 'Finality, Love, and Marriage' 19–23.

44 'Mission and the Spirit' 24.

45 See *Insight* 267.

46 See ibid. 451–54; 259–60.

47 Ibid. 129.

48 Ibid.

49 *Insight* 128. The notion of emergent probability as a relatively invariant basis for world process is explored at greater length and depth in Frank Braio, *Lonergan's Retrieval of the Notion of Human Being: Clarifications of and Reflections on the Argument of* Insight *Chapter's I–XVIII* (Lanham, MD: University Press of America, 1988).

50 It is this mechanist notion of science that many feminist critics have strenuously opposed. See, for instance, Merchant, *The Death of Nature* 164–90, 290–95, and Ruether, *New Women / New Earth* 186–211.

51 See *Insight* 130–32.

52 Ibid. 134–39.

53 Ibid. 209.

54 Ibid. 187. In chapter 15 of *Insight* Lonergan differentiates operators in human development on three distinct levels: the biological, the psychic, and the intellectual. As in non-human process, so in human affairs these levels constitute a hierarchy of ends, each level having an essential or horizonal finality of its own and a vertical finality to a higher level. Various organic processes such as digestion, the nervous system, and sexual reproduction are in place to ensure the continuance of individuals and the species. Neural demands, conditional by underlying systems, though unconscious, seek psychic representation and integration in sensitive consciousness. Both psychic and intelligent levels are conscious levels. Psychic representation occurs in dreams and in the contents of the conscious flow of internal experience. The sensitive psyche provides a flow of images that is subsequently operated upon by the recurrent schemes of human cognition. When successful, these intelligent operations mediate the subsequent flow of conscious presentations into a higher integration of human conscious living. A concise exposition of this complex 'formal dynamic' is presented in Kenneth Melchin, 'Ethics in *Insight*,' in Fred Lawrence, ed., *Lonergan Workshop* 8 (Atlanta: Scholars Press, 1990) 137–38. Melchin explores this dynamic more fully in *History, Ethics and Emergent Probability*.

55 For Lonergan an adequate differentiation of animal and human knowing is essential to his philosophical position. Moreover, it is the confusion of these two kinds of knowing that lies at the root of confusion on epistemological and metaphysical questions. See David Burrell, ed., *Verbum: Word and Idea in Thomas Aquinas* (Notre Dame: University of Notre Dame Press, 1967) 7.

56 On animal consciousness see *Insight* 182–85.

57 Lonergan writes the following in *Verbum*: 'A useful preliminary is to note that animals know, not mere phenomena, but things: dogs know their masters, bones, other dogs, and not merely the appearance of these things. Now this sensitive integration of sensible data also exists in the human animal and even in the human philosopher' (7). This sensitive integration is discussed at

length in Julian Peghaire, 'A Forgotten Sense: The Cogitiva, According to St. Thomas Aquinas,' *Modern Schoolman* 20 (1943) 123–40, 210–19.

58 Lonergan, in *Collected Works* 5:314–15, cites the experiments of Wolfgang Köhler, which indicate that higher vertebrates are capable of imaginatively linking images that are within their range of vision. See Wolfgang Köhler, *The Mentality of Apes* (Harmondsworth: Penguin Books, 1925; Pelican Books, 1957), 11–24.

59 See *Method* 194–96.

60 Lonergan's most extensive account of human cognition is in *Insight*. An excellent and concise rendering of the argument can be found in his article 'Cognitional Structure,' in *Collected Works* 4:205–21, and *Method* 3–25.

61 See 'Mission and the Spirit,' 25, on the distinction between instrumental and participatory finality.

62 Knowledge of the cognitional process is available to us through self-appropriation. Lonergan writes: 'Thoroughly understand what it is to understand, and not only will you understand the broad lines of all there is to be understood but you will also possess a fixed base, an invariant pattern, opening upon all further developments of understanding' (*Insight* xxviii).

63 Lonergan's *Insight* is itself the presentation of a series of higher viewpoints.

64 On Kohlberg's stages of moral development see Ronald Duska and Mariellen Whelan, *Moral Development* (New York: Paulist Press, 1975). Lonergan distinguishes three stages of meaning in the history of human intelligence. See *Method* 85–97. For a comparison of Kohlberg and Lonergan see Cynthia Crysdale, 'Kohlberg and Lonergan: Foundational Issues in Justice Reasoning,' *Église et théologie* 22:3 (1991) 337–57, and Elizabeth Morelli, 'The Sixth Stage of Moral Development,' *Journal of Moral Education* 7 (1977–78) 97–108.

65 Lonergan writes: 'All development is development inasmuch as it goes beyond the initial subject, but in man this "going beyond" is anticipated immanently by the detachment and disinterestedness of the pure desire. Again, all development is development inasmuch as it possesses a point of departure, a concrete material to be transmuted, but in man this concrete material is permanent in the self-centred sensitive psyche content to orientate itself within its visible and palpable environment and to deal with it successfully. Nor are the pure desire and the sensitive psyche two things, one of them "I" and the other "It". They are the unfolding on different levels of a single, individual unity, identity, whole. Both are I and neither is merely It' (*Insight* 474). Crucial to Lonergan's position here is that kind of insight that grasps the unity, identity, whole that is a 'thing.' See *Insight*) 245–54.

66 Lonergan writes: 'Accordingly, one might say that a single dialectic of community is related to a manifold of individual sets of neural demand functions

through a manifold of individual dialectics. In this relationship, the dialectic
of community holds the dominant position, for it gives rise to the situations
that stimulate neural demands and it moulds the orientation of intelligence
that preconsciously exercises the censorship' (*Insight* 218). This priority is
evident in the role belief has in the ongoing development of both persons
and communities. See *Insight* 703–18. Lonergan writes: 'Human knowledge,
then, is not some individual possession but rather a common fund, from
which each may draw by believing, to which each may contribute in the measure that he performs his cognitional operations properly and reports their
results accurately' (*Method* 43).

67 *Insight* 212.
68 See Lonergan, *Method* 47–52, for an account of the structure of the human
good.
69 *Insight* 213.
70 Ibid. *Insight* 236.
71 On cultural superstructure and infrastructure see Lonergan, 'Belief: Today's
Issue,' William F.J. Ryan and Bernard Tyrrell, eds, *A Second Collection* (Philadelphia: Westminster, 1974) 91–92.
72 A higher reflex control of culture emerges in the shift from the first to the
second stage of meaning in history. See *Method in Theology* 85–96.
73 This representation of human living as normatively cooperative distinguishes Lonergan's position from both Marxism and classical liberalism. Liberalism stresses the role of the autonomous individual, while Marxism,
though it recognizes the need for collective power, stresses the conflictual
character of social progress. For Lonergan, it is the liberty of the individual
that ensures the progress of the social order, but the personal growth that
liberty promotes occurs in the context of social cooperation. Intersubjective
groups work together for the attainment of particular goods. The social
organization of the division of labour ensures the recurrent provision of particular goods through the concretely operating good of order. Through
authentic personal relationships persons cooperate in accord with human
liberty to foster each other as principles of benevolence and beneficence.
74 *Insight* 215–16. Emphasis is mine.
75 Ibid. 237.
76 Lonergan writes: 'The principle of progress is liberty, for the ideas occur to
the man on the spot, their only satisfactory expression is their implementation, their only adequate correction is the emergence of further insights'
(*Insight* 234). Ultimately, the vertical finality of communities heads towards
an end that goes beyond the essential capacities of human beings, in which
human persons are embraced by a higher and supernatural order.
77 In this paper I have merely pointed to a dynamic context rooted in emer-

gent probability that is available in Lonergan's work. The understanding of *Insight* involves considerable labour quite beyond what I have detailed in a very elementary way in this paper. The following cautionary note from Philip McShane's unpublished manuscript 'Process: Introducing Themselves to Young (Christian) Minders' is appropriate here: 'But the elementary pointing invites the beginner to step backwards, from a description of the elusive worldview of chapter four of *Insight* to the intimation that that view requires one's constitution in meaning as Kanon through the inner illumination of one's own achievements in the four elementary zones of inquiry' (200). Those elementary zones are the physical, chemical, botanical, and zoological. McShane has explored these questions in botany and zoology in *The Shaping of Foundations: Being at Home in the Transcendental Method* (Lanham, MD: University Press of of America, 1976) 6–45, 79–95. Robert Doran explores the psychic zone in his works. See *Subject and Psyche: Ricoeur, Jung and the Search for Foundations* (Washington: University Press of America, 1977); *Psychic Conversion and Theological Foundations: Toward a Reorientation of the Human Sciences* (Chico, CA: Scholars Press, 1981); and *Theology and the Dialectics of History* (Toronto: University of Toronto Press, 1990). Patrick Byrne explores elements of the physical zone in 'Lonergan and the Foundations of the Theory of Relativity,' in Matthew Lamb, ed., *Creativity and Method: Essays in Honor of Bernard Lonergan* (Milwaukee: Marquette University Press, 1981) 477–94.

78 See Lonergan, 'Natural Right and Historical Mindedness,' in *A Third Collection* 169–83.

79 I discuss this expansion at length in *The Origins of Lonergan's Notion of the Dialectic of History*.

80 See 'Healing and Creating in History,' in *A Third Collection* 103.

81 On control of meaning see Lonergan, 'Dimensions of Meaning,' in *Collected Works* 4:309. The framework for the implementation of this larger control is suggested in chapter 18 of *Insight* and chapter 2 of *Method*.

82 See *Insight* 225–26.

83 What follows merely points to elements of chapter 15 of *Insight* relevant to the general problematic we have been discussing. A fulsome account of these pointers is beyond the scope of this paper.

84 See *Insight*, 471–72.

85 See ibid. 472–74.

86 Ibid. 477.

87 For Lonergan's account of bias, see *Insight* 191–206, 218–32.

88 *Method* 55.

89 *Insight* 228.

90 For Lonergan's treatment of the supernatural component in human history

see *Grace and Freedom: Operative Grace in the Thought of St. Thomas Aquinas*, ed. J.P. Burns, with intro. by Frederick E. Crowe (London: Darton, Longman and Todd, 1971) and *Insight* 687–730.

91 'Motherearth and the Megamachine' 62.

92 *Insight* 726.

From Mystification to Mystery: Lonergan and the Theological Significance of Sexuality

ABSTRACT *This essay addresses the problem of the use of sexual and gender analogies in theological discourse. Part 1 of the essay invokes Bernard Lonergan's notion of 'scotosis,' as well as the psychoanalytic theory of Jacques Lacan, to unravel the fundamental mystification enshrined in analogies that constellate maleness and femaleness in terms of hierarchical dualism. The argument asserts that such uses of sexual and gender imagery represent a dangerous short-circuiting of the tension towards transcendence that is engendered by the basic anxiety humans experience in the face of non-being.*

Part 2 is constructive; it employs Lonergan's basic anthropological and methodological principles to work towards a more adequate philosophy of human sex, gender, and sexuality. The key assertion here is that an explanatory insight into human sexuality requires us to define it, not in terms of physical sex or psychological gender, but in terms of a superrational orientation of the human spirit to self-transcendence in love.

Part 3 returns to the explicitly theological issues involved, proposing that sexual imagery is appropriately used within theological discourse when it orients the psyche towards 'mystery.' Correctly understood, the specifically Christian mysteries of cross/resurrection and Church do not short-circuit the anxiety of non-being, but rather transform it within a mystical communion with God.

In recent years Pope John Paul II, as well as other theologians following his lead, has been making increasing claims for the theological significance of sex and gender.[1] The positive context of this work has been the desire to

correct longstanding tendencies towards overt misogyny and the denigration of sexuality in Christian theology. As such, this is an agenda that feminists and others of a progressive bent can enthusiastically affirm.

This papal theology, however, has a second agenda that is anathema to
feminists: namely, the need to justify the restriction of the ordained ministry
to males. One approach to this involves renovating the old idea that the
male/female difference is constituted by God to represent the grace/nature
distinction. A recent article by Mark Frisby recruits Lonergan to this cause.[2]
Frisby concludes: '[I]t is at least *prima facie* sensible to regard the sexual
difference of husband and wife as the natural analogue, as a "mystery" of
the radical difference of the divine and the created parties to the order of
religion ... Just as the Christly activity is concretely necessarily masculine, so
any authentic priestly activities in the emergence of religion will be necessarily masculine.'[3]

The present essay will offer a very different reading of the contribution
of Lonergan's project to reflection on the theological meaning of sexuality.
The issue is not simply: What did Lonergan say about it? but, more profoundly: What are the implications of applying his form of reflection to this
issue? Without attempting to answer Frisby's arguments in detail, I will
indicate how, in my view, readings like his involve both a profound misunderstanding of Lonergan and a destructive mystification of themes essential
to Christian theology.

Part 1 of the essay invokes a 'hermeneutics of suspicion' to spell out what
is fundamentally wrong with the analogy of male/female with grace/nature.
Part 2 is constructive; it employs Lonergan's basic anthropological and
methodological principles to work towards a more adequate philosophy of
human sex, gender, and sexuality. Part 3 returns to the explicitly theological
issues involved, proposing an appropriate context for the recovery of sexual
imagery within theological discourse.

1   Mystification, Scotosis, and Myth

1.1 Lonergan on Scotosis, Myth, and Mystery

The term 'mystification' has been introduced above because it points
directly to what is at stake in this discussion. As employed here, 'mystification' refers to a largely unconscious but nevertheless pervasive effort to
obscure the fundamental anxiety of human existence by falsely resolving it
in a world-view structured by hierarchical dualisms. A profound dimension
of existential anxiety is endemic in human life because humans are conscious
of their own lack of being – physical, emotional, intellectual, moral, and
spiritual.[4] Power hierarchies aim to make up for the sensed lack of being by

asserting one group's dominance over another. Some feminists argue that all such hierarchies are analogies based on the first hierarchical dualism, that of male over female.[5] Feminist deconstructionists find that 'one of the major cornerstones that can be found in virtually every text, especially "master" texts, is a mystification of the problem of gender.'[6]

Lonergan himself did not pursue this kind of analysis of gender. His term 'scotosis,' however, offers a perspective on the phenomenon of mystification as it would be explained within his analysis of the dynamic structure of consciousness. For him, scotosis is the distortion of understanding that occurs when a given insight is systematically excluded from entrance to consciousness.[7] The root of scotosis, Lonergan wrote, is a displacement of the tension between limitation and transcendence.[8] Limitation refers to the structured concreteness of what, in fact, one currently is; transcendence refers to the seemingly unstructured region within which what one is capable of becoming is already straining to emerge through the discovery and/or creation of 'higher system.' This definition elegantly points to the dynamic tension that Lonergan sees powering all of reality.

Insight into the 'limitation' pole of the tension involves grasping the 'nature' of a thing. A thing's nature is the set of recurrent operations by which it interacts with other things in the world while maintaining its own unity, identity, and wholeness. Thus, nature is both conservative and dynamic: it operates to conserve established structure, but it does so through constant activity.

Insight into the 'transcendence' pole of the tension involves grasping the process of 'emergence.'[9] At any given time, the systematic schemes of recurrence that are in operation are unable to systematize everything that falls within their purview. Some unsystematized materials remain; and it is this dimension of non-system that provides fertile ground for the eventual emergence of a new set of schemes of recurrence that will provide a higher level of systematization. Once this occurs and becomes established, the higher-level system sublates and wholly recontextualizes the lower level. Insofar as the lower system is now part of a higher system, it is no longer a 'thing' of the same nature; it is, rather, a lower dimension within a higher 'thing' of a different nature.[10]

This tension between limitation and transcendence is operative throughout reality, but it comes to a peak of consciousness within human beings. The human being is not only an established set of schemes of recurrence but also 'a higher system on the move.'[11] Indeed, Lonergan calls the human person 'the being in whom the highest level of integration is, not a static system, nor some dynamic system, but a variable manifold of dynamic systems.'[12] What Lonergan calls 'genuineness' is living both humbly and creatively with that tension. To be genuine is to live with integrity within one's present self-structure and at the same time not to evade the doubts, questions, and anxieties that signal its impending breakdown in favour of something yet more true.[13] Since human beings are oriented towards the radical self-transcendence of communion with the absolute fullness of being, genuineness requires as much openness to the non-systematic dimensions of one's existence – and, therefore, to the existential anxiety of non-being – as to the currently systematic and secure.

The key insight here is that the problem that leads to scotosis is the encounter with data that does not fit within one's established schemas for understanding the world. One can falsely resolve this problem either by imposing the safe security of the currently known system even where it does not fit, or by making up a fantasy system that eliminates the disturbing elements without regard for empirical facts. Either of these is a scotosis of the true insight into the situation, which is that there is something here that cannot be accounted for within one's present world-view. This true insight would require one to accept the pain, insecurity, and struggle of waiting and searching for insight into the next higher-level system to emerge – a process that takes its own time and rarely can be forced.

When scotosis is fully entrenched, it generates what Lonergan terms 'myth.' For Lonergan, a myth is a story that enshrines insight that may not be wholly false, but is nevertheless dangerously incomplete. At bottom, says Lonergan, mythic consciousness is 'the absence of self-knowledge.'[14] For it, 'the real is the object of a sufficiently integrated and sufficiently intense flow of sensitive representations, feelings, words and actions,' rather than what has been affirmed as the conclusion of a conscious process of rational judgment.[15]

The positive and necessary role of imagistic expressions is their capacity to orient and motivate the sensitive psyche in relation to the 'known unknown' – the unintegrated but dimly perceived region towards which self-transcendence is currently striving.[16] In the operation of human consciousness, the coincidental manifolds of experience spontaneously form themselves into the symbolic images of the psychological level; and it is these that provide the materials for the emergence of intellectual insight.[17] Thus, stories and other imagistic expressions can function beneficially in human life as shorthand ways to communicate truths on occasions when laborious explication is inappropriate, or to express 'hunches' that have not yet been fully worked out. They are problematic, however, insofar as they enshrine and give credence to naïve, unreflective views of human reality.[18]

The greatest danger of mythic expressions is that when they are defended as an adequate statement of truth, they 'lock down' any movement towards self-knowledge and self-transcendence. Instead of orienting the psyche towards the emergence of adequate knowledge of the 'known unknown,' they proclaim that the unknown is already known – and that it is 'really' structured according to the story told in the myth. The myth, then, is an organized and affirmed scotosis. As such, it is a false resolution to the basic anxiety of human existence. The basic anxiety exists because we humans know that we are not yet what we long to be; we are interminably in the painful process of self-transcendence towards fullness of being. The false mythic resolution necessarily sets in place some form of hierarchy of dominance, because by lifting out and reifying one position within an intrinsically dynamic process it casts other positions into the margins.

The true resolution to basic anxiety, in Lonergan's view, is 'mystery.'[19] Mystery does not set up a hierarchy of dominance; rather, it draws us forward into self-transcendence with symbols of our fullest potential.[20] William Loewe summarizes Lonergan's definition of mystery as the 'affect-laden image or pattern of such images which ... symbolize man's constitutive orientation toward unrestricted being and value, toward the transcendent term indicated by the word God.'[21] Myth resolves the anxiety of non-being by setting a limit on human potential, and then striving to stamp out what lies outside the limit; mystery, by contrast, embraces non-being within the dynamic dialectic of self-transcendence.

1.2 Lacan and 'The Myth of the Phallus'

The question at hand is how sexual imagery becomes involved in what Lonergan terms 'scotosis' and 'myth.' Indeed, some feminists would assert that scotosis about the meaning of sexual difference is not just *a* scotosis, but the root of *all* scotosis. Though Lonergan never commented upon this explicitly, it is possible to find within his definition of scotosis a clue as to how this might be so. He said that scotosis was 'a displacement of the tension between limitation and transcendence.' In common human experience, a major experiential manifestation of limitation is the stubborn fact that as embodied persons we are irreducibly separate from one another, while a major experiential manifestation of transcendence is the longing for union with another. The anxiety generated by the tension between factual separateness and the desire for union, therefore, is one of the experiential roots of scotosis. Wanting to be at-one-with an 'other,' but in fact being separate, I may displace the tension in the direction of limitation by seeking to dominate the other (thus forcing a false 'worldly' union); or I may displace the tension in the direction of transcendence by denying in fantasy the fact of separateness (thus creating a false 'spiritual' union).

Stated in this abstract form, the problem that embodied individuality presents to union does not per se involve the question of sexual difference. In human psychological development, however, the discovery of separateness and the encounter with the bodily difference between the sexes occur in the same developmental period and become profoundly intertwined. At this point our exploration of Lonergan's contribution to understanding the theological significance of human sexuality will be aided by a quick detour through a psychoanalytical perspective on how this intertwining takes place.

The psychoanalytical work of Jacques Lacan, for example, supports the theory that scotosis about sexual difference is the root of all scotosis.[22] Lacan posits that the child begins life in what he calls the 'imaginary' world – a world in which the child's expectation in all situations is that he/she is the mother's one and only desire. The shattering of this expectation comes with the discovery of the mother's desire for the father. In the child's psyche the father's 'difference' grounds the symbol of Phallus, which stands for both the terrifying sense of 'absence' (of the imagined union with the mother) *and* the possibility of its one day being overcome through romantic reunion.[23]

It is the psychological construction of the Phallus, then, that casts the child out of the 'imaginary' world and inaugurates his/her entrance into what Lacan calls the 'symbolic' world.[24] Lacan's theory is that the symbol of the Phallus is the foundation of all human symbolic life, and boys and girls apprehend it differently. As boys lay claim to the symbol as their own, they claim hegemony in the world of culture. Girls feel themselves displaced to the margins by this symbol, and hence (Lacan says) are likely to retreat back into the 'imaginary' world of supposed unbounded union. Both positions, however, are illusory – that is, they are simply psychological constructions.

Lacan revises Freud's theory of the castration complex by asserting that the root of anxiety is not fear about a physical organ, but shock at the experienced loss of the imagined total relationship with the mother. Both the reality of the 'absence' this creates, and the possibility of its being overcome, become symbolized in the Phallus, since (in the world of the child's psyche) it seems that this is what the mother desires.

This Lacanian psychoanalytic perspective provides us with a way to gain some understanding of the problem of mystification and scotosis in relation to sexuality. In human psychological development the inevitable tension between limitation and transcendence takes the form of anxiety about 'absent' union with a beloved other, which becomes symbolized as 'absent' body parts. From the child's point of view, the sexual difference of bodies is a jarring experience of 'non-system' that, as it happens, correlates developmentally with the even more jarring insecurity instigated by loss of the sense of union with the mother.

The child's intense need to tame the consequent anxiety leads him or her to grasp onto a systematic resolution that presents itself imaginatively. This resolution can be termed the 'myth of the Phallus.' The myth is that the

Phallus defines both foundational difference *and* the path to overcoming it. More plainly: the myth is that the 'difference' between being and non-being – which is experienced psychologically as a raw emotional sense of absence – is fundamentally a question of sexually different bodies, so that overcoming it is fundamentally a matter of romantic pursuit culminating in ecstatic sexual intercourse.

Our initial claim in this paper was that the view that maleness represents divinity and femaleness represents nature is a mystification of reality. We can now spell this out more specifically: it is a myth generated by a basic scotosis – a displacement of the tension between transcendence and limitation, such that the myth-maker commits 'the blunder of attributing an explanatory power to the [imaginative] presentations and even to associated feelings and emotions.'[25] Lacan offers psychoanalytical insight into how and why this occurs developmentally, while Lonergan provides a philosophical analysis of its underlying cognitive dynamics.

2   Sexuality and Human Nature

Having gained insight into how the meaning of sexuality can become distorted within the context of basic psychological and cognitive dynamics, our next task will be to search for a more adequate theoretical perspective on sexuality. My proposal is that a careful application of the basic principles of Lonergan's method will enable us to reclaim sexuality itself, as well as sexual analogies to be employed within theological discourse, from the distortions that have plagued them.

First, to clarify the issues involved, let us define some terms. Herein I will use the term 'sex' to refer to physical maleness or femaleness; the term 'gender' to refer to the sexual component of an individual's psychological and social identity; and the term 'sexuality' to refer to the orientation of the whole human being (physical, emotional, intellectual, existential, spiritual) towards intimacy and union with an 'other.'

Very briefly summarized, Lonergan's method involves what he calls 'critical realism.' It is a method of realism because it starts from the data of experience and asserts that we can, in fact, ascertain truths about the real world. It is a critical method because it asserts that only by knowing and critically appropriating the dynamic structures of our own consciousness can we gain the tools necessary to sort fact from fiction when questions become complex (as they invariably do, since humans are intrinsically reflective beings who continually raise more questions).

Scotosis, we will recall, enters in exactly at the point where a higher system or higher viewpoint is struggling to emerge. The seeming absence of system (from the established, lower perspective) generates anxiety, to which the scotosis is a false resolution. Lonergan's method involves attending to *all* the relevant data, including that which seems non-systematic, until insight into the higher perspective has fully emerged. In the following pages we will briefly survey the results of applying this method to understanding human sex, gender, and sexuality.

2.1 Sex and Gender: From Common Sense to Explanation

Attending to the most basic level of the data of the senses, the difference between the sexes seems self-evident, fundamental, and thoroughly systematic. Even if we could be persuaded to prescind from cultural reinforcement of such differences, the physical differences between female and male bodies are factual. To recognize these physical differences, then, cannot be a scotosis. The scotosis, rather, lies in turning the image of this difference into a false system for the resolution of the more basic problem of the anxiety of absence. It is a scotosis because it systematically excludes some of the actual data; specifically, that which would raise doubts about the truth of this resolution. Instead of acknowledging the dimension of non-system within which a higher system will be discovered, scotosis locks in the system on the level of the imaginative presentations.

Chief among the data that is excluded is any evidence that the difference between the sexes is neither fundamental nor wholly systematic. Yet the facts are that some human beings do not fit into the systematic division; some are genetically and/or anatomically of ambiguous sex. Research on these phenomena reveals that human zygotes are originally sexually undifferentiated, and hence theoretically capable of differentiating with either male or female characteristics. Normally, the process leading to unambiguous maleness or femaleness is clearly programmed in the genes and proceeds unhindered. Certain genetic or environmental conditions can turn the process of differentiation in an unusual direction, however, so that the child is born with a mix of 'male' and 'female' characteristics. In some cases the sexual ambiguity is obvious at birth; in others it may be so subtle that it is not discovered until adulthood, if at all.[26]

Though such sexual ambiguity is a rare phenomenon, it calls our attention to the fact that even in the usual case one's maleness or femaleness is contingent (it could have been otherwise) and contains elements of ambiguity (all males have greater or lesser manifestations of female physiology, and vice versa). An accurate assessment of physical facts requires the judgment that division into two sexes is not absolute, but rather is a differentiation that admits of degrees.[27]

Lonergan's own description of sex points towards this assessment. He wrote: '[Sex] is a bias or orientation in a large number of potencies, a typical and complementary differentiation within the species, with a material basis in a difference in the number of chromosomes, with a regulator in the secretions of endocrinal glands, with manifestations not only in anatomical structure and physiological function but also in the totality of vital, psychic, sensitive, emotional characters and consequently, though not formally, in the higher nonorganic activities of reason and rational appetite.'[28] Here Lonergan says that sexual difference 'consequently, though not formally' affects the 'higher nonorganic activities.' With this statement he points to the emergence of the insight that will take us definitely beyond the common-sense perspective.

In *Insight* Lonergan discusses at length the question of the nature or 'central form' of the human being. The concrete human being is constituted by both material and spiritual dimensions. The material dimensions (organism and psyche) are simply intelligible, while the spiritual dimension is 'intelligibility that is intelligent.'[29] Lonergan's analysis indicates that it is not possible for the material to ground the acts of intelligence or 'spirit' that we discern in human beings. Spirit, by contrast, *can* ground the observed acts of organism and psyche. He concludes that, in human beings, the set of recurrent operations that makes each one a unity-identity-whole occurs on the level of intelligence or spirit.[30] The central form – that is, the defining nature – of the human being, then, is 'spirit.' This central form defines its own mediation within characteristic 'conjugate forms' in the material world.[31]

Our analysis, as well as that of Lonergan himself,[32] indicates that sex is a matter of organic and psychic life and, as such, is essentially on the level of the material. The spiritual, says Lonergan, 'neither is constituted nor is conditioned intrinsically by the [material dimension].'[33] Spirit is integration of the representations supplied by psyche; hence, it necessarily draws upon material that is influenced by sexual difference, but it itself is not intrinsically sexually differentiated. Sex, then, is neither a central form in itself nor an intrinsic condition placed on the human central form. It is, rather, one of the organic and psychic conjugates of the human being in his or her characteristic relations with other things in the world.

Thus, careful attention to the data on the physical aspect of sex leads to an 'inverse insight'[34] into the significance of the existence of two sexes. The inverse insight is that, at the level of human nature, the two sexes are identical; there is no difference. Whatever the significance of sex and sexuality may be, it is *not* that there are two definitively different types of human beings. Despite the heavy bias of common sense towards viewing physical sexual difference as basic and absolute, explanatory insight requires affirming a single human nature within which one set of conjugates is sexual differentiation.[35]

We can now briefly address the question of psychological differentiation – that is, gender. The non-systematic dimension within the physical nature of sex creates the space within which the psychological systematization of gender identity not only can, but must, emerge.[36] Though one's physical sex is given at birth, one's gender is not; it must be constructed. As Lonergan would put it, the human being does not live in the world of immediacy and instinct, but in a world mediated by meaning.[37] The meaning of the physical facts of one's bodily constitution is mediated by one's culture and by one's particular psychological trajectory.[38]

Among the many elements that enter into the shaping of gender identity are concrete experiences of one's body and its potentialities, experienced patterns of relationship with male and female persons in various roles, and expectations created by language and culture – each of which offers almost infinite possibilities for variation. Empirical researchers find no identity characteristics that always adhere to one sex or the other, although some statistical differences can be found.[39] The more the theorist struggles to find the system defining manhood and womanhood at this level, the more she or he is pushed towards acknowledging that the real 'system' is that characteristic of the human central form: the dynamic structure of cognitional process that is at work constructing the human world as mediated by meaning.

In short, the systematic pattern is not primarily in what is constructed (gender identity), but in the operation of the constructor (a human being). Gender differentiation differs from physical sexual differentiation in that construction of gender identity engages the spiritual dimension (that is, intelligence and will) in both its unconscious and conscious aspects. In Lonergan's technical language, gender is an intellectual conjugate.[40] As such, it is both formally and experientially closer to the core of human being than is the simply physical.[41] Nevertheless, the distinction between conjugate forms and central form is of the essence. Sex and gender are conjugates of human being, and as such are always present in the concrete individual; their specifics, however, neither constitute nor intrinsically condition the essential nature of the human being.[42]

2.2 Sexuality: From Explanation to Interiority

Our argument here is that a full intellectual conversion – that is, the completion of the shift from immersion in the world of immediacy to appropriated knowledge of the world as mediated by meaning – requires a radical re-evaluation of the 'common sense' understanding of sex, gender, and sexuality. The implications of this conversion, however, will not be fully spelled out until we have gone beyond the abstract explanatory viewpoint and returned to experience on the level of what Lonergan calls 'interiority.'[43]

Even at a common-sense level, it is obvious that in normal human life sex is integrated into the higher dimensions of human being. In 'Finality, Love, Marriage' Lonergan spelled this out in terms of 'vertical finality.' He wrote that while the horizontal and 'most essential' finality of human sex is towards procreation,[44] its vertical finality is towards relationships of friendship and, ultimately, of supernatural charity. Because these are the more 'excellent' ends, they 'enter more intimately into the significance of bisexuality than does the union on the level of nature.'[45]

Thus, even in 1942, Lonergan had clearly formulated the idea of the sublation of the physical aspects of sexuality within the more distinctively human aspects. By the time he wrote *Method*, his insight into the concrete dynamism of this 'vertical finality' had become more fully integrated into his holistic understanding of the self-transcending human subject. He wrote: 'The transcendental notions, that is, our questions for intelligence, for reflection, and for deliberation, constitute our capacity for self-transcendence. That capacity becomes an actuality when one falls in love. Then one's being becomes being-in-love. Such being-in-love has its antecedents, its causes, its conditions, its occasions. But once it has blossomed forth and as long as it lasts, it takes over. It is the first principle. From it flow one's desires and fears, one's joys and sorrows, one's discernment of values, one's decisions and deeds.'[46] Here we see Lonergan's growing awareness that, on the level of interiority, the ultimate dynamism and ordering principle of spirit is 'being-in-love.' This perspective enables us to rediscover sexuality as an integral dimension of the central human form. Earlier in the paper sexuality was defined as the holistic orientation of the human person towards intimacy and union with an 'other.' Prescinding from its material conjugates (that is, sex and gender), sexuality is the innate tendency to transcend oneself by 'being-in-love.'

What is important here is that sexuality has been thoroughly distinguished from sex. Note well that this is a *distinction* that is by no means a *separation*.[47] 'Being-in-love' is not some disembodied state of consciousness; it is an embodied response to embodied experiences. In practice, human beings live out their sexuality as persons physically differentiated by sex and, in most cases, as persons engaging in sexual intercourse. Nevertheless, an adequate theoretical analysis requires distinguishing between sex, which is defined by physical differences oriented to procreation, and sexuality, which is defined by a holistic and superrational orientation of the human person to love. Lonergan's theory of vertical finality undergirds insight into how it is the holistic orientation to love that conditions the human relationship to physical sex, not vice versa.[48]

By defining human sexuality in terms of superrational love, have we reached the end of our analysis? Not quite – especially since our original question has to do not only with the *human* significance of sexuality, but also with its *theological* significance. Although there is no more powerful organizer of human thought, feeling, and action than being-in-love, honesty requires us to acknowledge that here too there remains a troubling residue that raises questions about whether this is the final answer to the question of the 'system' of human existence. Being-in-love, after all, is notoriously unstable. Even when it is authentic, it can be devastated by rejection; it can fail in the breach; it can be so battered and crushed by events that it dies. If the highest possible fulfilment of human life were human love, the final truth about human life would be tragedy.[49]

The reply of biblical religion is that the final truth about human life is not tragedy, but God's offer of saving grace. At this point we can begin to address the core of our original question: What is the specifically *theological* significance of sexuality?

3   Theology, Sexuality, and Mystery

3.1   Theology and Mystery

Part 1 of the paper included a psychoanalytic perspective on the problem of scotosis and myth in relation to sexual imagery. If we left it at that, the reader might presume that our argument is that all use of sexual imagery in theology is inevitably a manifestation of the falseness of mythic consciousness. We must recall, however, that Lonergan clearly acknowledged that the psyche requires images to orient it into the 'known unknown' – that is, the unknown of whose existence we are aware through our unanswered questions. Though the danger of allowing one's use of images to be ruled by scotosis and myth is always present, it is equally dangerous to presume that one can do without images.

As noted in part 1, Lonergan gave the name 'mysteries' to images that offer the orientation to transcendence in an entirely beneficial and non-distorting manner. The essential difference between myth and mystery is that the mystery orients the psyche into the 'known unknown' without short-circuiting the process by grasping a facile, and in some way false, 'known.' Mystery presents its images humbly, acknowledging that they can only point to what is essentially beyond the psyche's capacity to comprehend; thus, the mystery frees the psyche's innate dynamism towards radical self-transcendence. Myth, by contrast, presents its images authoritatively, asserting that they are a correct picture of reality; thus, the myth locks the psyche's dynamism in at a lower level.

Of the physical world in general, Lonergan wrote: 'the world of sense is,

more than all else, a mystery that signifies God as we know him and sym-
bolizes the further depths that lie beyond our comprehension.'[50] These
words could perhaps be applied most of all to the sensual dimension of
human sexuality. Though sex as physical is *merely* physical, bodily sexual
experience as sublated within the spiritual life of a human being is not just
one source among many, but commonly a prime source of experiences,
images, and insights oriented towards radical self-transcendence. Sexuality
is, indeed, 'mystery' – if mystery is understood in Lonergan's technical sense,
as meaning a concrete dimension that is essential to orienting the whole
person towards 'unrestricted being and value.'

Sexuality, however, is what might be called a 'natural mystery.' In technical
Christian theology the term 'mystery' normally is employed to refer to the
concreteness of God's self-revelation, through which we can truly know
something of the transcendent One who would otherwise be almost entirely
inaccessible to us. Thus, the central Christian 'mysteries' do not derive
directly from natural phenomena, but from events of revelation.

The central Christian mysteries revolve around the Christ-event. What is
revealed in the Christ-event – most radically, in the event of the cross and
resurrection – is the full emergence of God's infinite and indestructible love
into communion with the human level of existence. Christian faith asserts
that this is the only genuine resolution to the basic human anxiety of non-
being. This resolution is radically distinct from the false resolutions offered
by the institution of power hierarchies; for the cross of Christ does not
annihilate suffering, emptiness, and evil, but instead transforms them within
the glory of God.[51]

The ongoing embodiment of the divine love that has emerged in cross
and resurrection is the communion of saints; and the earthly contingent of
the communion of saints is the Church. These, then, constitute the core
mysteries of Christian revelation. The principle of discernment for the
appropriate use of sexual imagery as a 'mystery' within Christian theology
must be its capacity to orient the psyche in harmony with the core Christian
mysteries of cross/resurrection and Church. These mysteries are concrete,
historical symbols of the grace of mystical communion – a communion in
which the totality of human being, with all its non-being, is embraced by the
divine Being.[52]

3.2 Sexuality: From Human Love to Mystical Communion

At the end of part 2 above we concluded that while a holistic orientation
towards superrational love is the defining context of human sexuality, this
does not quite complete the answer to the question about the theological
significance of sexuality. From a theological perspective it is God's love, not

human love per se, that fulfils the human orientation to love.

An article by James R. Price makes a distinction that is helpful in furthering our inquiry into the theological significance of sexuality.[53] Price notes that Lonergan's phrase 'being-in-love' refers to the activation of the dynamic ground of human being; when it is God with whom one is in love, this 'being-in-love' is the highest possible arousal of one's human intentionality. Lonergan's phrase 'God's love flooding our hearts,'[54] however, refers to an activity that is all on God's part. Price suggests that, while 'being in love with God' names the experience of religious intentionality, 'God's love flooding our hearts' names a mystical communion that is given at the level of the non-objectifiable ground of human consciousness.[55]

'Being-in-love,' like all human intentionality, is subject to vicissitudes, sin, and failure – even when the object of one's love is God. The grace of mystical communion, however, is a presencing of God, not as object, but as transcendent ground of one's being. Mystics articulate such experiences in the language of paradox, speaking of both astounding presence and terrifying absence.[56] Yet in this paradoxical experience, the human longing for the fullness of being finds the culminating rest that eludes it everywhere else – even in its highest exaltations of 'being-in-love.' In the famous words of St Augustine: 'Our hearts are restless, O God, until they rest in you.'[57]

If one's notion of sexuality limits it to being a dimension of intrahuman relationships, this discussion of mystical communion will appear to be off the topic. But if we return to the definition of sexuality as the holistic orientation of the human person to intimacy and union with an 'other,' we find that sexuality is profoundly called into play in the human relationship with God. On the level of 'being-in-love,' the passion, ecstasy, and commitment that human beings can feel in relation to a human lover pale before the passion, ecstasy, and commitment that can be evinced in the divine-human relation. And, ultimately, it is only in the grace of mystical communion that sexuality can find its ineradicable fulfilment – a genuine union with the absolute 'other' who is God.

Mystical communion, then, is the final – and ultimately defining – sublation of human sexuality. While this perspective obviously provides grounds for a positive theology of celibacy,[58] it also provides grounds for a wholly positive theology of physical sexuality.[59] Insofar as two Christians centre their union in God, they form a community that is in some sense a 'church.' Their sexual experience of joyous physical union is a climactic form of the concrete mediation of their spiritual communion.[60]

3.3 The Use of Sexual Imagery in Theology

At this point we can return to our initial question of the appropriate use of sexual imagery within theological discourse. All theological discourse – that is, any talk about God – has a fundamental problem: it is talk about a reality that radically transcends the dimension within which talk takes place. All talk about God, therefore, uses various forms of analogy, comparing God to aspects of reality that can be known by conventional methods. The use of sexual imagery in theology is such an analogy. The problem we are examining in this paper is a particular approach to using this analogy, which parallels the radical transcendence of God with the male role in sexual intercourse.

Like all symbols of any depth, sexual imagery is multivalent – that is, it has multiple connotations and interpretations, not all of which are in harmony with one another or with the core meaning of the phenomenon of sexuality. In certain rhetorical contexts, the comparison of God's transcendence with the male role in sexual intercourse and procreation could possibly have validity as one of many connotations of the symbolic imagery. Taken as explanatory meaning in a theological context, however, this comparison leads the thinker seriously astray.

The transcendence of God is, strictly speaking, not comparable to any other form of 'transcendence.' It is not a 'place,' distinct from any other place; it is not a 'part,' distinct from any other part; it is not even a 'system,' distinct from other systems. Rather, it is the ground of being, which transcends, includes, and is mediated in all places, parts, and systems. No place, part, or system can be independent of or 'over against' God's radical transcendence. It is only *because* God is radically transcendent in this sense that God can be the 'centre of the circle whose circumference is everywhere' – or, in more existential terms, the centre in whom each and all persons find perfect communion with God and one another.

The danger of the analogy between the physical aspects of the male role in procreative sexual intercourse and God's radical transcendence is that it reduces God's transcendence to a 'part' within a larger system. In doing so, it sets up a world-view structured by a fundamental hierarchy of dominance. God acts upon the world from 'outside,' while the world simply receives. Correspondingly, within the world, the male is understood as active power and the female as passive receiver. The mystery of God's radically transcendent mode of action-within-the-worldly is reduced to a form of merely worldly action.

The more appropriate analogy between sexual intercourse and God's radical transcendence would compare God to the spiritual communion that is embodied in the 'one flesh' of loving sexual union. This communion is not a part, nor a place, nor a system, but the spiritual ground that transcends, includes, and is mediated in all the acts of the marriage partners.

At this point we can return briefly to the ideas of Mark Frisby, who offers us a classic example of the 'myth of the Phallus' as applied to theological issues. As noted at the beginning of this article, Frisby wrote: 'it is at least *prima facie* sensible to regard the sexual difference of husband and wife as the natural analogue, as a "mystery" of the radical difference of the divine and created parties to the order of religion.'[61] Frisby's most basic error is to take the physical act of sexual intercourse, rather than sexuality as a dynamic and holistic orientation of the human person, as the analogue of self-transcendence. On the basis of that error he quickly moves to elevate the 'myth of the Phallus' – that is, the myth that the male/female difference represents the fundamental divide between being and non-being – to supernatural status.[62]

This whole development of thought is a classic example of scotosis – that is, the failure to complete the shift from viewing the real as the 'already out there now real'[63] to insight into the real as what has been verified by the operations of spirit. By locking in the meaning of gender difference at the biological and procreative level, views like that of Frisby short-circuit the most profound, creative, and spiritual dimensions of human sexuality – that is, its role in the vertical dynamism towards human and Christian perfection. The claim of this paper is that insistence on this interpretation of sexual imagery distorts both the true nature of sexuality and the true nature of God.

4   Conclusion

In sum, our conclusion is that the true meaning of sexuality is the orientation of the human person towards communion with other human persons and with God. Theologically, the most radical fulfilment of this communion is articulated in terms of mystical communion and Church. All human beings, regardless of sex, gender identity, marital status, or any other conjugate of human being, are called to the gift of this communion within human friendship, life in a community of disciples, and mystical communion with God. These, therefore, are the appropriate references of the theological use of sexual symbolism. When employed in theological contexts, romantic, sexual, and marital imagery is functioning appropriately as 'mystery' when it invokes resonances of these realities.

In the present context, the implication of this interpretation is that any use of sexual categories within theology or in ecclesial life must be controlled by reference to the holistic orientation to superrational love and the graced vocation to mystical communion, not by gender or sex. We must take seriously the biblical statement that 'in Christ there is no male or female' (Galatians 3:28). The human person as a subject and agent of communion is not defined by sex. Even in Christian marriage, the communion of persons as such transcends sex, gender, and the act of sexual intercourse. Insistence on a world-view of sexual hierarchy is a mystification that not only blocks the unfolding of sexuality in its true role as mystery, but also blocks true insight into the ultimate Mystery – the radical transcendence of God. In Lonergan's technical terminology, a theory of sexual hierarchy constitutes a counterposition that is bound to be reversed, because it identifies the real with the material, rather than with being.[64]

If this counterposition is reversed, with it will go the major justification for the exclusion of women from ordained ministry. The underlying principle of discernment in regard to any Christian vocation ought to be the proposed activity's potential for fostering the love of God and the love of the saints in God, for these are the final fulfilment of the human orientation to self-transcendence. Vocation to ordained ministry, then, ought to be discerned in terms of an individual's charism for fostering the concrete communion of persons within the Church. The latter is a category of sexuality, but not of sex or gender.

Notes

1 See, for example, John Paul II, *Original Unity of Man and Woman: Catechesis on the Book of Genesis* (Boston: Daughters of St Paul, 1981) and '*Mulieris Dignitatem*: On the Dignity and Vocation of Women,' *Origins* 18:17 (6 October 1988).

2 Mark E. Frisby, 'Lonergan's Method in Ethics and the Meaning of Human Sexuality,' *Proceedings of the American Catholic Philosophical Association*, 1990, 235–56. Frisby's argument begins by stating that marriage is the 'primary natural analogate or symbol' (p. 247) of the order of religion, because marriage – embodied in the act of sexual intercourse insofar as it is capable of producing an 'unrestricted unit of life' (i.e., a child; p. 244) – is the most unrestricted form of communion possible at the natural level. In the order of marriage, he continues, the male-female difference is the essential lower-level condition for the emergence of the higher-level good. Therefore, he asserts, the male-female difference must also have an analogous role in the order of religion. He then spells out the analogy in terms of the act of procreative sexual intercourse, in which the male 'acts in an outwardly directed *ad extra* manner' while the female 'acts in a receptive and then inwardly bearing/nurturing mode' (247).

3 Ibid. 247–48.

4 For a classic discussion of the problem of basic anxiety, see Paul Tillich, *The Courage to Be* (New Haven: Yale University, 1952). Tillich wrote: 'Anxiety, if

not modified by the fear of an object, anxiety in its nakedness, is always the anxiety of ultimate nonbeing' (38). For discussion of this issue in the psychological terminogy of 'absence,' see introductions by Juliet Mitchell and Jacqueline Rose in Jacques Lacan, *Feminine Sexuality* (New York: W.W. Norton, 1982).

5 See, for example, Rosemary Radford Ruether, *Sexism and God-Talk: Toward A Feminist Theology* (Boston: Beacon, 1983) 53–54.

6 Nancy J. Holland, *Is Women's Philosophy Possible?* (Savage, MD: Rowman and Littlefield, 1990) 10. For an example of this type of deconstructionist analysis applied to a eucharistic text of St Thomas Aquinas, see David Crownfield, 'The Seminal Trace: Presence, Difference, and Transubstantiation,' *Journal of the American Academy of Religion* 59:2 (1991) 361–71.

7 Bernard J.F. Lonergan, *Insight: A Study of Human Understanding*, 3d ed. (New York: Philosophical Library, 1970) 191f.

8 On the tension between limitation and transcendence, see *Insight* 472–79. On its relation to the root of scotosis, see p. 478.

9 Lonergan's philosophy of 'emergent probability' is an elaboration, within a modern scientific context, of the notion of vertical finality – which is a central notion for Lonergan's entire system of thought. All things have an absolute finality to God and a horizontal finality to the end entailed by each one's essential nature. In addition, however, within the fertile 'concrete plurality' of the world, things have a vertical finality inclining them to move towards the next higher level of integration. An example would be the evolution of multicelled creatures out of the banding together of the single-celled. See Lonergan, 'Finality, Love, Marriage,' in Frederick E. Crowe and Robert M. Doran, eds, *Collection*, 2d ed. (Toronto: University of Toronto Press, 1988) 19–23. On emergent probability, see *Insight*, chap. 4, esp. pp. 115–28, as well as the discussion in Michael Shute's contribution to this volume. Examples of emergence include the emergence of the chemical out of the physical; the biological out of the chemical; the psychological out of the biological; and the intellectual out of the psychological.

10 *Insight* 438–39. Frisby's argument, it is to be noted, depends on emphasizing the ways in which the nature of the lower system places restrictions on the higher integrations in which it becomes involved; cf. Frisby, p. 242. This is typical of classical nature-law theory, in which 'the natural tends to be seen as something absolute and sufficient in itself to which the supernatural is added' (Charles E. Curran, 'Natural Law,' in *Themes in Fundamental Moral Theology* [Notre Dame: University of Notre Dame, 1977] 29). My argument, by contrast, depends on emphasizing the transforming potential of the higher integrations; my claim is that this is also Lonergan's emphasis.

11 *Insight* 476.

12 Ibid. 508.

13 Ibid. 475–78.

14 Ibid. 542.

15 Ibid. 538.

16 Ibid. 531–34.

17 On development from neural to psychic to intellectual as the series of higher integrations, see *Insight* 454–79. On the insight as prototype of emergence, see *Insight* 481.

18 Lonergan, 'Reality, Myth, Symbol,' in Alan M. Olson, ed., *Myth, Symbol and Reality* (Notre Dame: University of Notre Dame, 1980) 33. See also *Insight* 546–49.

19 Cf. *Insight* 546–47.

20 See Michael Shute's article in this volume for further discussion of the difference between impoverishing hierarchies of domination (which limit the potential of the dominated) and enriching hierarchies of differentiation (which enhance the potential of the sublated).

21 William P. Loewe, 'Lonergan and the Law of the Cross: A Universalist View of Salvation,' *Anglican Theological Review* 59 (1977) 167.

22 See Lacan's essays in *Feminine Sexuality*, as well as the introductions by Mitchell and Rose.

23 It is important to emphasize here that in Lacan's system the Phallus is a symbol, not the physical reality of the penis. The Phallus represents the 'difference' and the desirability of the father in relation to the mother. This is typically associated with the penis, but there is not a one-to-one correspondence.

24 Though Lacan uses the term 'symbol' here, what he refers to seems to explain only the genesis of the worlds of ideology and myth; it offers little hope that symbols can function as 'mystery,' opening the psyche to fulfilment in genuine self-transcendence. For use in Christian theology, the term 'symbol' must be open to the latter. I find the work of Paul Ricoeur useful here, for it spells out in great detail the relation of 'is / is not' that is essential to the symbol. Though the symbol is concrete (and therefore 'is'), it 'is not' what it expresses, nor can it fully exhaust the deeper meaning that it presences. Hence, symbols incarnate a paradox of presence and absence. This way of using the term symbol opens it to the entire range from myth to mystery. See, for example, the essays in *The Philosophy of Paul Ricoeur*, ed. Charles E. Reagan and David Stewart (Boston: Beacon, 1978).

25 *Insight* 539.

26 For a popular but very thorough discussion of the physiological possibilities, see Jared Diamond, 'Turning a Man,' and Denise Grady, 'Sex Test of Champions,' both in *Discover* 13:6 (June 1992).

27 To clarify this point: I am not suggesting that human physiology exhibits a continuum of even distribution between the extremes of 'male' and 'female.'

The great majority of people – perhaps as high as 99 per cent – have physiological characteristics that quite clearly place them near one end of the continuum or the other. The cases of those who do fall in between, however, provide the clue that forces us to re-examine the assumption that there is a radical distinction between 'maleness' and 'femaleness.'

28 'Finality, Love, Marriage' 42–43.

29 *Insight* 516. It is important to note here that Lonergan's distinction between material and spiritual does not involve a hierarchical dualism. There is only one 'thing' – a human being – and one location – the electrochemical processes of a living body. Spirit is not an entity, but the capacity for a set of recurrent activities – the 'operations of intelligence.' Spirit is distinct from organism and psyche neither in location nor in the materials that it organizes, but in the new and transforming level of organization that it brings to the materials they present.

30 *Insight* 514–20.

31 On definitions of central and conjugate form, see *Insight* 434–37.

32 Lonergan explicitly identifies sex with the 'lower manifolds' of organism and psyche, as distinct from the 'higher integration' of intelligence (*Insight* 474).

33 *Insight* 517. The term Lonergan uses here instead of 'material dimension' is 'empirical residue.' In his thought this term refers to the brute totality of the material dimension, including all that defies human efforts to discover its intelligibility.

34 Of inverse insight, Lonergan says: 'While direct insight grasps the point, or sees the solution, or comes to know the reason, inverse insight apprehends that in some fashion the point is that there is no point, or that the solution is to deny a solution, or that the reason is that the rationality of the real admits distinctions and qualifications.' *Insight* 19.

35 Elizabeth A. Johnson has summarized the emerging consensus of feminist thought on this question as affirmation that there is 'one human nature celebrated in an interdependence of multiple differences.' She continues: 'Not a binary view of two male and female natures, predetermined for ever, nor abbreviation to a single ideal, but a diversity of ways of being human: a multi-polar set of combinations of essential human elements, of which sexuality is but one.' Elizabeth A. Johnson, 'The Maleness of Christ,' in *The Special Nature of Women?* (*Concilium* 1991:6), ed. Anne Carr and Elisabeth Schüssler Fiorenza (Philadelphia: Trinity Press International, 1991) 110.

36 As we are using the term here, the notion of gender includes more than simply basic identification as man or woman. It also comprises the personal characteristics and behaviours one associates with one's manhood or womanhood, as well as the affects and behaviours involved in one's pattern of sexual interaction.

37 Bernard J.F. Lonergan, *Method in Theology* (London: Darton, Longman, and Todd, 1971), esp. 73–99.

38 See, for example, Sherry B. Ortner and Harriet Whitehead, eds, *Sexual Meanings: The Cultural Construction of Gender and Sexuality* (Cambridge: Cambridge University Press, 1981). Ortner and Whitehead assert that 'natural features of gender, and natural processes of sex and reproduction, furnish only a suggestive and ambiguous backdrop to the cultural organization of gender and sexuality' (p. 1).

39 See Eleanor E. Maccoby and Carol N. Jacklin, 'Summary and Commentary,' in *The Psychology of Sex Differences* (Stanford, CA: Stanford University, 1974). My argument is that if there is any systematic pattern of gender identity at all, it is at best of a statistical (not classical) type. Classical laws articulate the necessary patterns of conjugation; statistical laws articulate only patterns in the frequency of concrete events (cf. *Insight* 108). 'Complementarity' theories, I believe, are based on the perception of statistical patterns.

40 For this terminology, see *Insight* 515.

41 The existential intimacy of one's sense of one's own gender identity is, no doubt, a major factor in the high level of emotion that often pervades debates on topics related to the philosophical and theological meaning of sex, gender, and sexuality.

42 To put this another way: the central form of human being is constituted by the pattern of operations that is the same regardless of the specificity of the materials it integrates. The concrete integration that constitutes each human individual is certainly 'conditioned' by sex and gender, as well as by many other specifics of the individual's heritage, locale, and history. Our explanatory insight into essential human nature can (indeed, must) prescind from this; our description of the concrete human person cannot.

43 In *History, Method, and Theology: A Dialectical Comparison of Wilhelm Dilthey's Critique of Historical Reason and Bernard Lonergan's Meta-Methodology*, AAR Dissertation Series no. 25 (Missoula, MT: Scholars Press, 1978) 290, Matthew Lamb defines interiority as 'an experience of consciousness as a state which is its own act of awareness.' Somewhat more simply, it is our concrete experience that whenever we are aware of any object, our awareness transcends the object. We 'stand' in our subjecthood, even though the subject-as-subject always transcends objectification.

44 Limitations of space prevent the present essay from attempting to come to terms with the many complex theological and ethical issues surrounding the question of procreation. With Lisa Sowle Cahill, I would agree that while the Catholic tradition affirms an intrinsic unity among physical sexual intimacy, committed love, and parenthood, 'The necessary correction to the traditional way of stating this unity is to add that [these three] ... are all to be understood as ongoing *personal relationships*, rather than as isolated acts or

qualities of acts' (*Women and Sexuality* [New York: Paulist, 1992] 70). Hence, the present argument would place the emphasis on parenting as formation of the child within a community of love, rather than on procreation as the physical engendering of the child. A child can be conceived without love, but it cannot be parented without love; hence, even for parenting the love-dimension of physical sexual intimacy is more significant than its strictly procreative aspect.

45 'Finality, Love, Marriage' 46, fn. In the context of theological debates in the 1940s, Lonergan's nuanced, explanatory affirmation of *both* procreation *and* friendship as 'ends' of sex and marriage was brilliant and perhaps even daring. In the 1990s, Frisby's affirmation that procreation is the *only* complete fulfilment of the orientation of sex and marriage to 'unrestricted community of life' (p. 244) seems retrogressive.

46 *Method* 105. An earlier reader of this paper noted that, in *Caring About Meaning: Patterns in the Life of Bernard Lonergan* (Montreal: Thomas More Institute Papers no. 82, 1982), Lonergan is quoted as saying that the 'situation in life' in which this insight came to him occurred when he was asked to speak with the daughter of a woman who was upset about the fact that the daughter was going to marry a Protestant. In speaking with the daughter, Lonergan observed that she was in love, and that everything else flowed from that fact.

47 Another way of saying this is to note that the more fundamental distinction is between 'spiritual' and 'material' dimensions. Spirit is not *separate* from matter, but it is a *distinct* level of organization that cannot be reduced to the material.

48 In other words, 'sex' and 'gender' are descriptive terms, while 'sexuality' is explanatory. Lonergan wrote: 'Description deals with things as related to us. Explanation deals with the same things as related among themselves' (*Insight* 291). We cannot help but describe human bodies and feelings and behaviours in terms of sex and gender, but we cannot adequately explain them except in terms of sexuality (as defined here).

49 The term 'tragedy' is employed here in its classical Greek sense, to refer to a plot in wihch the hero's fidelity to his/her own deepest identity inexorably leads to his/her destruction.

50 *Insight* 692.

51 Bible and tradition present many variations on the theology of cross and resurrection. Most pertinent here is the theology of the gospel of John, for whom Christ's 'lifting up' on the cross *is* his exaltation to glory. Cross and resurrection are not two historically separated events, but a single mystery of the revelation of God's glory (John 3:14–15; 12:31–33; 13:31–32; 17:1–5; 19:30). Cf. Francis J. Moloney, 'Johannine Theology,' in *The New Jerome Biblical Commentary* (Englewood Cliffs, NJ: Prentice-Hall, 1990) 1421.

52 In the 'mystery,' the paradoxical potential of the symbol to incarnate both

presence and absence comes to its climax. (On symbol, see above, n. 24.)

53 James R. Price III, 'Lonergan and the Foundation of a Contemporary Mystical Theology,' *Lonergan Workshop* 5 (1985) 163–95.

54 See, for example, *Method* 105.

55 My position, like that of Price, is that this 'mystical' communion is not something limited to extraordinary mystics, but rather is the basic reality of grace. People whom we term 'mystics' are extraordinary not in the basic reality of God's presence, but in the differentiation of consciousness with which they appropriate it. My book, *The Intersubjectivity of the Mystic: A Study of Teresa of Avila's Interior Castle* (Atlanta, GA: Scholar's Press, 1994), develops this point in detail. See also Karl Rahner, 'Mystical Experience and Mystical Theology,' *Theological Investigations* 17 (1973), esp. 95–99.

56 See, for example, John of the Cross, *The Dark Night*, chap. 5, no. 2: 'Why, if it is a divine light, ... does one call it a dark night? ... First, because of the height of the divine wisdom, which exceeds the capacity of the soul. Second, because of the soul's baseness and impurity; and on this account the wisdom is painful, afflictive, and also dark for the soul.' In Kieran Kavanaugh, ed., *John of the Cross: Selected Writings* (New York: Paulist Press, 1987) 201.

57 Augustine, *Confessions*, Book I, chap. 1.

58 In 1942 Lonergan himself still affirmed the traditional negative justification for celibacy. That argument stated that because of original sin, concupiscence has made it almost impossible for humans to exercise physical sexuality within sin ('Finality, Love, Marriage' 49–51). My reading of his work suggests that it can support a much more profound and positive approach to the question.

59 See Charles A. Gallagher et al., *Embodied in Love: Sacramental Spirituality and Sexual Intimacy* (New York: Crossroad, 1989), for a credible popular presentation of a theology of marriage based in a similar view. It is noteworthy that this text, while consciously building on John Paul II's notion of the 'nuptial' meaning of the human body, does not find it necessary to take up his heavy-handed emphasis on the difference between masculine and feminine natures.

60 Physical sexual union is *a* mediation of spiritual communion, not *the only* such mediation. Any concrete act that manifests and builds up the communion of God and the people of God is equally a mediation of mystical communion. The same principle applies to sexual activity as to other forms of activity.

61 'Lonergan's Method in Ethics' 247.

62 Frisby's position seems to depend implicitly on a metaphor of God as phallus; for him, God is 'that which comes in from outside.' The image is based not on sex as mutuality and communion, but on sex as active penetration of passive vagina, for the purpose of planting the seed of a child. Lisa Sowle

Cahill notes that, in women's accounts, 'sex as an act or activity tends to be subsumed within a more holistic relational view' (*Women and Sexuality* 58). Women's analogies tend to view God as 'that which is most inside' – and so enables us to recognize our own deepest being in the other.

63 This is Lonergan's term for 'concepts uttered by an intelligence that is grasping, not intelligent procedure, but a merely biological and non-intelligent response to stimulus' (*Insight* 251).

64 Cf. *Insight* 387–88.

On the Possible Relevance of Lonergan's Thought to Some Feminist Questions in Christology

ABSTRACT *Christology, the theological explication of Jesus Christ's person and work, has often, and with good reason, been seen by feminist theologians as highly problematic. This essay aims at discovering whether Lonergan's Christology throws any light, first, on the question of Christ's maleness, and, second, on the meaning of his crucifixion. These topics are closely related, for as Lonergan understands them each depends on the way in which consciousness is conceived. The argument is that when appropriate distinctions have been drawn between different ways in which Christ 'assumed our humanity,' his being male need not be thought of as intrinsically conditioning his redemptive work. But since for Lonergan the essence of redemption, and hence the properly Christian ethic, is the 'Law of the Cross,' the question whether his Christology as a whole is compatible with feminism ultimately turns on the value of power and the implications of religious conversion.*

At the risk of appearing quite insolently obvious, I shall say that if the Church is to make any impression on the modern mind she will have to preach Christ and the cross.

Dorthy L. Sayers

'The nub of the question as to whether feminism is compatible with Christianity is that of whether a Christology can be found of which it may be said that at least it is not incompatible with feminism.'[1] Many feminist theologians would concur with this judgment. Even those who do not regard Christology

as the single most estimable problem could probably agree that it is problematic, and that in two main ways. First there is a cluster of questions
summed up in the subtitle of a well-known essay by Rosemary Radford
Ruether: 'Can a Male Savior Save Women?' Questions of this sort belong to
Christology in the strict sense, in so far as they regard the *person* of Christ.
But they usually shade over into a second set of difficulties regarding Christ's
work. Here, as Anne Carr has pointed out, the chief problem lies in the way
the passion and death of Christ have been used 'to legitimate family, church,
and societal structures that support gender roles for women of nonassertiveness, passivity, and sacrifice of self.'[2]

Can Lonergan's thought throw any light on either or both of these concerns? I shall try to develop that question in the pages that follow, and to
suggest some tentative answers, by drawing on Lonergan's Christology –
not, that is, on his philosophy or methodology. These will of course enter
the discussion that follows, but only ad hoc, since it is meant to be a discussion within theology, more or less centred in what Lonergan calls the functional speciality 'systematics.' My reasons for this approach are two. In the
first place, it seems to me that feminist questions about Christology such as
those I have mentioned are, at bottom, questions about how the person
and/or the work of Christ are to be *understood*; questions, in other words,
for systematics in the sense laid out in *Method in Theology*. Then, in the
second place, Christology is one topic on which we have in Lonergan's work
not only methodological considerations but also his own theological performance. It is true that most (though not all) of what he wrote on Christology he wrote in Latin, true that the Roman textbooks that contain it were
published before *Method*, and true that much of their content is as jejune
and outdated as their form, so that he was understandably reluctant to have
them translated. All this notwithstanding, the treatises *De Verbo Incarnato*
and *De constitutione Christi*, used with discrimination and in the light of
Lonergan's more recent writings, do speak to the contemporary theological
situation as regards Christology in general. Whether, in particular, they offer
resources for elaborating a Christology 'of which it may be said that at least
it is not incompatible with feminism' seems a worthwhile question.

The first section of my essay will spell out in greater detail the two-sided
Christological problem I stated above, drawing chiefly on the work of
Daphne Hampson, whom I have already quoted and who has articulated
both sides of the problem in clear and trenchant terms. The second section
turns to Lonergan's systematic understanding of Christ as the subject of a
thoroughly human consciousness. The third goes on to his account of
Christ's redeeming work as consisting in and mediated by acts of meaning.
I believe all three parts are accurate, as far as they go, but for none of them
would I claim exhaustiveness. An essay is an essay.

1   Articulating the Questions

Hampson does not count herself a Christian. She is, however, a woman of prayer who speaks movingly of her love for God; and the position she presents is consistent, nuanced, and clearly argued. Not for her the easy refuge of ambiguities and half-measures and the use of names from which most of the meaning has been drained. Theism, for instance, if it is properly so called, involves something beyond believing that the universe is not malevolent or indifferent, and theology thus has to include more than a political agenda promoted by a 'God-concept.' Likewise, Christianity worthy of the name needs a firmer basis than the view that Jesus was someone deeply in tune with God or that his was a very fine moral teaching.[3]

This last is the issue at present. For Hampson a theology is Christian theology, and a theism is Christian theism, just in so far as it holds that Jesus was unique.[4] But the uniqueness that Christians have traditionally ascribed to the relationship between Jesus and God also gives Hampson two reasons for rejecting Christianity as a whole. One reason is that uniqueness *as such* is untenable. This is Hampson's line of thought when she denies 'that there could be particular events ... which interrupt the normal causal relationships persisting in history and in nature,'[5] since if no particular historical person or event can possibly be related to God in a way that makes it different from all other people and events, then obviously Christianity's central tenet cannot be true. God does not 'do special things'; conversely, no one, male or female, can be held to have a relationship to God that abrogates the causal nexus of the universe. For the most part, though, Hampson does not rely on this sort of a priori argument, and I shall not be concerned with it here. It is more a philosophical than a theological objection; Bultmann is the proximate source, as Hampson notes, but behind him stands Kant's first *Critique*. And while Lonergan certainly has something to say on the question whether the universe is a closed nexus of causes and effects, the (counter) position that it is does not seem to have any intrinsic connection with feminism.

Hampson's second objection to Christ's uniqueness is another matter. What is unacceptable about Christianity, considered from a more specifically feminist viewpoint, is not that it is inextricably rooted in one particular history but that the history in which it is rooted is a history of patriarchalism. So, even if the philosophical and a priori objection to Jesus' uniqueness were to be answered, an objection on ethical grounds would remain, namely that because the person to whom Christianity ascribes a unique and saving relationship with God was a male, the symbols that convey Christian meaning have been, and cannot help being, such as to exclude women and deny their equality with men. This is an important objection. If the uniqueness that Hampson rightly holds to be part and parcel of Christianity is inextricably bound up with the fact of Christ's maleness, it does seem she is also right in holding that feminism and Christianity are irremediably at odds. For, in that case, it would have to follow that symbolic mediations of the meaning and value that were incarnate in Jesus' life and death *must* include, as in fact they have included, his maleness.

In this connection it should be pointed out that the Christianity in relation to which Hampson is a post-Christian is a sacramental Christianity. The symbolic mediations she is concerned with are predominantly ecclesial, liturgical, and above all eucharistic; and the concrete issue she returns to again and again is the ordination of women – not as a matter of abstract right, but because of the meanings and values that are, or are not, concretely embodied in the celebrant of the eucharist. Christology is relevant to these concerns in so far as the exclusion of women from ordained sacramental ministry is defended on the ground that Jesus was a male, for implicit in such arguments is a judgment as to what the qualities and characteristics are that constitute Christ as uniquely the mediator of redemption.

Such is the context within which Hampson weighs a number of Christological positions and finds them wanting. It goes without saying that Christologies for which maleness is essential to Christ's nature are unacceptable,[6] but the Christologies proposed by some feminist authors are not ipso facto valid. Hampson has little good to say about the compensatory manoeuvre of adopting Mary (or the Spirit) as a female counterpart of the male Christ. A 'low' Christology in which 'we see God through a Christ-shaped window' may well be Christocentric but, paradoxically, disqualifies itself as Christian.[7] The same is true of 'message' Christologies in so far as they refer only incidentally to the person of Christ. As for 'high' Christologies that stress a cosmic Christ in whom alienation and division are overcome, they do not address the problem so much as ignore it by de-emphasizing Christ's humanity.

There is, however, one Christology that promises to meet feminist objections. Interestingly enough, it is the classical Christology of the Patristic period. The Patristic writers, Hampson observes, do not hold that the doctrine of Christ's divinity means he was a god – a male deity, that is, which would of course disqualify the doctrine for almost any feminist. Rather, they hold that he was one of three persons who are the only God there is, and that he was constituted as such not by his humanness, much less his maleness, but by relatedness to the other divine persons. On this construal women and men alike, having been baptized into Christ, are baptized into the death and risen life of someone who, as one of the persons who are God, has no sex. Jesus did live a human life also, and in that regard he was certainly a man and not a women, just as he was a Jew and not a Gentile.

But in Patristic Christology nothing is made of these further characteristics. The important thing is what Christ shared with other humans, because, as Gregory Nazianzus put it, 'what has not been taken on is not healed.' Construing this maxim in light of the fact that women have never been denied baptism, Hampson writes: 'If it is to be held that both women and men find salvation in Christ, then it must be simply "humanity" which is of significance as having been taken on.'[8] In Christ God took on that which every woman and every man has in common with each other and with Jesus. At the same time, Hampson also notes that an emphasis on commonness with respect to Christ's 'humanity' does not rule out, but on the contrary makes possible, a celebration of the diversity and particularity of other persons. Patristic theology passes no judgment whatever on the relative significance of these differences, including even differences between the sexes, except in so far as to say that none of them precludes participation in Christ.

Having found in classical Christology so much that is consonant with a feminist position, it might be expected that Hampson would herself embrace some version of its basic tenets. At one point in her career she did just that. In the end, however, she has come to relinquish the classical view as hopelessly antiquated. When Patristic authors spoke of 'humanity,' she now considers, they were thinking in terms of a 'universal' conceived along Platonistic lines as more truly 'real' than the particulars that instantiate it. But now that the whole philosophical framework of Platonism has collapsed, people invariably think of individuals as truly real, rather than as instances of something else that has its own real existence. 'So the question then becomes for them how this particular human being is God, rather than their thinking in terms of a humanity in which he too participated.'[9] In short, what seemed a promising Christology fails to deliver the goods because it is unintelligible.

If the classical doctrine of one person in two natures could be understood today, Hampson implies that it would go a long way towards answering the question whether a male saviour can save women, because from that doctrine it follows that God in Christ saves, not as male but as human. Moreover, turning to the second aspect of the Christological problem mentioned at the outset, it would therefore be not only possible but imperative to ask, with Carr, whether the received interpretations of Christ's saving work, especially his death, present it as meaningful in human terms or as meaningful only within a patriarchal horizon. If it is indeed as human that Christ saves, interpreting his role in exclusively male terms would have to be regarded as an aberration, though not necessarily an incorrigible one.

Such is the problematic. There is a question about Christ's constitution, about how he was what he was; and there is a question about the effect that his being thus constituted has on what he has done as saviour. With these questions, respectively, the next two sections will attempt to deal from the standpoint of Lonergan's theology.

2   Lonergan on Christ's 'Humanity'

The 'systematics' that *Method in Theology* advocates is 'quite a homely affair. It aims at an understanding of the truths of faith, a *Glaubensverständnis*,' where the 'truths of faith envisaged are church confessions.'[10] If Lonergan's Latin textbooks are any indication, the homeliness that distinguishes systematics from grandiose speculation is compatible with a high degree of precision and differentiation. Yet even so the aim remains modest. Systematics is a quest for understanding, not judgment; the question is not *what* is so but *how* it could be true that what is so is so. As we have seen, Hampson's assessment of classical Christology raises two such questions: how, if at all, Christ can be understood as having taken on 'humanity,' and how this taking-on of 'humanity' can be understood as effecting salvation. But in order to find out whether Lonergan offers any answers it will be necessary to begin further back, with some account of how he regards the 'church confession' from which his own systematic theology of Christ takes its bearings.

Where Christology is concerned there is not much dispute as to which church confession above all others must be reckoned with. It is the *Definitio fidei* framed at the council of Chalcedon. There is, however, dispute as to exactly what the definition defines, largely because it uses the seemingly philosophical language of 'person' and 'nature.' Lonergan's position on the dispute could be called minimalist. He regards the Chalcedonian doctrine as a heuristic rule of speech grounded in a dogmatic – not, that is, a Platonic or otherwise explicitly metaphysical – realism. In effect, the definition marks the entry into Christian discourse of the principle of non-contradiction, which the bishops at Chalcedon invoked performatively, though not explicitly, in order to say what the Nicene creed does and does not say. That creed makes two sorts of statements about Christ, using human predicates on the one hand and divine predicates on the other. Since no finite creature, as such, is God, the two sets of predicates are contradictory. But contradictory predications cannot be truly asserted of the same thing in the same respect without violating the principle of non-contradiction, and the Chalcedonian definition embodies that principle by declaring that while both sets of predicates do apply truly to 'one and the same' Christ, they do not apply in the same respect. One set belongs to him *as* human; in Chalcedonian terminology, as having a human 'nature'; the other belongs to him *as* divine, that is, in virtue of his divine 'nature.' Christ himself is not two, however, but identically one; and the definition gives the name 'person' to that because of which he is himself and no other.

That, for Lonergan, is the minimal, open-ended meaning of the definition's central and much-debated terms. They might almost be place-holders, X and Y. 'What is a person or hypostasis? It is ... in the Incarnation what there is one of. What is a nature? ... in the Incarnation it is what there are two of.'[11] Difficulties arise only in so far as other meanings seep out of different contexts of common sense or theory and into the merely logical context within which the council's implicit definitions function. But the seepage is all but impossible to prevent, and to avoid the endless confusion that has resulted Lonergan prefers to substitute a different vocabulary while maintaining the same functional definitions. As he puts it in a précis of the position developed in his Latin Christology, 'the doctrine of one person with two natures transposes quite neatly into a recognition of a single subject of both a divine and a human consciousness.'[12]

With the transposition itself we need not be concerned here. Consciousness is clearly the key, and it is of course his own analysis of conscious intentionality that gives Lonergan a thoroughly modern framework for understanding the classical doctrine. In that analysis, 'subject' means 'subject of conscious acts' and 'conscious acts' are those that make the subject present to himself or herself as performing them. 'Consciousness,' then, is both the presence to oneself *of* oneself *as* sensing, feeling, thinking, judging, deciding, loving, and so on, and the presence of these same acts to oneself. In light of these definitions, Lonergan's transposition of the Chalcedonian formula means that Christ, as the subject of *divine* consciousness, was (and is) present to himself in a divine way. Such an unrestricted self-awareness is not something that anyone understands, short of the beatific vision. But neither does it bear on the question of redemption, because it is *ut homo* – as a human or, in Lonergan's terms, as the subject of a human consciousness – that Christ is redeemer. And it was human consciousness, his finite self-presence, that made him, in Chalcedon's phrase, 'like us in all respects apart from sin.'

Does 'us,' then, refer to all human subjects, or only to those who also, like Christ, are male? If the question is to be given a sufficiently differentiated answer, some distinctions need to be drawn.

The first point to note is that it is through conscious acts, acts of experiencing, understanding, judging, and deciding, that a conscious subject 'lives a life,' humanly, historically, and as conditioned (extrinsically) by space and time. The sequences and groupings of these acts can be understood in relation to any number of other conjugates. According to Carol Gilligan, for example, there are several ways in which schedules of probability differ significantly as between women and men. For Lonergan, however, there is a distinction that, without negating such differences, cuts across them. It is a distinction between two ways in which it is possible to understand conscious operations, not in relation to anything else, but in relation to each other.

The first of these intelligible unities is familiar, at least notionally, to anyone who has even a casual acquaintance with Lonergan's work. It is the unity of a recurring, dynamic structure in which the elements structured are conscious activities as occurring on qualitatively different levels. Verifying this pattern in one's own experience is what Lonergan means by self-appropriation, and it is a pattern that presumably belonged to Christ the first-century rabbi just as it does to any other subject of human consciousness. It has to be distinguished, however, from the historical, biographical unity of conscious operations over time, a unity that 'already is teleologically what it eventually is to become,' and that is thus unique to every conscious subject as 'the first and only edition' of herself or himself.[13] There is a distinction, in other words, between the self-assembling structural unity of many-levelled conscious activity, and the self-constituting unity of cognitional and moral self-transcendence.

At the same time, these two intelligible unities are intimately related. The clearest analogy is the way a differential equation is related to a function. As there can be any number of different functions (relationships among variable quantities) that will satisfy the same differential equation, so there are any number of different ways to live a human life by being attentive, intelligent, reasonable, and responsible. As the differential equation regards from a higher viewpoint all the functions that fulfil the requirements it expresses, so the structure of conscious intentionality is verifiable in every biography constituted by an individual's conscious intending. As further determinations are needed in order to specify which of many possible functions is in fact relevant to a particular range of data, so the unfolding of a particular human life depends on the myriad concrete circumstances, the historical 'givens,' within which it unfolds.

However it is conceived, the distinction I have just drawn is quite relevant to the problem at hand. In respect of the first, structural unity, there is 'neither Jew nor Greek,' but one human nature in all.[14] Nor, in the same respect, is there male or female – until it can be affirmed on the basis of self-appropriation that women's conscious acts manifest among themselves an intelligible unity different from the one Lonergan articulates. Meanwhile, granted that the pattern itself is *not* gender-specific, Christ as a humanly conscious subject was 'like us' in such a way that 'us' does mean every woman and every man. He conducted his life by experiencing, understanding his experience, and arriving at judgments of fact and of value. In respect of the second, teleological, existential unity, by contrast, every person is different from every other. So, for example, it might be that the thinking and judging and deciding that constitute some particular human life would characterize it not only as the life of a Jew, say, but as that of a literate, male, Aramaic-speaking, Galilean Jew of the first century with a fondness for food and drink and a penchant for a fortiori argument. Those are the lines along which Lonergan takes account in *De Verbo Incarnato* of modern historical-mindedness as it bears on the way in which human personality is conceived. Whereas Thomas Aquinas accepted cognitional development in Christ rather hesitantly and only in his latest writings, Lonergan can fully acknowledge all the historical particularity and change that contemporary theologians rightly insist on as entailed in Christ's being truly human.

Now, does the distinction between the structural and the biographical unity of conscious acts help to make intelligible the idea that Christ took on 'humanity'? Not yet. In fact, it seems to make matters worse. Either of the two unities could perhaps be thought of as 'humanity' in the sense that each is verifiable in every human. And certainly neither of them involves the kind of Platonism that Hampson detects in Patristic Christology. Even so, neither of them qualifies as the *what* in Gregory's heuristic statement that *what* is not taken on is not healed. On the one hand, in so far as Christ's 'humanity' is common to all humans, it consists in the dynamic pattern of cognitional and moral activity; but that structure, as structure, is not what needs healing.[15] On the other hand, in so far as the 'humanity' taken on by God the Word was historical and particular, his own and nobody else's, it was precisely not a 'humanity' common to all humans, and so its being taken on has none of the soteriological consequences that Hampson would have liked to retrieve from Patristic Christology as relevant to feminist concerns.

Fortunately, the distinction outlined above between two senses in which the ambiguous term 'humanity' might be understood in terms of consciousness is not the whole story. It prescinds from yet another sense in which 'humanity' is unitary. In Lonergan's published writings the place where this further oneness is perhaps most evidence is the end of *Insight*. For the point he has been leading up to all along is that progress and decline, and therefore also redemption, pertain neither to a concrete particular nor to an abstract universal 'humanity' but to the concrete universal for which the only English word available is 'man.' Correspondingly, in the Latin theology, Christ is redeemer in virtue of his being head of the human race, where 'human race' denotes not merely the sum total of women and men but an explanatory unity that is both genus and species. To put it another way, Lonergan's soteriology takes its bearings from his understanding of human solidarity. Humans are redeemed in so far as 'man' is redeemed, and the 'moment' or 'instant' in which redemption occurs is the whole of human history. This calls for some elaboration.

To understand a living being it is necessary to understand that being's development, and to understand human being it is necessary to understand the development that Lonergan sometimes calls 'man's making of man.' If it is true that I am the agent of my own becoming, that by my conscious acts I make myself what I am and am to be, it is equally true that I am at the same time both drawing on and contributing to the ongoing self-making of the human race. From the moment of anyone's entry into the world mediated by meaning and motivated by value – a moment that there is reason to think begins at birth if not before – that person is cooperating in schemes of recurrence that will in part determine, and will in part be determined by, his or her more or less attentive, intelligent, reasonable, responsible performance over a lifetime. Human development, then, the achievement of the human good, 'is a personal function of an objective movement in the space-time solidarity of man.'[16] The acts that constitute such a development are conscious and intentional; that is, they *mean*. Accordingly, 'one can apprehend mankind as a concrete aggregate developing over time, where the locus of development and, so to speak, the synthetic bond, is the emergence, expansion, differentiation, dialectic of *meaning* and of meaningful performance.'[17]

This is the third sense in which 'humanity' is to be thought of as *one*. The first was that conscious operations have a unitary structure, a dynamic oneness common to all human subjects; the second, that any individual's life-story has a teleological unity that is unique to that individual. But this biographical oneness has only the descriptive intelligibility of a narrative. For an *explanatory* account of personal existence, of what it is to be myself and no one else, I need an understanding of the meaning I have made my own; and for an explanatory account of *that*, I need an understanding of the unitary human reality that is constituted by meaning – an understanding, that is, of the whole of history in its progress, its decline, and its redemption. Of that objective movement, no individual is more than an instrument, not even the incarnate Word. But every individual *is* an instrument, including the incarnate Word, who became incarnate for just that reason – so that God, the first agent of every event, might also be a secondary cause and as such contribute, directly and in person, to the 'emergence, expansion, differentiation, dialectic of meaning' that unifies all men and women. Because of the Incarnation, humans are united through meaning with the person of God the Word, who has entered, and altered, human meaning by performing the same kind of conscious operations that other women and men perform.

I have already pointed out that whatever Christ did in the world mediated by meaning he did *ut homo*, as a human. Nothing he thought or said or suffered bypassed his human consciousness, which had the same structure as ours; nor did it abrogate the particularity of his historical life, which was his alone. Still, as Lonergan emphasizes in his only English-language writing on redemption, the Incarnation was 'not simply the fact of the Second Person of the Blessed Trinity assuming human nature, it was an act of communication,' the 'outstanding expression' of God to human persons.[18] Lonergan's is a Christology of revelation, quite as much as Karl Barth's. It was the *Word* that became flesh, and it is in what the incarnate Word contributed to the human race's making of the human race – in the meanings and values he communicated to the space-time solidarity of the concrete human universal – that his saving presence is real and effective. Human solidarity is a fact, whether the Incarnation occurred or no; but if the Incarnation too is a fact, then any attempt at understanding human reality that leaves that fact out of account is radically defective.

Supposing the rapid-fire overview I have been presenting to be faithful to the main lines of Lonergan's thought, there are two conclusions to be drawn.

1. The first returns to the idea, which Hampson found so promising, expressed compactly in the maxim 'what is not taken on is not healed.' Conceiving Christology in terms of conscious intentionality entails conceiving the Word as having 'taken on' a human consciousness, through the operations of which he made himself become what he was. But it also entails conceiving the Word as having 'taken on' human history, in the sense that his conscious self-constituting was a function not only of a common cognitional structure but also of a common enterprise, 'man's making of man.' That enterprise was mediated to him, as to anyone else, historically – in art, symbol, language, gesture, and through traditions, language, customs, stories, interpersonal relations. It was by making these mediated meanings and values his own that Christ enacted his human selfhood; conversely, it was by transforming them to enact his own self-meaning that he healed them. Living and dying as one of us was the way God the Word communicated the 'outstanding expression' of meaning and value to the world that meaning mediates and value motivates. In a Patristic phrase that Lonergan himself adopts, 'God the Word became a human so that in taking on what is ours he might give us what is his.'[19]

2. All of which leads to the other conclusion that can be drawn from Lonergan's Christology, a conclusion regarding the second part of Hampson's objection to Christ's being unique. From what has been said so far, it follows that on Lonergan's view the uniqueness of Christ, in the soteriologically relevant sense, does not lie in the physical, chemical, organic, or psychic particularities of his humanity. Nor does it lie in the social, cultural, linguistic, or conceptual particularities of his historical situatedness. In all these ways Christ was, to be sure, unique; but they bear on the economy of salvation to just the same extent that they were subsumed, in keeping with the structure of a consciousness like ours in every respect, into the incarnate

meaning that has been his unique and saving contribution to the human project.

What that meaning *is* has yet to be discussed. So far as Christ's constitution is concerned, I have tried to show that Lonergan does take a position 'of which it may be said that at least it is not incompatible with feminism.' But that position entails conceiving Christ's work as well as his person in terms of acts of meaning, so that whether this further aspect of Lonergan's Christology is objectionable from a feminist viewpoint depends on whether his construal of the Incarnation as expression, meaning, 'word' is compatible with those meanings that define a feminist position as such.

3   Lonergan on Christ as Redeemer

The first section of this essay raised a question: Can the 'classical' Christology of the Patristic writers and the early councils be conceived in a way that (1) does justice to the particularities of the human Jesus, while at the same time it (2) maintains that he shares with other humans, male and female alike, 'humanity' in a sense that is real and intelligible as such, yet (3) does so without resorting to a defunct ontology? The second section outlined Lonergan's answer, which is affirmative on all three counts, only to raise a further question: Are the meanings and values consciously introduced by the incarnate Word into humankind's self-constitution such as can be embraced by feminists? The answer proposed in this final section begins as *yes* and turns into *maybe* – a very inconclusive conclusion, but one that may nevertheless serve to narrow the range of questions that need to be explored by Christian theologians who are in sympathy both with feminist thinking and with Lonergan's.

The account of the psychological constitution of Christ that *De Verbo Incarnato* offers as consistent with the classical Chalcedonian doctrine says nothing about the extent to which, in point of fact, the 'outer word' that has its source in him is intrinsically conditioned by his sex. Everything depends on what the word itself amounts to. That is the question that comes to the fore at the end of Lonergan's treatise, in its three theses on 'Redemption.' They concentrate on what has always been regarded as the climax of Christ's redeeming work, the Paschal mystery of his passion, death, and resurrection, which Lonergan sets out to understand as the definitive expression of meaning and value intended in Christ's conscious acts of understanding, judging, deciding, and loving. It is a topic with many aspects, two of which warrant attention here. One is Lonergan's treatment of the doctrine that by dying Christ made a 'satisfaction' for sin; the other is his discussion in Christological terms of what in *Insight* he had called God's solution to the problem of evil.

The thesis on Christ's satisfaction, as I have tried to suggest elsewhere,[20] is one place where Lonergan's Latin theology transcends to some extent the cumbersome idiom in which he had to cast it. Yet a thesis it is, and a technical one at that. In order to relate it to the topic of the present essay a broader and more basic startingpoint is needed – symbolic meaning. Christ crucified is first of all a symbol and, as Lonergan has said, 'a symbol of endless meaning.'[21] As such it makes 'mind and body, mind and heart, heart and body communicate,'[22] and theology exists, not to replace, but only to regulate this immediate and highly personal communication.

Now, what the symbol of the cross communicates to women has been studied in very concrete terms by several feminist writers. In particular they have pointed out from different angles how deeply and how variously the imagery of the crucifixion has affected the thinking and feeling of women as regards their own suffering. A much discussed case in point is 'Christa,' Edwina Sandys's sculpture of a woman with arms outstretched as though crucified. One sort of reaction appears in the anonymous poem quoted by Susan Brooks Thistlethwaite:

> I have known you as a vulnerable baby,
> as a brother, and as a father.
> Now I know you as a woman.
> You were there with me
> as the violated girl
> caught in helpless suffering.

Other women, however, have found the statue repulsive. Such was Thistlethwaite's own first response. "This," she said to someone when she saw it, 'will tend to legitimate violence against women.'[23]

For the most part it has been the destructive impact of the cross as symbol that feminist writers have emphasized. Perhaps the most thorough and penetrating study in this regard is an article by Joanne Carlson Brown and Rebecca Parker with the pointedly punctuated title, 'For God So Loved the World?' Christianity, they write, 'has been a primary – in many women's lives *the* primary – force in shaping our acceptance of abuse.' Behind this force stands Christianity's central image: 'Divine child abuse is paraded as salvific and the child who suffers "without even raising a voice" is lauded as the hope of the world.'[24] The cross of Christ, on this reading, 'upholds actions and attitudes that accept, glorify, and even encourage suffering.'[25]

While the charge of 'divine child abuse' may be exaggerated, it is not unfounded. What Brown and Parker allude to is a way of construing Christ's death that has, in fact, informed much if not most of the preaching and piety of Western Christianity, Protestant and Catholic alike, since the Middle

Ages. In theological parlance this view goes by the name 'substitutionary penal atonement.' Christ is portrayed as effecting salvation in that he was punished by God in the place of sinners whose just deserts the punishment would have been. Stated in everyday language, the point is that the cross has 'settled the score' or 'made things even' between God and humankind; stated more technically, it is that Christ's suffering was the 'satisfaction' demanded by divine justice.

Lonergan will have none of it. He is willing to keep the *term* 'satisfaction,' which carries the authority of Anselm, but his long and painstaking analysis of its meaning concludes that the tradition of interpreting Christ's death in penal-substitutionary terms has been one long aberration. The very idea that divine justice demands the suffering of an innocent victim, or that only such a death as Christ's could placate the wrath of an offended deity, is either immoral or amoral. Broadly speaking, Lonergan thus concurs with Brown and Parker in rejecting what they call a bloodthirsty God. But his own negative critique is only a beginning. On the positive side, he argues that what the passion and death of the incarnate Word display, far from being God's imposition on Christ of the punishment others deserve, is Christ's own expression of detestation and sorrow towards all human misdeeds. The cross as symbol thus stands for something Christ did, more than something he suffered. But his outward expression proceeded from an inward judgment of value passed on those misdeeds *as* sins against the God he loved. In that what he did was expressing this love, siding with the offended rather than the offenders, his deed was pleasing to God; and in that sense, which has nothing to do with punishment or substitution, Christ made a real 'satisfaction' for the sins of others.

Redemption, then, as mediated by the death of Christ, is for Lonergan no juridical transaction but a personal communicative act rooted most basically in Christ's love for God and for other persons. How this constructive interpretation bears on the problem at hand will perhaps be clear. Detestation and sorrow are not gender-specific; neither is the judgment of value they rest on, nor the prior judgment that moral evils are also sins, nor the love of God that grounds all these. All these conscious acts, the ingredients of 'satisfaction' as Lonergan conceives it, pertain to Christ as human – not as male. From a feminist viewpoint this would seem to be a major point in Lonergan's favour, but there is another. He also interprets Christ's sacrificial love in exactly the way Anne Carr holds it must, for women, be interpreted: 'as a free and active choice' in the face of evil, and not as 'passive victimization.'[26] A separate thesis in *De Verbo Incarnato* is devoted to arguing that Christ was free in accepting his suffering and death, where 'free' has the same full and nuanced sense analysed in *Insight* and *Grace and Freedom*. What Christ did, he did as a human who was 'like us in all respects.'

In sum, the thesis on Christ's satisfaction achieves what Lonergan would call a higher viewpoint. What is permanently valid in the theological tradition gets sorted out and carried forward into a richer context where the basic terms and relations can be verified irrespective of geography, language, or gender. In reaching such a viewpoint, Lonergan dismantles any theology that would depict the atonement as a matter of vengeance, retaliation, or arbitrary wilfulness. So far, so good. But two qualifications must be added.

1. The first is that the level at which Lonergan addresses one problem that feminist theologians such as Brown and Parker have raised is the level of systematic, explanatory theory. He is concerned with basic principles. But it is one thing, though an important one, to show that an idea like penal substitution is untenable in principle, and something else to change the commonsense, symbolic mediations of what redemption is all about. It takes more than theory, however admirable, to shift the probabilities that the cross will be presented in ways that lead to alienation on the part of women (and men) and to ideology on the part of men (and women). Which is simply to say that systematics is not the whole of a functionally-specialized theology. Until it is complemented by the functional specialty of communications it has not made its contribution to humankind's making of humankind. An authentic theory of redemption *ought* to help reorient common sense; that is what it is for. Whether it actually does so will depend, however, on the decisions of those who have a hand in educating a new generation. Even if Lonergan has shown how a major theological aberration might be corrected and replaced with something better, one may ask whether it is worthwhile to work out the further transitions to a better praxis. The answer finally depends on a more searching question: whether the story that Christian theology seeks to understand, a story neither for nor about winners, is true – a question to which even a functionally specialized theology, by itself, can give no answer.

2. The second qualification is that in some sense Lonergan's dialectical retrieval and transposition of the notion of satisfaction is a preliminary step. It clears the way for what he himself, to judge by his later writings in English, viewed as *De Verbo Incarnato*'s lasting contribution to theology. This is the final thesis, entitled 'Understanding the Mystery.' The question Lonergan asks there is again the kind of question that belongs to systematic theology; a question, that is, for understanding. *Why* has the Word became incarnate, suffered, died, and been raised again? Granted the truth of these articles of faith, what is their intrinsic intelligibility? The answer is the Law of the Cross: 'Divine wisdom has ordained, and divine goodness has willed, not to do away with the evils of the human race through power, but to convert those evils into a supreme good.'[27]

Here, if anywhere, Lonergan's Christology will turn out to be at odds with feminist positions.

I have tried to show that for Lonergan asking, 'What think ye of Christ?' comes down to asking, 'What think ye of the word, the meaning, enacted in the passion of the Word incarnate?' Given the culminating thesis of *De Verbo Incarnato*, feminists might reply, putting it mildly, 'not much.' Why should the Law of the Cross be seen as anything but another form of the same interpretation of Christ's death that, to quote Carr again, has been used throughout Christian history 'to legitimate family, church, and societal structures that support gender roles for women of nonassertiveness, passivity, and sacrifice of self'?[28] It is a fair question. A fair answer depends, in the first place, on what exactly Lonergan is referring to under the rubric of *lex crucis*, often mentioned but not always explicated. Then, in the second place, it would seem fair to examine Lonergan's own estimate of the significance and implications of this 'law.'

1. First, what the Law of the Cross says. Like any other law, it expresses a grasp of many things in a single view. In this case what is grasped is a sequential pattern comprising three steps. In the first step, to state it using *Insight*'s vocabulary, basic sin gives rise to moral evil. Contraction of consciousness, lack or failure of self-transcendence, not only raises the probability of further basic sin but also accelerates the systemic evil that Lonergan conceives as longer and shorter cycles of decline. The second step is voluntary acceptance of moral evil. 'Sin is the source of evil in this world insofar as this world is a human creation and a human product. It involves an objective surd, and that surd is stopped, it is absorbed, only insofar as there is suffering ... it is only insofar as suffering is accepted in the spirit in which Christ accepted it that the surd of sin is, as it were, wiped out.'[29] In the third step a greater good ensues, to which suffering, by being accepted, has been the means. The Law of the Cross thus involves a reversal of roles. For Christ, death becomes the means of life; for others, death, understood in physical, ascetical, moral, or sacramental terms, becomes the 'principle' of salvation, the first term in an ordered series that constitutes the 'whole Christ' and converges on the vision of God.[30]

2. Next, the significance of the Law of the Cross. Lonergan has two ways of describing it. The Law of the Cross adds the 'strictly theological complement' to *Insight*'s 'general analysis of the dynamic structure of human history' and it states 'the proper Christian ethic.'[31] The operative words are 'strictly' and 'proper.' As they indicate, the Law of the Cross pertains to the order of realities that are disproportionate to any finite nature – the supernatural order. This is not to say that either the philosophy of history in *Insight* or the foundational ethics there and in chapter 2 of *Method* is being called into question. Both are preserved, though both are also comple-

mented and contextualized. Redemption, of which Lonergan writes that the Law of the Cross is the essence, is no apocalyptic reversal; it occurs in and as a shift of probabilities. Under the 'reign of sin' the ratio of alienation to authenticity and of decline to progress is high, and the probability of self-transcendence is low; and if we ask from any but a theological standpoint how such a situation can be remedied, we come up against the fact of moral impotence. The 'problem of evil' does not admit of a sheerly natural solution. Accordingly, to say that the redemptive shift of probabilities does happen whenever evils are willingly endured for the sake of a greater good is to say it is a mystery, in the exact sense of the word: it makes no sense except within the horizon of religious conversion.

Still, it will not do simply to assert mystery in order to cut off debate. The Law of the Cross, both as a statement of what does happen and as a prescription of what can and ought to happen, is entirely general. In itself it neither enjoins particular decisions nor forecasts particular outcomes. Further determinations are necessary before this law can be applied to a given situation. The situation has to be understood and dialectically evaluated in all its concrete detail; and precisely because God does not overpower sin, human efforts at applying the Law of the Cross are subject to their own dialectical distortions. The danger that Lonergan warns against in the very last sentence of *De Verbo Incarnato* – that those who learn of the excellence of the cross will end up following not Christ but Pilate, by laying the cross on others – can become a terrible reality.

That, of course, is just what many feminists would say has been happening to women throughout most of Christian history. There is no dearth of critiques of patriarchal culture meant to show the extent and subtlety of Christian men's subordination of Christian women on the pretext of inculcating Christian humility, self-sacrifice, and the like. In the present context, however, the question is whether the fact that what Lonergan calls the proper Christian ethic can be, and has been, made into an ideology is a fact that sooner or later must lead anyone whose identity is mediated by a feminist horizon to reject the Law of the Cross itself and, with it, the meaning of God incarnate. Anything more than a tentative answer would be inappropriate here, if not impossible, first because the question is one that must in the last resort be addressed by women, each for herself, and second because any answer will turn on what is meant by *power*, a difficult notion in itself and one towards which feminists appear to be ambivalent.

Lonergan is by no means the first to say that wielding power is not the way God deals with evil. The ethical as well as the ontological significance of Christ's *kenosis*, his emptying himself to take the form of a servant, has always been part of what Christianity teaches. Daphne Hampson, reviewing this tradition in an article 'On Power and Gender,' sums up as follows its central theme of powerlessness voluntarily embraced: 'instead of a model of the self which is isolated, self-sufficient, and independent in its power, we have a model of the self broken for others, connected, and indeed not a "self" existing in itself at all. It is a paradigm of sacrifice of self leading to nurture of others.'[32] Taken on its own this quotation could suggest that in finding the essence of redemption in the Law of the Cross Lonergan was anticipating several characteristically feminist themes. Despite the apparently approbatory tone of the passage, however, Hampson goes on to say that while for men such a model may be appropriate, for women it is not. Her judgment is one with which many other writers would concur, especially those who have stressed a parallel between feminist and liberationist theologies. The image of the suffering servant, it is often said, does not speak to the condition of those who struggle to be liberated from oppression. For women, more especially, the problem has not been a prideful self-sufficiency but its opposite, a lack of self-affirmation. Hampson herself concludes that, either way, 'the only possible response to being discriminated against, if one is to retain a sense of one's own integrity, is to fight the discrimination with all one's might.'[33]

If this were her final word there would be nothing left to say. The alternatives would be pretty much what they were for Jesus in Gethsemane, and what for Hampson is the 'only possible response' would be a response he decided against. But her rejection of the model of powerlessness willingly embraced is not, perhaps, so complete as some of her statements suggest. The militant strain in her article is not the predominant one. Quite the contrary. For when she discusses the non-hierarchical practice of women's groups, contrasting it with the impersonal objectivity and efficiency that characterize men's ways of operating; when she describes friendship in terms of cooperation and confidence, as contrasted with the competitive, adversarial relationships that define success in the masculine world; when she speaks of the Quakers, with whom she herself worships, as the only mixed groups she has seen operating successfully according to what she calls women's ways; when she writes that 'empowerment,' as distinct from both power and powerlessness, 'implies a different understanding of the self from either the self-enclosed self which dominates others, or the destroyed self which lives outside itself in a mistaken service of others'[34] – when all this is taken into account, Hampson's basic stance appears more complementary than antagonistic to the horizon of meaning and value that Lonergan describes as 'being in Christ' in the moving paragraphs at the end of his paper on *Existenz* and *Aggiornamento*.'[35]

How far this possible complementarity might actually extend I will not presume to say. What I can, however, do is suggest where the possibility may perhaps be explored to best advantage. My discussion of Lonergan's position on the person and work of Christ has led – inevitably, I think – to the protean notion of power. Towards clarifying that notion Lonergan offers his most important indications in the strangely neglected essay 'Dialectic of Authority.' As might be expected, he speaks of redemption 'from within the Christian tradition, in which Christ suffering, dying and rising again is at once the motive and the model of self-sacrificing love.'[36] But he connects this love explicitly with community, and thus with common meaning and with the cooperation that is the source of power in the relevant sense. 'Legitimate power' is his definition of authority, and what makes power legitimate is authenticity – fidelity to the familiar transcendental precepts of attention, intelligence, reasonableness, and responsibility.[37] If these precepts are truly transcendental, gender is one thing they transcend. Conversely, linking them with one gender would seem to be a source of inauthenticity and might, indeed, be a definition of patriarchy, parallel to Lonergan's own definitions of alienation and ideology. In any case, the point to which the present essay has brought the question of Lonergan and feminism, in its Christological aspect, regards the further, religious transcendental precept, Be in love. Here Romans 5:5, the text so often cited in Lonergan's later writings, is not the whole story. 'Without the visible mission of the Word, the gift of the Spirit is a being-in-love without a proper object; it remains simply an orientation to mystery that awaits its interpretation.'[38]

What the Christian interpretation is, as Lonergan understands it, I have tried to show. On the one hand, it would seem to be an interpretation that implicitly calls into question many of the values that have motivated Western culture for hundreds of years, including at least some of the values that have been adopted by at least some feminists. If the Law of the Cross means anything it means that neither retaliation nor yet even-handed justice alone can reverse the inauthenticity, the oppression, the violence of our day. On the other hand, the mysterious alternative that Christ died to communicate would also seem to be, in some measure, compatible with and even supportive of at least some feminist positions. Exactly what measure is for others to say. But it will be in just that measure that Lonergan's is a Christology of which it may be said that at least it is not incompatible with feminism.

Notes

1 Daphne Hampson, *Theology and Feminism* (Oxford: Basil Blackwell, 1990) 50.
2 Anne Carr, *Transforming Grace: Christian Tradition and Women's Experience* (San Francisco: Harper and Row, 1990) 174.
3 Hampson, *Theology and Feminism* 160, 29, 8, 50.
4 Ibid. 43, 65.

5 Ibid. 8; see also p. 42.
6 Ibid. 52, 66.
7 Ibid. 63.
8 Ibid. 55.
9 Ibid. 57.
10 Lonergan, *Method in Theology* (New York: Herder and Herder, 1972) 350.
11 Lonergan, 'The Origins of Christian Realism' (1972), in W.F.J. Ryan and B.J. Tyrrell, eds, *A Second Collection* (Philadelphia: Westminster Press, 1974) 259.
12 Lonergan, 'The Dehellenization of Dogma' (1967), in *A Second Collection* 25.
13 Lonergan, 'Christology Today: Methodological Reflections' (1975), in F.E. Crowe, ed., *A Third Collection* (New York: Paulist Press, 1985) 92; and 'The Subject' (1968), in *A Second Collection* 83.
14 See Frederick E. Crowe, 'Neither Jew Nor Greek, but One Human Nature and Operation in All' (1965), in his *Appropriating the Lonergan Idea*, ed. Michael Vertin (Washington: Catholic University of America Press, 1989) 31–50. The whole discussion is relevant to the present topic.
15 Basic sin, for Lonergan, is a failure of *act*, a negation of the norms inherent *in* the self-assembling pattern itself.
16 Lonergan, 'Finality, Love, Marriage' (1943), in F.E. Crowe, ed., *Collection* (*Collected Works of Bernard Lonergan*, vol. 4; Toronto: University of Toronto Press, 1988) 45.
17 'The Transition from a Classicist World-View to Historial-Mindedness' (1966), in *A Second Collection* 5–6; emphasis added.
18 Lonergan, 'The Redemption' (1958), in R. Eric O'Connor, ed., *Bernard Lonergan: Three Lectures* (Montreal: Thomas More Institute, 1975) 4.
19 Lonergan, *De Verbo Incarnato* (Rome: Gregorian University Press, 1964) 313.
20 See Charles C. Hefling, Jr, 'A Perhaps Permanently Valid Achievement: Lonergan on Christ's Satisfaction,' *Method: Journal of Lonergan Studies* 10 (1992) 51–76.
21 Lonergan, 'The Redemption' 7.
22 Lonergan, *Method in Theology* 67.
23 Susan Brooks Thistlethwaite, *Sex, Race, and God: Christian Feminism in Black and White* (New York: Crossroad, 1989) 92–93. Note that, in the light of 'the healing these statues seem to evoke in women who have survived sexual and domestic violence' (p. 93), she has revised her initial view.
24 Joanne Carlson Brown and Rebecca Parker, 'For God So Loved the World?' in Joanne Carlson Brown and Carole R. Bohn, eds, *Christianity, Patriarchy and Abuse: A Feminist Critique* (New York: Pilgrim Press, 1989) 2.
25 Ibid. 4.
26 Carr, *Transforming Grace* 174.
27 *De Verbo Incarnato* 552.
28 *Transforming Grace* 174.

29 Transcribed from a discussion in Lonergan, *Understanding and Being* (*Collected Works of Bernard Lonergan*, vol. 5; Toronto: University of Toronto Press, 1990) 373.

30 See Lonergan, 'The Transition from a Classicist World-View to Historical-Mindedness' 8–9.

31 Ibid. 7, 9. The latter quotation occurs in a question, but Lonergan is pretty clearly asking it rhetorically.

32 'On Power and Gender,' *New Theology* 4:3 (1988) 239.

33 Ibid. 240.

34 Ibid. 246.

35 '*Existenz* and *Aggiornamento*' (1964), in *Collection* 249–51.

36 Lonergan, 'Dialectic of Authority' (1974), in *A Third Collection* 10.

37 Ibid. 5–7.

38 Lonergan, 'Mission and the Spirit' (1976), in *A Third Collection* 32.

Contributors

Denise Lardner Carmody is Bernard J. Hanley Professor in the Department of Religious Studies at Santa Clara University. She and her husband, John Tully Carmody, have published more than sixty books in the areas of world religious and Christian theology, all of them shaped foundationally by both Lonergan and feminism.

Frederick E. Crowe is Professor Emeritus of Regis College, Toronto, and Director Emeritus of Lonergan Research Institute, which he cofounded with Robert M. Doran. He has written extensively on Lonergan's work, most recently in a 'Rethinking' series of theological articles in *Science et Esprit*. He is currently coediting with Robert Doran the *Collected Works of Bernard Lonergan*.

Cynthia S.W. Crysdale is an Assistant Professor in the Department of Religion and Religious Education at the Catholic University of America. Her research interests include moral and religious development and feminist ethics. She is the author of 'Lonergan and Feminism,' *Theological Studies* 53 (1992) 234–56.

Tad Dunne is an Adjunct Professor of Medical Ethics at Marygrove College in Detroit and a management consultant for Blue Cross and Blue Shield of Michigan. His publications include *Lonergan and Spirituality* (Chicago: Loyola University Press, 1985), *Spiritual Mentoring*, and *Spiritual Exercises for Today* (San Francisco: Harper, 1991).

Mary Frohlich received the Ph.D. in Spirituality from the Catholic University of America in 1990. She is currently Assistant Professor of Spirituality at the Catholic Theological Union in Chicago. Her book *The Intersubjectivity of the Mystic: A Study of Teresa of Avila's Interior Castle* was recently published by Scholars Press.

Charles C. Hefling, Jr teaches philosophy and systematic theology at Boston College, where he is the Coordinator of the Lonergan Center. He is the author of *Why Doctrines?* and an editor of *Method: Journal of Lonergan Studies*.

Paulette Kidder is an Assistant Professor of Philosophy at Seattle University, where she was hired in 1989 after completing her doctoral studies at Boston College. Her research interests include philosophical hermeneutics, ethics, Lonergan, and feminist theory.

Elizabeth A. Morelli is an Associate Professor in Philosophy at Loyola Marymount University. Under the direction of Lonergan, she co-edited with Mark Morelli *Understanding and Being: An Introduction and Companion to* Insight (Toronto: Edwin Mellen Press, 1980). She collaborated with Frederick E. Crowe, s.j., on his revision of these lectures, *Collected Works of Bernard Lonergan*, vol. 5: *Understanding and Being* (Toronto: University of Toronto Press, 1990). She continues to teach and write in the area of existential phenomenology.

Michael Shute is Assistant Professor of Religious Studies at Memorial University of Newfoundland, where he teaches courses in religion, ethics, and culture. He is the author of *The Origins of Lonergan's Notion of the Dialectic of History*. He holds an S.T.D. from Regis College, Toronto.

Michael Vertin teaches philosophy and theology at St Michael's College in the University of Toronto. His central interests include the philosophical presuppositions of interdisciplinary dialogue. He is the editor of *Appropriating the Lonergan Idea*, a collection of essays by Frederick E. Crowe (Washington: Catholic University of America Press, 1989).

Index

161–62, 185, 191, 200, 205–206,
208; and object, 51, 53–54, 57, 59, 68
n. 21; substance becoming, 23–24
Subjectivity. *See* Objectivity, and subjectivity
Surd, 162–63, 214

Tarule, J.M., 88, 91
Tennyson, Alfred, 27
Thatcher, Margaret, 120
Theory, x, 4, 84, 153, 158, 164; cognitional, 6, 40, 44, 54–55, 117, 134,
205, 213
Teresa, Saint, 77
Thistlethwaite, Susan Brooks, 211
Thillich, Paul, 4, 192 n. 4
Toynbee, Arnold, 14, 16, 28 n. 5, 129
Tracy, David, x, xi
Tradition, 24, 120, 128, 147
Transcendence, 161–62, 177–81,
186–87, 189, 191. *See also* Self,
-transcendence
Transcendental, 17, 43, 54; method, 3,
4; notions, 18, 30 n. 13, 185; precepts, 6, 43–44, 47 n. 46, 121–22,
128, 130, 134–37, 140–43, 163, 217.
See also Consciousness, transcendental
Truth, 16, 57, 79, 93, 94, 95, 102–103,
108 n. 27, 118, 121, 139–42, 155,
159, 178, 181, 182, 186, 204, 213
Tuana, Nancy, 35
Twohig-Moengangongo, Cora, 148

Understanding, ix, 5, 16, 18–19, 39, 53,
89–91, 129–30, 137, 140, 155–56,
165, 177–78, 200, 204–205, 208,
210, 213
Universal, 207. *See also* General

Vertin, Michael, 6
Voegelin, Eric, 120

Wittgensstein, Ludwig, 36
Wollstonecraft, Mary, 75
Women, and knowing, 6, 34, 64,
72–76, 78, 80–83, 86 nn. 34 and 35,
88–90, 92–95, 98–104, 111 n. 45,
112 n. 50, 155; and Lonergan, 82–84;
and men, 6, 21–22, 24, 27, 40, 74–75,
77, 89, 108 n. 30, 110 n. 38, 111 n.
46, 114, 130, 143, 149, 161, 201–202,
205–208, 213 (*see also* Female, and
male); oppression of, x, 3, 4, 33, 35,
38, 45, 76–77, 91–93, 106 n. 15, 108
n. 29, 110–11 n. 44, 111 n. 47, 115,
146–48, 200, 215–16; spirituality of,
211 (*see also* Experience, mystics'). *See
also* Consciousness, women's
wonder, 123, 124
world, 7, 34, 37, 40–41, 53, 90, 91, 93,
94, 117, 123, 125, 129, 146–48, 160,
163–64, 176, 178, 180, 184, 187, 189,
208; of immediacy/meaning, 59, 101,
127; process, *see* Emergent probability